ADIRONDACK ODYSSEYS

Exploring Museums and Historic Places From the Mohawk to the St. Lawrence

Elizabeth Folwell and Amy Godine

The Adirondack Museum
Blue Mountain Lake, New York

Berkshire House Publishers
Lee, Massachusetts

Adirondack Odysseys
Exploring Museums and Historic Places from the Mohawk to the St. Lawrence

Copyright © 1997 by the Adirondack Museum

Editor: Sarah Novak
Front cover: Steamboat cruising on Lower Saranac Lake.
              Photograph by Nancie Battaglia
Cover design: Pamela Meier
Text design and layout: Jane McWhorter
Maps: Matt Paul/Yankee Doodles

Library of Congress Cataloging-in-Publication Data
Folwell, Elizabeth, 1953-
Adirondack odysseys : exploring museums and historic places from the Mohawk to
the St. Lawrence / Elizabeth Folwell and Amy Godine.
        p.   cm.
Includes bibliographical references and index.
ISBN 0-936399-78-3
1. Adirondack Mountains Region (N.Y.)—Guidebooks. 2. Historic sites—New York
(State)—Adirondack Mountains Region—Guidebooks. 3. Historical museums—New
York (State)—Adirondack Mountains Region—Guidebooks. I. Godine, Amy. II.
Title.
F127.A2F56   1997
917.47′50443—dc20   96-43863
                                                              CIP

ISBN 0-936399-78-3

10 9 8 7 6 5 4 3 2 1

Printed in the United States of America

CONTENTS

MAPS

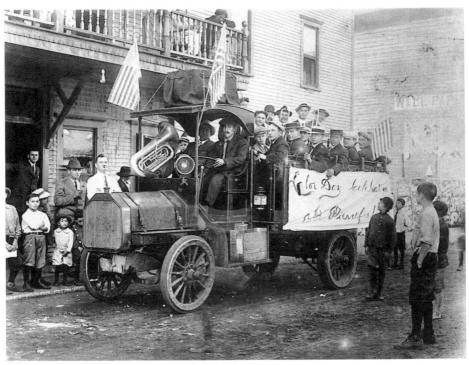

Labor Day celebration in Piercefield.
Courtesy of the Adirondack Museum, Blue Mountain Lake

THE ADIRONDACK HISTORICAL ASSOCIATION

THE ADIRONDACK MUSEUM
ROUTE 28 NORTH & 30 * POST OFFICE BOX 99
BLUE MOUNTAIN LAKE, NEW YORK 12812-0099
518-352-7311 • FAX: (518) 352-7653
Director, JACKIE DAY

Dear Friends:

Most visitors to the Adirondacks today travel through miles of heavily forested, sparsely populated land. To many, this land may appear to be an uninhabited wilderness. In fact, the Adirondack landscapes that we see today along roads, trails, and waterways reflect the history of the interaction between people and place. The Adirondack region is a highly humanized landscape. Study it carefully and you can learn much about the lives and values of the people who settled, farmed, logged, mined, and recreated here.

This book unlocks the door to the rich human history of the Adirondacks. Armed with it, the time traveler can look beyond spectacular lakes, rivers, and forests, and learn about the people who have lived in and passed through this region. The book will help you see the region with new eyes, and will train your vision in a way that uncovers connections, ties, and relations between past and present.

At the Adirondack Museum, we use historic artifacts, photographs, and works of art to explore the complex interaction between people and the land that has shaped the nature of work, recreation, community, and creative expression in the Adirondacks. Throughout the region, other large and small museums and historic sites preserve the distinctive stories and cultural heritage of their locales. Together these cultural institutions preserve and interpret the region's past.

With this book as a guide, you can discover this past for yourself. You can wander main roads and remote byways, and, in every corner of the region, you will meet its people and learn their history.

I would like to thank everyone who worked so hard to bring this project to completion, especially authors Betsy Folwell and Amy Godine, and editor Alice Gilborn.

Jacqueline Day

Jacqueline Day
Director

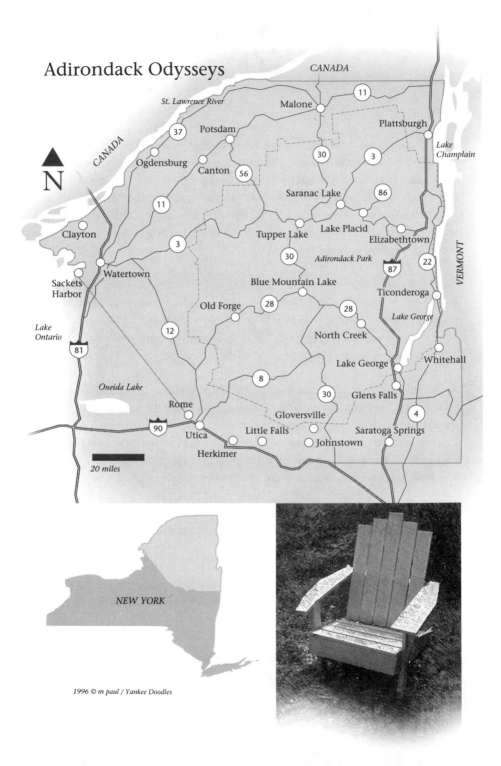

Adirondack Odysseys

CANADA

St. Lawrence River

Malone

11

Potsdam

Plattsburgh

37

Ogdensburg

Canton

56

30

3

Lake Champlain

N

CANADA

11

Saranac Lake

86

Clayton

3

Tupper Lake

Lake Placid

Elizabethtown

Watertown

30

Adirondack Park

87

22

VERMONT

Sackets Harbor

Blue Mountain Lake

Ticonderoga

Old Forge

28

28

Lake George

Lake Ontario

12

North Creek

81

Lake George

Whitehall

Oneida Lake

8

Glens Falls

Rome

30

4

90

Gloversville

Saratoga Springs

Utica

Little Falls

Johnstown

Herkimer

20 miles

NEW YORK

1996 © m paul / Yankee Doodles

INTRODUCTION

A few years ago, while crisscrossing New York's North Country in search of unique places to share with readers of *The Adirondack Book*, I became reacquainted with the state's fascinating political and social history. One spring morning I was led to the spot where, in 1609, Samuel de Champlain is reputed to have met a band of Iroquois and fired a shot that resonated for centuries. With his arquebus the chevalier killed several native men, and for years to come, the Iroquois hated the French and sided with the British. (Or so the story goes — the fact that Champlain was guided by Algonquin and Huron men may have had more to do with developing alliances and adversaries.)

Later, on a July afternoon, in the cool recesses of a stucco cottage, I learned the life story of an opera diva who was once the toast of the world, adored by composers, kings, and commoners; just beyond the shade of the tall pines, water skiers jumped the wakes of droning speedboats. Late on an autumn day, I followed an old railroad grade through a long-deserted iron-mining center, with a walking tour in hand that pointed out the overgrown foundations of a huge enterprise. The roar of industry had once echoed across the hillsides, but that day only chipmunks chattered from second-growth woods.

In *The Adirondack Book*, I could sketch those places — the King's Garden, at Fort Ticonderoga; the Marcella Sembrich Memorial Studio, in Bolton Landing; and the Penfield Homestead Museum, in Ironville — but space dictated that I couldn't divulge more than just the essential details. It seemed to me that by learning more of the story, people might come to appreciate these special places just as I had.

The more miles I traveled, the more I found historic sites that had distinct relationships to each other: forts that served as different stages of military campaigns, industrial enclaves that fit together to give a concrete picture of the region's nineteenth-century economic development. I envisioned short tours that could link these spots in intriguing ways and build a meaningful, in-depth look at a particular landscape and a particular slice of time.

Also, the more miles I traveled, the more I realized that locating all the historic spots north of the Mohawk Valley and south of the St. Lawrence River was an overwhelming undertaking that could take me so long that by the time I was finished I would only have to start over again, to bring the information up to date. I enlisted social historian and writer Amy Godine to serve as co-author, and the task became more manageable and timely. Better still, we could share ideas about how to make these jumbled patches of information into a well-pieced quilt.

History on the printed page is often inert, disconnected, undeniably someone else's story. But history viewed from the spot precisely where it happened can become something alive, relevant, and personal. Fun, even. The intent of this book is to encourage fellow explorers to make their own discoveries about our past, to participate in their own Adirondack odysseys.

Elizabeth Folwell

It's easy enough to write about what's in a museum. You just list the artifacts and name all the exhibits. Same thing with a historic site, a home, battlefield, fort. Thus and so fought here, lived here, sallied forth from here, and multiplied. It's the drab, meager, sternly uninflected stuff of roadside markers and brochures. It's not, we hope, what *Adirondack Odysseys* is about.

A list of museum holdings, an inventory of the sights, bears about as much relation to a good collection as do Cliff Notes to a novel. Even the humblest, most unassuming of museums or historic places is always more than the sum of its parts. It has a spirit, a personality, here earnest and pedagogical, almost schoolmarmish, there coy and playful, or lordly and remote. That's what stays with me when I think back on some historic site I loved: not any one artifact or caption tidbit but this coloring or spirit. The haunted serenity of Oriskany Battlefield when I found myself in the same weedy, sunstruck gully as the Palatine patriots when they were ambushed by the Mohawks and the British. The lonely funhouse weirdness of the maze-like Musical Museum. The fierce, forlorn pride of place of the small village historical museum with its hay rake and its class pictures of squinting, nameless schoolchildren from the long-gone one-room school.

With a few notable exceptions these are not museums that stitch together a usable regional portrait. Their job is to localize, make you believe that this town, fort, historic gristmill, is nothing like the town, fort, or gristmill down the road. They tell us, *this* is how we see we're special. In Fulton County, *we* made gloves, the most and finest in the land. In Plattsburgh, we licked the Brits, rolled cigars. We carved duck decoys in Clayton. Wove the sweetgrass Indian baskets your grandparents used to pick up for a song at Akwesasne. Played the cowgirl and hooked a husband at a summer dude ranch in Lake Luzerne.

What's thrilling is the moment when these discrete snapshots and images start to come together in the traveler's mind to map a social landscape of the world we call the North Country — when we see what links the Polish or Italian glove cutter in Gloversville to the Irish tanner in Griffin to the French-Canadian logger who stripped the hemlock bark that fed the tanning vats, and so on. Then local historic places become more than local. They gain a context. They're in the big picture.

Our pocket-size accounts of historic places, for reasons of space, have omitted much. Still, even when descriptions falter, we trust we've managed to invoke the spirit of a place, something of that quality that makes a visit resonate long after it's done. And if travelers find in our descriptions some hint of the wider historical context that holds these sites in one unifying, brilliant web, we'll know we did our job.

Amy Godine

THE WAY THIS BOOK WORKS

A*dirondack Odysseys: Exploring Museums and Historic Places from the Mohawk to the St. Lawrence* covers the area roughly bounded by the Mohawk Valley to the south, Lake Champlain and New York's state line to the east, the St. Lawrence River to the north, and an imaginary line extending from Sackets Harbor to Rome on the west. Within that huge territory — bigger than the states of Vermont and Massachusetts combined — there are a hundred or more historic sites and museums, ranging from Victorian mansions to humble homesteads, impregnable fortresses to tumbledown ruins. You'll find scores of them described herein, in individual sections with pertinent information — address, hours, admission price, phone number — right up front.

Chapters are organized primarily along chronological lines, with political and social themes. For example, Chapter One, "The First People," gives an overview of native American sites and collections in the region, and Chapter Two, "Wars in the Woods," covers eighteenth- and early nineteenth-century sites, right up to the War of 1812. Places that are near each other — chronologically and geographically — are generally close to each other in the text, although that doesn't work out perfectly in every case. Chapters One through Seven open with an introduction and a map, which shows the towns where museums and historic sites are located. Numbers on the map correspond to sites named in the key. Next are listings that describe sites in some detail, including whether we think children may find the place interesting and how many hours you might expect to spend during a leisurely look around. You'll also find information about special events that make history really come alive, and in the section headed "Exploring Further," interesting nearby places to visit — including even more museums mentioned in brief — as well as books that give important background.

In Chapter Eight, you'll find a section covering permanent exhibits at the Adirondack Museum and where to find specific sites, like the blast furnace of the MacIntyre Mine, that are described in permanent exhibits. The last section includes a calendar of annual events plus lists of educational organizations, travel-information numbers, and "works in progress" — exhibit spaces that are just beginning or expanding. You'll also find our "best bets" — a highly subjective collection of our favorite spots for looking at art, enjoying a picnic, learning about colonial life. Finally, you'll see a master list of all the towns and historic sites so that, for example, if you were planning to visit Lake Placid, you'd know there are three museums in the village.

While we've made a good-faith effort to ferret out countless non-profit museum and historic sites, we know that we've missed a few. While researching this guide we discovered there's no single list that includes all the small museums and historic sites, even trying on a county-by-county basis. In the introduction this project is likened to a quilt, but perhaps an Oriental rug is a better analogy — in that no such tapestry is perfect. We appreciate your suggestions for places to include in future editions and information about sites in development.

What you won't find described in detail within these pages are strictly commercial establishments that — while they may imply or even state outright that the enterprise is a "museum" — don't have real collections and aren't actively involved in education and preservation. These places have different resources and exist for different purposes than historic sites, which have distinct responsibilities to their constituencies and communities.

ADIRONDACK ODYSSEYS

**Exploring Museums and Historic Places
From the Mohawk to the St. Lawrence**

CHAPTER ONE

The First People

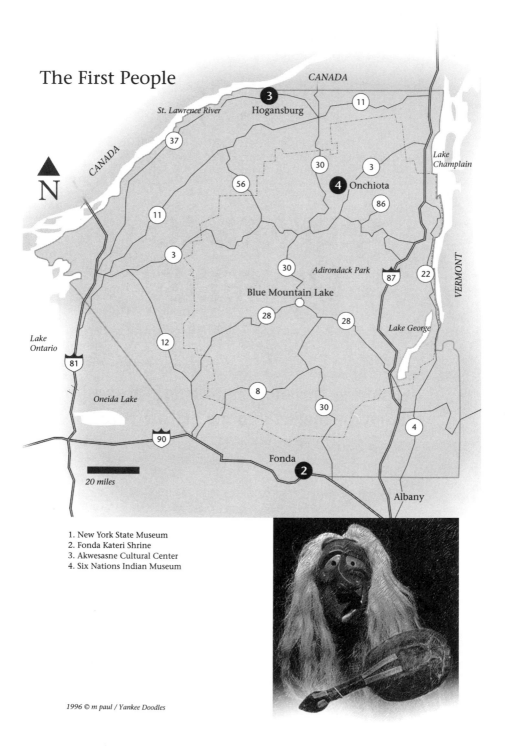

CANADA

St. Lawrence River

3 Hogansburg

11

37

CANADA

Lake Champlain

N

30

3

56

4 Onchiota

11

86

3

30

Adirondack Park

87

22

Blue Mountain Lake

VERMONT

Lake Ontario

28

28

Lake George

12

81

8

Oneida Lake

30

4

90

Fonda

2

20 miles

Albany

1. New York State Museum
2. Fonda Kateri Shrine
3. Akwesasne Cultural Center
4. Six Nations Indian Museum

1996 © m paul / Yankee Doodles

THE FIRST PEOPLE

■■

For a long time, generations of historians found it useful to describe the Adirondack region as a trackless wilderness, a land unsullied by the tread of moccasins and the smoke of campfires. And it is a fact that the evidence that might point to permanent, year-round American Indian encampments in the Adirondack region is virtually nil. But maybe in a culture that did not particularly value Western notions of permanence, property and land ownership are not the point. Maybe the better idea is to ascertain native presence here on its own terms — that is, in terms of seasonal and occasional usage. In these terms, native Americans, from the Ice Age hunters to the Iroquois, have made a home of upstate New York for some thirteen thousand years — a fact that should not surprise visitors to the North Country, where it seems every general museum, from the most professional and best endowed to the one-room corner in the basement of the town hall, boasts a harvest of arrowheads and other native artifacts gleaned from nearby fields.

Long before the seventeenth-century *coureurs de bois* of New France traversed the watery highways and thoroughfares of the North Country, Indian villages beaded an uneven necklace along the silted, temperate valleys of the St. Lawrence and Mohawk rivers and Lake Champlain. First to leave evidence of their stay were Paleo-Indians some eleven thousand years ago, whose large projectile spear points — so useful for hunting big game — would be greatly modified over the millennia as the climate warmed, megafauna died out, and smaller, less densely hided animals grew more prolific. The longest period of human development in the New World was the

Treaty with the Iroquois, 1750s. From *A Pictorial History of the New World*, 1870

seven-thousand-year-long Archaic period, the age that gave rise to the bark longhouse and stone technology. The period between the start of the Modern Era (1 AD) and the first contact with Europeans was the Woodland period. In this time, native Americans developed pottery; moved from spears to fleet, portable bow and arrow; and embraced agriculture — a development that helped centralize once far-ranging populations and to stabilize tribal identity and turf.

By the arrival of the Europeans, North Country tribal spheres of influence were well established. To the south along the Mohawk River were the Iroquois, who around 1570 were populous and organized enough to form a confederation, and one of those nations, the Mohawks, would emerge on European maps as the chief overseers of Adirondack lands. To the north and on both sides of Lake Champlain roamed the traditional enemies of the Iroquois, the Algonquin group known as the Western Abenaki, the westernmost extension of the Abenaki nation of northern Vermont, New Hampshire, and southern Maine. One of the Iroquois nations, the Oneidas, used a relatively small part of the Adirondack territory in the southwest, around what is now Utica and Rome. Beside the Mohawks and Oneidas, the Six Nations of the Iroquois included Senecas, Onondagas, Cayugas, and, last to be absorbed, the Tuscaroras.

The impact of the European discovery of upstate New York on native life is immeasurable. Indians knew how to get Dutch, French, and English traders exactly what they wanted — the prized beaver pelts that grew dense and glossy in the long, cold Adirondack winters — and the Europeans, in turn, introduced them to woven fabrics, steel knives, trade axes, metal kettles, glass beads, and, after 1640, firearms. As the available store of furs radically diminished and competition stepped up between traders from warring European nations, Indian tribes were compelled to ally themselves with one side or another, to lead raiding parties and serve as scouts. Tribal warriors took up arms for colonial powers at Fort William Henry, Fort Edward, Schuylerville, and Oriskany, to name a few. Inevitably, of course, this drew them into conflict with each other, and the incidence of intertribal skirmishes increased.

The Abenaki, for example, sided with the French; the Iroquois, and the Mohawks in particular, with the English — thanks, in no small part, to the brilliant and respectful negotiations of the crown's Superintendent of Indian Affairs, Sir William Johnson, who himself was adopted into a Mohawk clan and cohabited with the granddaughter of a Mohawk sachem. But if this was good news for the Tories, it was bad news for the Mohawks, when at the conclusion of the American Revolution they were driven north or west from the ancestral valley domain and eventually assigned to reservations straddling the Canadian border only fractionally as big as their original domain.

An Abenaki family weaving and selling baskets in Old Forge, circa 1920. Courtesy of the Adirondack Museum, Blue Mountain Lake

Yet while disease, dispersion, and the ravages of war did much to deplete the Adirondack region of its native American sojourners, Indians continued to drift into the area for seasonal employment. In the early nineteenth century, Adirondack Indians led white American speculators to hidden iron deposits and served as backwoods guides. All-Indian crews were represented in logging camps, tanneries, and road and rail work. Many Mohawk families in the St. Regis Akwesasne Reservation farmed. And as tourism and recreation overtook conventional extractive industries as a mainstay of the Adirondack economy, native American artisans and entrepreneurs swiftly secured a niche with Indian encampments in town parks and roadside crafts stands from Saratoga Springs to Plattsburgh.

A recent surge of general interest in the native American role in Adirondack history has led some historical societies and museums to develop special programs and exhibits. But most collections have still to catch up or even recognize the richness of this heritage. Neatly organized cases of projectile points tell us more about the zeal and commitment of the collector/donor than they do about the cultures that used these ancient tools. Happily, however, there are notable exceptions to the more parochial displays — ambitious, lovingly curated exhibits like the ones at the New York State Museum or the Akwesasne Cultural Center or the Kateri Shrine, in Fonda, that go far to flesh out the ancient story and in so doing leave a far deeper impression on us than the usual cotton-lined trophy case full of arrowheads or beads.

NEW YORK STATE MUSEUM
Cultural Education Center
Empire State Plaza
Albany NY 12230
Open: Daily 10am–5pm (closed Thanksgiving, Christmas, New Year's Day)
Admission: Suggested donation $2 adults, $5 family
518-474-5877

The gleaming heart of a seemingly impenetrable knot of exit lanes and overpasses in downtown Albany is the Empire State Plaza, home to the New York State Archives, the state library, and on the first floor, the oldest and largest state museum in the nation. Why include a page on a museum so far afield of the North Country? Two reasons — two exhibits: "Native Peoples of New York State" and "Adirondack Wilderness." Neither presumes to be comprehensive, but each offers an ambitious and dramatic introduction to its material that beats much of the competition farther north. And, with lots of splashy, blown-up images, atmospheric lighting, piped-in loggers' songs, and a minimal script, these exhibits create a mood and feel for the North Woods tailor-made for the traveler about to embark on a first Adirondack tour.

The more engaging and child friendly of the two is the smaller native American display toward the back of the museum rooms, just past "Birds of

New York." At the first diorama of the giant mastodon and fuzzy calf, turn right and keep walking. Children like these life-size, exquisitely detailed tableaux because there always seems to be a kid in them, and a mangy family dog. Additionally, they have recognizable backgrounds, like the Hudson and Mohawk river valleys, and two-tier captions pitched to two levels of interest: big and simple for those who just want the facts, and fine-print details for the pundits.

In "New York's First People: Ice Age Hunters" a thirteen-thousand-year-old family sitting around chipping flints and skinning caribou is interrupted by an excitable young man in skins who's just sighted a herd of distant game. In "The Growing Field" a wiry boy perched on a platform looks out for unwelcome blackbirds while family women harvest the "three sisters," corn, beans, and squash. The nursing baby is especially fascinating to younger viewers. Overheard on a recent visit: "There's that mommy holding the baby! Dis*gusting!*" "That's not disgusting, honey, that's what mommies *do.*" "Diz-GUST-ing!"

Reconstruction of an Iroquois longhouse, part of the permanent exhibits at the New York State Museum, Albany. Courtesy of the New York State Museum, Albany

But the pride and joy of the Native Peoples section, the part local kids return to with the faithfulness of Holden Caulfield's pilgrimages to the Museum of Natural History, is the model Iroquois longhouse. At first it just looks like sort of an upside-down empty hull with a lot of bunks and some scratchy mats to lie on. Then you get in deeper where it's all dark and there's a life-size diorama behind Plexiglas, and suddenly it's like the coolest clubhouse in the world, with all this stuff: bows and arrows hanging on poles, braided corn, a family with a dog sitting around a fake bed of coals that actually glows, and it's so mysterious and cozy you could hang out here all day.

The Iroquois longhouse accommodated as many as twenty families. Each tended its own cook fire; smoke drifted up through the bark roof. In the tribe's cosmology, a longhouse was more than a home, it was the ruling metaphor for unity and cooperation among the Six Nations — who even called themselves People of the Longhouse. At the western door of this symbolic longhouse stood the Seneca; at the east, the fearsome Mohawk; in the middle, guarding the fire, the Onondaga.

Political organization among the tribes was highly sophisticated, and you can admire those organizing skills at work in the other popular diorama — as tiny and meticulous as the longhouse is huge — of a seventeenth-century Mohawk village at Caughnawaga (see Kateri shrine, page 7). Here, Mohawks the size of bees clamber over the bowed roofs of longhouses in the making. Timber is felled with small, controlled fires (actually splashes of bright paint), glowing at the base of trees. Every ten or twenty years, when surrounding cropland was depleted, Mohawks pushed on to fresher fields elsewhere. The diorama plainly shows that these moves were as planned and well rehearsed as any Amish barn-raising two hundred years anon.

Notwithstanding the vagaries of the layout and an undernourished script, the second permanent exhibit, "The Adirondacks," has much to recommend it, starting with the incredibly high ceilings that allow for humongous photographs and artifacts as big as the 1930s plane used for spotting forest fires. The scale of this material impresses the visitor with a sense of the range and wilderness of the Adirondack Park as no mingy eight-by-ten print ever could. Here's a wall-size poster of a pile of logs that dwarfs the clapboard house beside it, a model of a tower used by state surveyor Verplanck Colvin, and a full-size installation of a fishing camp, complete with guide, guideboat, creel, pack basket, and a lounging sport. Particularly popular is a resolutely unpicturesque diorama of an iron-mining town, back when it took an acre of hardwood a day to feed a blast furnace, and the decimated, stumpy landscape was blanketed by smoke and dust.

Even if all the jigsaw pieces don't add up to a completely cohesive, easy-to-follow Adirondack history, they do showcase key North Country moments with a lot of flair. Folk songs of lumberjacks serenade your look at a typical loggers' bunkhouse. A full-scale logjam with river drivers treading precariously on tossing timbers seems to surge right at you. And there's a persuasive, if cursory, explanation of how a preservationist philosophy evolved in response to the catastrophic depletion of Adirondack forests and wildlife, something any visitor needs to know to understand the rationale behind the creation of the Adirondack Forest Preserve and, later, the Adirondack Park.

If You Go: Before your start, get clear directions on how to get there and where to park, or else, like Charlie on the MTA, you might find yourself eternally circling city cloverleafs. An hour and a half will do the two exhibits justice. The third permanent exhibit, "New York Metropolis," and the hands-on "Discovery Place" for kids, will add another hour to your stay. The state museum is very accessible for the mobility impaired.

Special Events: Events are keyed to changing exhibits; for instance, in fall 1996 the special show was "Backyard Monsters" — bugs. In October 1997 the famous Cohoes mastodon, unearthed in 1866, comes home to the museum, buffed and refurbished from trunk to tail.

Exploring Further: In 1995 Governor George Pataki gave the state museum funds to begin collecting contemporary Iroquois crafts from around New York. These fine works are displayed in changing exhibits near the Native Peoples entrance and show how traditions remain relevant in modern times. For other native American collections, visit the three other sites listed in this chapter. The Adirondack Museum (page 183) is the logical next — and far more informative — step for a big picture of the Adirondack Park.

FONDA KATERI SHRINE
Route 5
Fonda NY 12068
PO Box 627, Fonda
Open: Daily May 1–Nov. 1, 9am–4pm
Admission: Donation
518-853-3646

The Kateri shrine commemorates the site of a one-time Mohawk village and home (for eleven years, anyway) of a seventeenth-century native American woman, Kateri Tekakwitha. In 1676 the twenty-year-old Kateri, whose Mohawk and Algonquin parents had died in a smallpox epidemic, was converted to Catholicism by Franciscan missionaries. Persecuted for her new faith by fellow Mohawks, she fled to another, friendlier Mohawk settlement in Canada, where she took a vow of perpetual virginity. The story goes that upon her death in 1680 at the age of twenty-four, the smallpox scars vanished from her face. Three hundred years later, Kateri was blessed (not a saint, but close) by Pope John Paul II and named patroness of peace and ecology.

Others besides religious pilgrims may find things of interest in this Catholic shine. On the hill behind the two-hundred-year-old barn that houses a museum and a chapel, visitors can discern the excavated outlines of the twelve longhouses and stockade that once made up the Mohawk village of Caughnawaga — an easy, pleasant hike. And with its emphasis squarely on

American Indian history and culture, its vintage photographs and clear displays of Paleo-Indian tools, clay pipes, and pottery, the museum is a happily informative surprise.

Above the museum, frontier artifacts like pelts and snowshoes, and a mural depicting key moments from Kateri's life, adorn a woodsy, timbered chapel. And do poke your head into "Kateri's Castle," a tiny building near the entrance that houses a push-button light-up diorama in which facsimiles of wigwams look like nothing so much as plump, orderly cocoons.

If You Go: Thirty minutes to an hour should be ample time to see the museum and visit the Mohawk village, which is believed to be the only completely excavated Iroquois site in the country. Children are welcome, of course; you might want to visit when something special, like the blessing of the animals, is going on. The site is handicap accessible; you can drive to the excavation as well as walk.

Special Events: The shrine also serves as headquarters for numerous Catholic and Mohawk-related festivals, healing liturgies, and conferences, such as the Iroquois Planting Day, in May; Indian Weekend, in July; the blessing of the animals, in October; and the Iroquois Fallen Leaves Service, in late October.

Exploring Further: The Auriesville Shrine of North American Martyrs (518-853-3033) is just three miles away; it's near the Mohawk village known as Ossernenon and marks where three Jesuit missionaries, including Isaac Jogues, the discoverer of Lake George, were slain. In Liverpool, the re-created mission Sainte Marie among the Iroquois (315-453-6767) is a living-history center with costumed interpreters presenting a glimpse of seventeenth-century life for Europeans and Iroquois.

The biography *Lily of the Mohawks* (Bantam Books, 1984) by Jack Casey introduces Kateri to young readers.

AKWESASNE CULTURAL CENTER
Route 37
Hogansburg NY 13655
Open: Mon.–Thurs. 8:30am–4:30pm, Fri. 8am–4pm, Sat. 11am–3pm
Admission: $2 adults; $1 6–16; under 5 or native American, free
518-358-2240/2461

Straddling the Canadian border at Hogansburg, right on Route 37 in the St. Regis Mohawk reservation, is the Akwesasne Cultural Center, home to a library on the first floor and a fine small museum below. The St. Lawrence River valley was a meeting place for indigenous tribes of the Northeast long before the arrival of the Europeans, but it was the Mohawks' allegiance to the British during the Revolutionary War that forced their eventual exile to the northern reaches of their former kingdom. In a few wide rooms is a large, engaging collection — not just the obligatory arrowheads, but well-captioned artifacts and photographs that bring this two-hundred-year-old community to vivid life.

At the start of the exhibit is a brilliant display of Mohawk-style head-dresses, nothing like the familiar cascading feathered bonnets of the Plains. Finely carved "revelation canes" show covert intelligence of military advances and retreats during the colonial era. And a vast display of Mohawk basket-work reveals a stunning range of technique, style, material, and usage: here are baskets for trapping fish, bearing grain, and luring tourists, baskets that look like pineapples, urns, wedding cakes, and pillows. Note especially the handiwork of basket weavers Mary Adams and Margaret Torrance, masters of their craft.

The traditional Mohawk game lacrosse also gets a lot of play here, with a glassed-in lacrosse diorama, and a display of different gear and sticks. There's a small model of a bark-walled longhouse in the Iroquois style (a favorite with children), a case of the fine silverwork that evolved as a Mohawk craft after contact with the Europeans, an array of the painted cradleboards on whose reliable stiff backs Mohawk infants spent their first seasons, and a display of "snow snakes," long, polished maple poles with sharp points that Mohawk athletes hurled along a track in the snow to see how far they could make them glide. A side room celebrates the bicentennial of the Treaty of Canandaigua with photographs, poetry, and art.

Best of all is the extensive collection of captioned photographs on reservation life before the Depression and after the transition from a migratory culture to farming. These pictures will come as a mild shock to anyone whose image of American Indian culture is informed by the Wild West imagery of Hollywood. Here's a well-kept, prospering, wholly familiar North Country farm town. Gingerbread trim brightens Mohawk farmhouses. Fringed surreys bear Mohawk women in stylish hats. A Mohawk farm boy in a slouch cap lofts his new brother in a cradleboard, and another boy nuzzles the same-age colt he was given on his birthday to grow up with and learn to tend. The visit of Governor Franklin Delano Roosevelt to the reservation in 1930 is proudly documented, too. Affectionate and informed captions alert us to subtleties we might otherwise miss, like the movement of Mohawk men from side places in the photographs to the center, signaling a changing familial role.

If You Go: Allow a half hour or more. The museum is accessible.

Special Events: Ask about music, dance, and storytelling programs sponsored by the Native American Traveling College, which is based at Akwesasne.

Over Labor Day weekend, there's a pow-wow on Cook Road in Hogansburg, with dancing, music, crafts, traditional foods, and games.

Exploring Further: For literature about the Mohawks, try the library upstairs. For handicrafts, the museum has a gift shop, and there are shops selling Mohawk wares on Route 37, too. Many town and county historical societies contain some native artifacts, but another site that explores Iroquois culture from a native perspective is the Six Nations Museum, about an hour's drive away (described next).

SIX NATIONS INDIAN MUSEUM
County Route 30
Onchiota NY 12968
Open: July 1–Labor Day, Tues.–Sun. 10am–6pm
Admission: $2 adults, $1 children
518-891-0769

This roadside museum consists of several rooms dazzlingly packed with Iroquois artifacts on the walls, in glass cases, and hanging from the ceiling. Even the floor is painted with Indian symbols. There are fine historic pieces, such as intricate bead-work belts and tiny birch-bark baskets embroidered with moose hair, next to modern reproductions. Story belts describing events and legends line the walls, as do numerous illustrated posters explaining American political history from a native point of view. One display explains different arrows, how they were made, and why they were used for particular purposes. For some artifacts, the labels are quite informative, while others are sketchy. In corners and high on the walls, dim light sometimes makes it hard to know what you're looking at.

The initial effect can be overwhelming, especially if you're one to tour a place by the numbers; there are so many objects to see that all compete for your attention. The key to getting the most out of Six Nations is to ask questions of John Kahionhes Fadden, whose father, Ray, began the museum in 1954. John may launch into a legend or draw an evocative sketch to explain an object, a custom, or a traditional skill. He'll also explain how and why this place presents its material from a holistic native American point of view rather than a static, institutional, European approach.

If You Go: Six Nations Museum can be hard to find; follow the signs for New York State's Buck Pond Campsite from Route 30 in Gabriels, and you'll reach the museum before the campsite entrance. It's a one-story brown building. Park on the shoulder of the road. Allow about an hour for a visit. Children are welcome here and will probably get into the spirit of the place, discovering artifacts that have special appeal. The building is accessible, but displays outdoors might be difficult to reach over the dirt paths.

Exploring Further: Although the native American presence in the Adirondacks dates back thousands of years, there's little material on display in the park's major museums; many historical societies described in these pages contain displays of artifacts found locally. At Hogansburg, in the Mohawk Reservation on the St. Lawrence River, the Akwesasne Library and Cultural Center (the preceding section) showcases fine contemporary and historic crafts, and offers occasional performances and programs. The New York State Museum in Albany (page 4) has an extensive permanent exhibit dedicated to the Six Nations and other tribes. The Iroquois Museum in Howes Cave (518-296-8949) is informative and recently renovated to high standards. At the New York State Historical Association, in Cooperstown (607-547-1400), the Thaw Collection contains exceptional Indian artifacts from around the country.

In 1988 the Clinton County Historical Society, in Plattsburgh, put together an excellent temporary exhibit on the subject; the catalog *The Original People: Native Americans in the Champlain Valley* is still available from a few Adirondack booksellers and at regional libraries. For American Indian tales, read *Iroquois Stories: Heroes and Heroines, Monsters and Magic* (Crossing Press, 1985) by Joseph Bruchac, and *Go Seek the Pow-Wow on the Mountain and Other Indian Stories of the Sacandaga Valley* (Greenfield Review Press, 1993) by Don Bowman.

CHAPTER TWO

Wars in the Woods

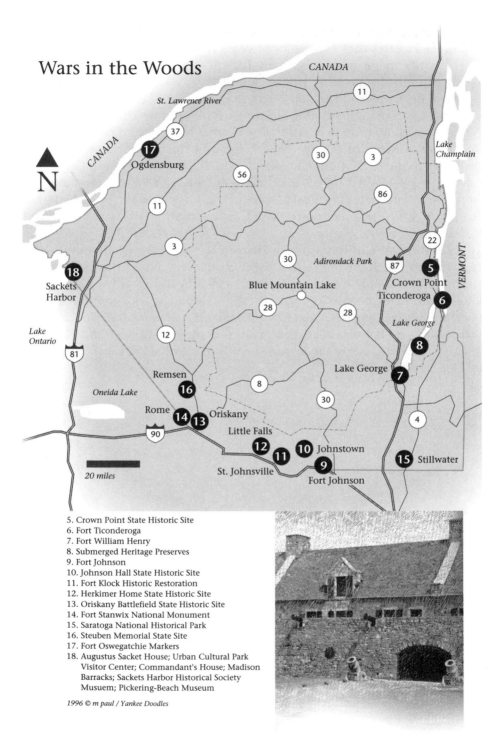

CANADA

St. Lawrence River

CANADA

N

Ogdensburg

Lake Champlain

VERMONT

Sackets Harbor

Lake Ontario

Adirondack Park

Blue Mountain Lake

Crown Point
Ticonderoga

Lake George

Remsen

Oneida Lake

Rome   Oriskany

Little Falls

St. Johnsville

Lake George

Johnstown

Fort Johnson

Stillwater

20 miles

5. Crown Point State Historic Site
6. Fort Ticonderoga
7. Fort William Henry
8. Submerged Heritage Preserves
9. Fort Johnson
10. Johnson Hall State Historic Site
11. Fort Klock Historic Restoration
12. Herkimer Home State Historic Site
13. Oriskany Battlefield State Historic Site
14. Fort Stanwix National Monument
15. Saratoga National Historical Park
16. Steuben Memorial State Site
17. Fort Oswegatchie Markers
18. Augustus Sacket House; Urban Cultural Park
    Visitor Center; Commandant's House; Madison
    Barracks; Sackets Harbor Historical Society
    Musuem; Pickering-Beach Museum

1996 © m paul / Yankee Doodles

WARS IN THE WOODS

■■

I t is impossible to read a history of the Adirondack region without bump-
ing into the cautionary tale of explorer Samuel de Champlain's failed
encounter with a small party of Iroquois in 1609. Wending south on the
great tapered lake that would someday bear his name, the French navigator
came ashore on a broad plain and encountered a group of unfamiliar Indians whose territory this evidently was. Possibly urged on by his anxious
Huron guides, Champlain let fly with his muskets, killing several Iroquois,
dispersing the rest, and managing to earn for New France the enmity of
the powerful Iroquois nation for the next century and more.

Would that the tangled history of the conflict between New France and
the British Empire was so tidily encapsulated, but it seems that the power
struggles that play out on the overlapping fringes of expanding empires are
rarely simple or short-lived. If this thumbnail sketch of the military history
of the North Country from 1609 to the resolution of the War of 1812 inevitably short-shrifts the complexity and drama of that battle-riven age, at the
very least it can alert the visitor to the larger context in which the many
sites and museums of the region should be understood.

The seed of the feud was a dispute between the French and English over
domination of the fur trade. So aggressive was this competition that the
Northeast region had "run out" of beaver as early as 1650. Inevitably, Europeans on either side sought the assistance and allegiance of American Indians from different tribes. To the French went the loyalty of the northernmost
tribes, the Hurons and Algonquins; to the English, thanks to already-in-place
alliances of the Dutch trappers and traders who preceded them and from

Champlain and the Iroquois near Fort Ticonderoga, July 30, 1609.
From *Fort Ticonderoga: A Short History*, 1946

whom they won New Netherlands in 1664, went the allegiance of the Iroquois Five Nations: the Onondagas, Oneidas, Cayugas, Senecas, and Mohawks. (Not until the 1720s was the sixth nation, the Tuscarora, admitted to the Iroquois Confederacy.)

For seven tedious years in the last decade of the seventeenth century combatants on either side, aided by their Indian proxies, raided each other's North Country forts and settlements with no gain in military advantage. The winds of Queen Anne's War didn't reach New York from Europe until 1709, some seven years after it began, and even then, its local influence was only incidentally felt. The 1713 Treaty of Utrecht was supposed to fix the borders between the competing empires once and for all, but no paper treaty could convince France, proud claimant to rights of discovery to the region, that it shouldn't build Fort St. Frederic on the promontory the English called Crown Point, or mustn't garrison French regiments that could and did swoop down on British settlements at Old Saratoga (Schuylerville today) and Schenectady. Bluntly, each side saw the other as a conniving, opportunistic aggressor, and each side was probably right.

If England did little for some decades to combat the French breach of the treaty, it had good cause. Busy fending off the Spanish, French, and their sundry allies back in Europe, the mother country had troubles of its own. Resources to wage an all-out war on the Adirondack frontier were hard to come by. When William Pitt came to power in the 1750s, however, things changed. Unhappily for the French, the British war minister was of the opinion that the American colonies were not only worth defending, but must be defended with all the resources Britain had in its power to command. The prize between the pincer tips of the rival powers was control of that strategic thoroughfare, Lake Champlain, and, now that the fur was depleted, the workable farmland and endless timber on either side. After a Pitt-directed blockade of French ports that made it impossible for France to provide Canada with supplies and reinforcements, Canada went on the defensive. Pitt also dispatched thousands of regulars to the colonies with an eye toward recapturing all French-controlled forts in the North Country, Fort St. Frederic, at Crown Point, and Fort Carillon, at Ticonderoga, among them.

Most of these campaigns, like Jeffery Amherst's siege and capture of Louisbourg, were resoundingly successful. One stunning failure that any visitor to the Champlain Valley ought to know about, however, was Commander James Abercrombie's ill-conceived and bootless effort to take the French stronghold at Ticonderoga from the Marquis de Montcalm and his four thousand men. Safely entrenched behind their breastworks and sharpened abatis, the French troops, who were outnumbered four to one, managed to stave off wave after wave of hapless Highlanders and other regulars until Abercrombie finally ordered a retreat. A few years earlier Montcalm had captured Fort William Henry and, before that, had razed the English fort at Oswego. But in 1759, when the British general Amherst steamrolled north with a army of eleven thousand, the frustrated Montcalm, too long denied badly needed reinforcements, withdrew his troops to Canada. That same year James Wolfe breached French defenses at Quebec, and an English and American army routed the French on the Plains of Abraham. By 1760, all that stood for the domain of New France was the city of Montreal, and that beleaguered holdout surrendered that same year. The changing of the Canadian guard from French to English hands was now essentially complete.

What did this portend for New York's North Country? The French and Indian War had exposed thousands of soldier-adventurers, many Scots and Scotch-Irish among them, to the Champlain and Hudson river valleys, and when the Crown offered land grants to veterans with an itch to settle, hundreds of them did indeed. The empire of veteran Philip Skene began in this fashion, and Skene's contemporary and fellow land baron William Gilliland was a veteran of the French and Indian War as well. The same war also introduced American militias and British regulars to unorthodox native American styles of guerrilla warfare — small, mobile, lightly armed units who moved single file through the woods and delivered not formal European-style synchronized volleys, but carefully aimed fire.

One legendary American guerrilla fighter was Robert Rogers, an irascible New Hampshire man and son of Scotch-Irish immigrants from Ulster. Rogers' Rangers, as his hand-trained units were called, scorned the lobster-red British uniforms for camouflage gear, and sometimes snowshoed and even skated their way into enemy fire, pressing as far north as Abenaki strongholds in Canada. Later, during the War of Independence, veteran Rangers who had trained under Rogers fought gallantly at Bunker Hill and Bennington. (Rogers himself, who cast his lot with the Loyalists, spent his last days in boozy penury in and out of debtors' prisons here and abroad.)

The War of Independence, which really began in 1765 in the first phases of colonial rebellion, populated the old Adirondack forts and historic sites of the French and Indian War with a whole new cast of ghosts: Tories, Patriots, and their native American proxies on either side. A few names overlap, of course. Although the ubiquitous French and Indian War veteran William Johnson died before the outbreak of American resistance, his self-exiled son John Johnson led raids from Canada on patriot settlements in the Mohawk Valley. The fabled Adirondack land barons Skene and Gilliland lost their fledgling empires to the American government after the Revolution, even though Gilliland, unlike Skene, was not a Loyalist. And in some Tory-ridden domains of upstate New York, like modern-day Saratoga and Washington counties, neighbor took up arms against neighbor, and skirmishes raged well after the war was resolved.

In 1775 Ethan Allen and Benedict Arnold put Ticonderoga on the map again when they stormed and took the famous fort "in the name of the Continental Congress and the Great God Jehovah." That same year, Bostonian bookseller-turned-soldier Henry Knox dragged captured artillery from Fort Ti and Crown Point 300 miles east to Boston in the dead of winter, which ordnance George Washington used to scare the British right out of the city. Ticonderoga was also a point of retreat for a badly demoralized, starved, and disorderly American army on its way south from a failed attempt to storm Quebec. Also hoping to move south on Lake Champlain was the British Navy, which Benedict Arnold attempted valiantly to cut off at Valcour Island. The Americans lost that battle, but unnerved the Royalist command sufficiently to delay the British advance for another season, just time enough for the Americans to muster an army to meet the British at Saratoga in the summer of 1777.

The British and Hessian army of General "Gentleman Johnny" Burgoyne had to slog through miles of tangled Adirondack wilderness before it found its weary way to Bemis Heights, south of present-day Saratoga Springs. Meanwhile, a patriot army under General Nicholas Herkimer stalled a British advance on Albany from the west at Oriskany in one of the most horrific battles of the war. All this continued to buy the patriots' needed time to build up troops and supplies, and when Americans won the Battle of Saratoga in October of 1777, British home support for the war plummeted at the same time that French respect for the Americans' resilience soared.

Perhaps the greatest impact the American Revolution had on the North Country, however, wasn't military but demographic. As long as the colonists perceived the Champlain and Hudson valleys as a war zone, settlement was slow. But when the war concluded, and the stone-broke American government offered compensation to veterans through grants of wilderness land, the rush was on. Yankees poured across Lake Champlain to stake out homesteads along the lakefront and the fertile watersheds within.

Indeed, so many New Englanders thronged the upstate wilderness in the latter part of the eighteenth century, there was talk of renaming it New Vermont. Town after Adirondack town was founded by these restless, land-hungry, eminently practical pioneers. They farmed, built mills and small, waterpowered factories, speculated avidly in land, and, if they lived close enough to the Canadian border, smuggled. They also moved back and forth across the border to the extent that by 1812, some 80 percent of the people of Upper Canada were American born.

Many factors informed the American decision to wage war on Britain in the War of 1812, but no reason was good enough to persuade most upstate New Yorkers that "Mr. Madison's War" was worth fighting or supporting. It wasn't just that the United States, without a regular army, with an aging and undependable army leadership, and with inconstant popular support at best, was unprepared. The Canadians were the New Yorkers' neighbors, after all. True, the provocation was not imagined. In an effort to stem the United States' free trade with its French enemy, Britain had seized more than 500 American vessels between 1803 and 1807, to which Congress, under Jefferson, had responded with an embargo. But more than a defensive war was not a happy prospect in a region as trade- and smuggling-dependent as upstate New York. In the end, it took direct British assaults on American homesteads and farm towns to mobilize the militia of the St. Lawrence and Champlain valleys — and in *this* war, as distinct from battles previous, the armies of the North Country met on water.

At Plattsburgh, American naval commander Thomas MacDonough, assisted by the motley army of Alexander Macomb, decimated the British flotilla. Shipyards at Sackets Harbor on Lake Ontario turned out light, fast-moving vessels to meet the British challenge; Sackets would remain a base of American naval operations well into this century. In the end, the war concluded with little change in the border, but on either side a heightened sense of nationalism and even paranoia was the outcome. Britain quit violating neutral rights. The U.S. gave up its ill-engendered plan to take over its northern neighbor. And in the fact that half a million Canadians had faced down almost eight million Americans, Canada could take rightful pride.

The sheer number of historic sites in the North Country beggars description. Add to this the fact that the same fort was often rebuilt, renamed, and re-used by opposing sides, and that some very big forts, like Crown Point, saw hardly any action, while some comparatively small ones — Fort Schuyler or Fort Ann, for instance — were the scenes of momentous raids, and the picture grows still more confused. Count on the Urban Cultural Park exhibits in Whitehall and Sackets Harbor for some of the best-written, most engaging accounts of various raids and battles, and never hesitate to ask a guide at any site to help you sort things out.

It's a foregone conclusion that *every* museum or historical society frames its hometown battle as *the* key military turning point of a larger war — and why not? The truth is, the turning points were legion. You couldn't have the American victory at Saratoga without the earlier Battle of Valcour in Lake Champlain. And without the patriots' rise to power and the dispersion of the Tories north to Canada, you wouldn't have the stand-off at Oriskany or the vengeful Tory raids that put German Palatine and patriot settlements in the Mohawk Valley to the torch even *after* the War of Independence.

The chain is there. The trick is recognizing all the links, and getting them squared away in your mind's eye in the right order. You'll come out reeling, but the connection to the sites you tour will be that much more powerfully felt for knowing their wider context, and why they mattered, and why they matter still.

This chapter begins with the earliest site, Crown Point, and proceeds in rough chronological order — which means we jump from the eastern Adirondacks to the Mohawk River to pick up the story of Sir William Johnson, then return east for the Battle of Saratoga, and finally head north for the War of 1812. Note that town and county museums described in chapters Five and Six also contain significant military history exhibits.

CROWN POINT STATE HISTORIC SITE
Off Routes 9N and 22 at Champlain Bridge
Crown Point NY 12928
Mail: RD 1, Box 219, Crown Point
Open: Visitor Center open third Sat. in May–last Sat. in Oct., Weds.–Sun.;
    grounds open daily 9:30am–one hour before sunset; remainder of year
    grounds open Mon.–Fri. 8am–4:30pm
Admission: $4 per passenger vehicle; group visits need two weeks' advance
    notice
518-597-3666

In 1731, the French picked *Pointe à la Chevelure* (Crown Point) for a strategic spot to place an occupying force in the New World because of its commanding view up and down Lake Champlain. Three years later, construction began on Fort St. Frederic, a massive four-story-high octagonal chateau designed by the leading military architects of the day. The fort had walls some twelve feet thick and cannons on every floor. Garrisoned by a hundred officers and nearly a thousand enlisted men, the post was used as a base for raiding parties aimed at British settlements to the south; troops from Fort St. Frederic burned old Saratoga (now Schuylerville) in 1745, and ranged as far as Deerfield, Massachusetts, and Charlestown, New Hampshire, to butcher civilians and soldiers alike. Beyond military activity, the fort was a true outpost of French culture in the Champlain Valley for about twenty-five years, supporting artisans such as blacksmiths, carpenters, farmers, stonemasons, and their families, and functioning as an Indian trading post. Today a white flag waves above the grass-covered remains of Fort St. Frederic.

The windswept ruins of Crown Point barracks. B. Folwell

Because of Crown Point's prime location, the British also coveted the site and repeatedly attacked from the water, beginning in 1755. In 1759, the French abandoned the fort and exploded the redoubt before an overwhelming force of twelve thousand colonial and British troops could get there. While the French beat a retreat to Montreal, the British immediately set about building their own better, bigger fort, just west of St. Frederic's ruins.

His Majesty's Fort of Crown Point was the largest British stronghold ever created in the colonies: three thousand men worked three years to build trenches, barracks, blockhouses, and roads. Within the redoubt, walls encircled more than eight acres; the entire complex carved almost four square miles from the surrounding wilderness. The officers lived in comfortable stone barracks, the walls of which still stand. Conditions for the ordinary soldiers were rather different, according to Lord Jeffery Amherst's papers: "[Sick Provincial carpenters] will not Voluntarily Stir out of their Hutts, but live in dirt & Nastiness which they are vastly careful never to wash off from them, that & fryed Pork would kill off half of the Provincial troops if they are not forced to be cleanly." The British flag still flies over the ruins of that fort.

Surprisingly, Crown Point did not play a major role in the American Revolution. In 1773 a chimney fire close to stored ammunition blew much of the complex to smithereens and little was rebuilt; only a small force of redcoats stayed on to protect the remnants. In a daring maneuver, patriots captured the well-armed British garrison and gained cannons and heavy weapons for their cause, and in 1776 Crown Point served as a much-needed resting point for exhausted American troops returning from the disastrous attempt to conquer Quebec. Within another year, though, the fort was once again in British control and remained so until the end of the war.

More than eighty years ago New York State was given the Crown Point ruins. It's clear that this deserted spot was a popular stop with nineteenth-century tourists; graffiti etched into the soft limestone outcrops in front of the walls records dozens of names in elegant script.

If You Go: To find Crown Point State Historic Site, follow the brown-and-white signs visible from Route 22. The park is on the access road to the bridge over Lake Champlain, about four miles east of Route 22.

Allow at least an hour and a half for a visit; choose a sunny day so that you can enjoy the lakeshore (launch a canoe here, even), and bring a picnic. Crown Point is a fine place to bring children of any age since there's plenty of room to roam. You can walk atop the rounded walls of the redoubt, high above the surrounding fields; imagine those manicured green lawns filled with soldiers' tents. Asphalt-paved paths make much of the outdoor site accessible (the interpretive building is completely accessible), although getting into the barrack ruins involves a couple of steps.

Do visit the interpretive building first, which was substantially redesigned in 1986. Exhibits depict the succession of armies occupying the location; comparisons are made between Fort St. Frederic and Louisbourg, in Nova Scotia. Don't miss the slide show; it presents a great deal of information in an entertaining way. The program is followed by a sound-and-light map display that outlines the routes that visitors should take in order to see the ruins in chronological order.

Special Events: In recent years, the site hosted eighteenth-century reenactments and demonstrations of skills, but state budget cutbacks have put these lively and informative programs on hold. Before you go you may wish to see if any living-history events have been rescheduled. The free *North Country Chronicle*, available in Champlain Valley towns and shops during the summer, lists events with eighteenth-century focus sponsored by museums in Quebec, Vermont, and New York.

Exploring Further: Fort Ticonderoga, just fifteen miles south, was originally built as a French fortification on Lake Champlain (see page 22).

Lake George is another logical stop in a French and Indian War tour. General Montcalm's troops left from Fort St. Frederic in 1757 to attack Fort

William Henry (page 24). A full-scale reconstruction of the fort is next to the Fort William Henry Motor Inn and open daily from May through October. It's more like a theme park than a museum; the bona fide historical materials take a back seat to musket smoke and cannon fire. Lake George Battlefield Park, at the southern end of town, across from the steel pier where the tour boats dock, was the site of a major battle. There's little interpretation of the various statues and barely visible ruins, but in the state campground, which connects with the park, you can see the remnants of old Fort George.

A self-guided driving-and-walking tour, "Colonial Wars of Lake George," explains and maps events of the French and Indian War and the American Revolution. Recently published by Bateaux Below (see page 27), it's an excellent introduction to the southern basin of the lake. Stop by the Lake George Chamber of Commerce office, Canada St. (518-668-5755), for a copy. Scholarly papers of a statewide archaeological conference have been collected in *Military Sites of the Hudson River, Lake George and Lake Champlain Corridor*, edited by David Starbuck; the spiral-bound book includes research on underwater sites and digs at Rogers Island, Fort William Henry, and Vermont's Mount Independence.

A self-guided tour brochure, "The Mohican Trail," maps and mentions scores of eighteenth-century sites from Ticonderoga to Saratoga. The tiny text is hard to decipher in places, but the maps give you an excellent idea of the quantity and quality of all the monuments, forts, cemeteries, and such. Copies are available for a dollar from the Adirondack Regional Chambers of Commerce (136 Warren St., Glens Falls NY 12802; 518-798-1761).

For a truly hands-on exploration of the era, Adirondack Community College (ACC) runs two summer archaeology programs around the Lake George–Glens Falls–Fort Edward region. Experts in different disciplines meet with students and volunteers each day, and college credit is available. Call Professor William Gehring at ACC at 518-743-2236 or write to the Adirondack Field School, ACC, Bay Road, Queensbury NY 12804.

Originally published in 1938, Guy Omeron Coolidge's *The French Occupation of the Champlain Valley from 1609 to 1759* (Harbor Hill Books, 1989) is still the best chronicle of the earliest military settlements. Books about the French and Indian War are plentiful: for nonfiction, try *Reminiscences of the French Wars with Robert Rogers' Journal and a Memoir of General Stark* (Freedom New Hampshire Historical Society, 1988); *Robert Rogers of the Rangers* (Fort Ticonderoga Museum, 1988) by John Cuneo; *Sails and Steam in the Mountains: A Maritime and Military History of Lake George and Lake Champlain* (Purple Mountain Press, 1992) by Russell Bellico. A diary kept by a young British ensign, *The American Journals of Lt. John Enys* (The Adirondack Museum/Syracuse University Press, 1976) gives a first-hand account of battles fought on these waters during the American Revolution.

Aerial view of Fort Ticonderoga. Courtesy of Fort Ticonderoga Museum, Ticonderoga

FORT TICONDEROGA
Fort Road
Ticonderoga NY 12883
Mail: Box 390, Ticonderoga
Open: Early May–late June, early Sept.–late Oct., 9am–5pm;
    July–Aug., 9am–6pm
Admission: $8 adults, $6 children 7–12; under 7 free
518-585-2821

Gibraltar of the North was one name bestowed upon Fort Ticonderoga, acknowledging the site's key role in European struggles to claim North America. The French built a star-shaped stone fort on a bluff overlooking the narrows of Lake Champlain in fall 1755 and named it *Carillon*; the spot is almost within sight of Lake George, where the French had been defeated by the British earlier that same year.

Carillon was at the far-flung edge of France's fur-trade empire in the New World, close to British forts along the Hudson River. The redcoats attacked it repeatedly, with the penultimate battle coming in 1758, when the Marquis de Montcalm trounced a far superior force that included the Black Watch regiment. The next year, though, Lord Jeffery Amherst captured Carillon —

but not before the French blew up the powder magazine and left much of the bastion in ruins.

Amherst rebuilt the partially destroyed site and the British held the fort — renamed Ticonderoga, from a Mohawk word for "place between great waters" — until May 1775, when Ethan Allen and Benedict Arnold made a daring raid with their guerrilla forces, claiming the fort "in the name of the Great Jehovah and the Continental Congress." After securing Ticonderoga — which was used to launch a raid on Canada — the Americans constructed a long floating bridge eastward across Lake Champlain to Mount Independence (now Vermont), where another fortification was built of wood and earth that gave them control over the waterway. In 1777, though, General John Burgoyne reclaimed Ticonderoga for the British by setting cannons in place atop Mount Defiance, a steep hillside overlooking the fort. Working feverishly for just twenty-four hours, his troops and engineers carved a road up the mountain. Ticonderoga was abandoned by the Americans exactly a year and a day after the signing of the Declaration of Independence and lay neglected for decades. Settlers helped themselves to stones and timbers for building homes and fences, while cows grazed where the summer bivouac had been.

Early in the nineteenth century William Ferris Pell (whose ancestors settled Pelham Manor in the Hudson Valley) bought the fort and fields to protect the stony ruins. Even before the Civil War, Ticonderoga was a destination for tourists who traveled up Lake George by boat, then crossed over to Lake Champlain. Stephen Pell oversaw rebuilding of the barracks and *place d'armes* beginning in 1908, thus making Fort Ticonderoga the country's first major restored historic site, predating Colonial Williamsburg by two decades.

Now Fort Ticonderoga is a remarkable artifact, handsomely kept, and a fitting place to display thousands of artifacts from the two eighteenth-century wars. There is an exceptional collection of guns, swords, cannons, and other pieces of armament, as well as surgeon's kits, hats, drums, maps, books, portraits, letters, and personal items displayed in the south and west barracks. Beneath the northeast bastion are the ovens, great yawning stone hearths that had to supply bread for the standing army. Guides — in period costumes that show appropriate snags, stains, and wear and tear — explain their roles within the fort's hierarchy; ask questions to get a unique and articulate historical perspective. The fort bustles with activity every day in the summer. Cannons fire, muskets blaze, the fife-and-drum band marches and plays, adding a spirited accent to the hallowed stone walls.

If You Go: Fort Ticonderoga is easy to find; follow the signs from Route 22 or Route 74 just east of the village of Ticonderoga. Allow at least two hours for a visit. Bring the kids, and don't forget sunscreen, binoculars, and a picnic lunch to enjoy on a grassy redoubt outside the fortress. Most of the site is wheelchair accessible, although the below-ground oven area is not. There's a snack bar on the premises and an excellent bookstore.

Special Events: On weekends from May through October there are eighteenth-century encampments, military tattoos, living-history events, and gatherings of bagpipe bands from the Northeast and Canada. Lectures on everything from military history to gardening are scheduled from time to time, and occasional Elderhostel programs take place at the fort.

Exploring Further: Mount Defiance, where Burgoyne's artillery so effectively intimidated the Americans, is open to visitors of the fort. The parking area is a short drive away (follow the signs once you get back to Route 22), and it's a short, steep hike to the top. The view is terrific; there are picnic tables as well as a small shelter.

Also on fort property is the King's Garden, one of five so-called "masterpiece gardens" in this country recognized by the Garden Conservancy. Research has shown that this peaceful spot on the lakeshore has probably been under cultivation for several thousand years; it is possibly the very place where Samuel de Champlain came ashore on his 1609 voyage and had a fateful encounter with an Iroquois band. During the eighteenth century the spot supplied food for three armies at different times. In the 1920s, a wonderful walled garden was created here. The King's Garden opened to the public in summer 1995; research and restoration are ongoing. A tour of the garden (offered three days a week, for a small extra fee) gives visitors a chance to glimpse the Pavilion, the Pell family's Greek Revival summer home, which was built in 1826. Other special tours available by reservation include in-depth visits to the Lotbiniere Battery and the French lines.

From the dock below the fort, you can also take a narrated cruise aboard the *Carillon*, an enclosed tour boat; call 802-897-5331 for information about their fort-to-fort excursion.

Crown Point State Historic Site (see page 18) is just a twenty-minute drive away. Mount Independence, which can be reached by a short ferry ride near the fort, is preserved jointly by Fort Ticonderoga and the State of Vermont. A visitor center there opened in 1996. The village of Lake George — home to Fort William Henry and a park dedicated to the battle of Lake George — is about twenty-five miles away.

FORT WILLIAM HENRY
Canada Street
Lake George NY 12845
Open: May 1–Oct. 15, 9am–9pm
Admission: $8 adults, $6 children, plus sales tax
518-668-5471

In 1755, as the hit-and-run conflicts of the French and Indian War escalated to pitched battles, Sir William Johnson and his troops hewed a military road through the wilderness from Fort Edward northward toward the waters then known as *Lac du St. Sacrement.* When he arrived at its shores, Johnson promptly named the lake for King George, thus proclaiming it as British territory. That fall, the sloping shore was the scene of three brutal episodes known collectively as the Battle of Lake George, in which Mohawk, provincial, and British forces trounced the French.

While raids continued up and down the lake in 1756–57, the Americans erected a massive log-and-earth stockade that Johnson named Fort William Henry, after a brother of King George. The bastion withstood a prolonged siege by the French during five cold, wet days in March, but that summer General Montcalm and his army attacked the fort. This time, the English surrendered, on the promise of safe passage to Fort Edward; instead, Algonquin and Huron warriors slaughtered soldiers and their families, in a tragedy now known as the Massacre of Fort William Henry, and an abiding blight on Montcalm's otherwise gallant and illustrious career.

Today's Fort William Henry dates back to the 1950s, when the complex was imaginatively re-created from original plans drawn by British army engineers. Visitors cross a bridge, pass a huge souvenir mart, and end up in the dusty parade grounds between the walls.

A costumed soldier explains the fine points of eighteenth-century battle at Fort William Henry. B. Folwell

Actual artifacts are skimpy and exhibit spaces on the first floor are dark and gloomy, perhaps in keeping with the site's gruesome past; on the second floor are wax-museumish tableaux showing officers' quarters, a surgeon's office, and the like. Follow your ears and nose to demonstrations of musket and cannon firing because these may be the most interesting part of your visit. Reenactors here have a solid grasp of eighteenth-century battle protocol and the not-so-glamorous life of enlisted men.

If You Go: Try to avoid visiting on a rainy day; the fort can get overrun. Bring the family and plan to link up with a group following a soldier in order to get more bang for your buck. The ground levels are wheelchair accessible, but not the second story. Before you go to this for-profit attraction, check out Fort William Henry's home page on the World Wide Web (www.adirondack.net/tour/fwh.html) and rent *The Last of the Mohicans*, which, though it was filmed in North Carolina in 1992 (warmer than the Adirondacks, for one thing, and not so blackfly infested, for another) and takes some major liberties with James Fenimore Cooper's plot, captures some of the flavor of the times.

Exploring Further: As long as you're mixing popular culture and twentieth-century spin with your history, you might as well step aboard one of Lake George's numerous tour boats. The discovery tour, scheduled daily for summer mornings on the *Mohican* (518-668-5777), goes as far as Baldwin, Ticonderoga's landing on Lake George. The ship has maps and some displays, and the narration sketches American Indian and military history. Shoreline Cruises (518-668-4644) runs several boats, including smaller vessels that maneuver close to shore for glimpses of mansions and historic spots.

Sites such as Fort Ticonderoga (page 22) and Crown Point (page 18) represent the period more thoroughly; it's unfortunate that Lake George's role in this country's past isn't particularly well interpreted within the village limits. A short distance from Fort William Henry is Lake George Battlefield Park, with bronze statues and nice pathways, but at present there's no printed guide or map to help you understand the place.

For a first-rate history, read *Betrayals: Fort William Henry and the Massacre* (Oxford University Press, 1990) by Ian Kenneth Steele. Russell Bellico's *Chronicles of Lake George: Journeys in War and Peace* (Purple Mountain Press, 1995) relies on journals from soldiers and travelers to give a well-rounded picture of the place.

SUBMERGED HERITAGE PRESERVES: SHIPWRECKS IN LAKE GEORGE

(Sunken vessels on the National Register of Historic Places)
Mailing Address: Department of Environmental Conservation, Region 5,
    Route 86, Box 296, Ray Brook NY 12977-0296
Admission: Free
Register for diving for the *Land Tortoise* at the New York State Department
    of Environmental Conservation facility at Lake George Beach, early
    June–Labor Day; diving for the *Forward* and the "Sunken Fleet of 1758"
    is first-come, first-served, Memorial Day–Oct. (depending on weather).
518-897-1200

During the French and Indian War, in 1757, after the British lost Fort William Henry and then failed to take Carillon, they got busy beefing up their navy by building boats. And not just some boats — hundreds of them. The great majority were the double-ended, flat-bottomed, easy-to-manufacture vessels called *bateaux*, and some, precursors to the modern aircraft carrier, were the seven-sided, armored gun batteries called *radeaux*. When the war zone shifted to Lake Champlain, the British had a choice: leave the boats for the French to capture or destroy, or scuttle them so they would be sealed and protected under ice. Thus were sunk some 260 of these brand-spanking-new bateaux in the fall of 1758 and, thanks to sonar and the dogged work of the not-for-profit local diving group Bateaux Below, several wrecks have been identified and spruced up for underwater viewing. The sites are marked with buoys bearing mooring cleats (for fair-weather mooring only) and, please, one vessel at a time.

Of the so-called "Sunken Fleet of 1758," seven bateaux are visible, of which mostly only bottom planks remain. The Wiawaka Bateaux Cluster, as it's called, is about 150 feet northeast of the Wiawaka Holiday House boathouse, on the east side of Lake George. Twenty-five hundred feet northeast of Tea Island is the radeau *Land Tortoise*, the oldest intact warship in North America, the only surviving vessel of its kind, and unique to eighteenth-century naval warfare in the Champlain Valley, with seven cannon ports buried in its seven sides. Only in 1990 was the bizarre seven-sided image sighted on a Bateaux Below sonar screen; until that time the fate of the much-described vessel was unknown. As for the 1906 pleasure launch the *Forward*, no one knows why it was sunk in the 1930s east of Diamond Island. From the Bolton Landing estate of William Bixby, the *Forward* was the first gas-powered vessel on the lake. You can still make out the name on the bow.

If You Go: Registration with the DEC is required for the *Land Tortoise*; don't forget it's first-come, first-served, so be prepared to wait a bit before you take your turn. To quote from the *Land Tortoise* brochure: "This is a cold, deep dive. A safety/decompression stop is recommended. The nearest recompression chamber is over 150 miles away. Keep this in mind!" Somewhat less expertise is required for the other two dives. The Sunken Fleet site is in only 25 to 40 feet of water, and the *Forward* in 35 to 45. Volunteer members of Bateaux Below, who monitor for zebra mussels, patrol sites, and undertake historical documentation, urge hopeful divers to acquaint themselves with the history of the region, the better to savor the significance of these watery remains.

Exploring Further: Also in Lake George is the for-profit built-to-scale restoration of Fort William Henry, some nearby remains of the original Fort George, and the village museum in downtown Lake George, next to a lovely park.

Suggested reading? Again, Russell Bellico's 1992 *Sails and Streams in the Mountains* from Purple Mountain Press. Also look for *Lake George Boats* by Betty Ahearn Buckell, and *The Great and the Gracious on Millionaires' Row*, by Kathryn E. O'Brien (1978), both from North Country Books. Pick up brochures about the shipwrecks at various locations around Lake George.

FORT JOHNSON
Route 5 and 67, one mile west of Amsterdam
Fort Johnson NY 12070
Open: May 15–Oct. 15, Weds.–Sun. 1–5pm
Admission: $2, children under 12 free
518-843-0300

Fort Johnson, home of Sir William Johnson from 1749 to 1763. Courtesy of
Montgomery County Historical Society, Fort Johnson

William Johnson came to upstate New York from Ireland in 1737. Barely out
of his teens, he was handed his uncle's vast lands to manage near present-
day Amsterdam. Trading with the Mohawks, an enterprise that proved ex-
tremely successful because the charismatic young man was quick to learn the
tribe's language and customs, was his next career move. By 1749, Johnson
was wealthy and prominent, so much so that he erected the grandest home
for miles around, Fort Johnson.

From this imposing Georgian-style three-story stone house with rust-red
shutters, Sir William, "Superintendent of all the affairs of the Six Nations and
other Northern Indians" made his fortune as a land baron, fur trader, and
overseer of numberless tribal council assemblies that routinely gathered on
his extensive grounds.

Today those sylvan holdings, once as far-reaching as the banks of the
Mohawk River, are cropped to the depth of a suburban lawn. Where Senecas
and Mohawks awaited an audience with the sympathetic and popular com-
missioner, diesels rumble on a dull arterial highway. But the house that was

Johnson's home from 1749 to 1763 still stands, as does his later mansion, Johnson Hall, to the north (see page 30), both lost legacies of an empire builder who would die before the outbreak of the American Revolution, and whose Tory dependents would be forced to flee to Canada, never to return to their beloved estates.

Visit Fort Johnson and you can understand how painful this exile must have been. The house itself, which he designed, is said to be modeled on the family manse in Ireland's County Meath. Dutch craftsmen were the builders; their handiwork is still visible in the attic, where the beams and joists bear the Roman numerals of their original alignment. While few furnishings in today's Fort Johnson actually belonged to Sir William (most were confiscated after his death), their replacements movingly evoke his taste and time. Delft china gleams in a corner cupboard. Muskets lean against the mantel. A tall-case Clisbe clock stands sentinel in the parlor. Display cases scattered throughout the manse hold powder horns carved with mermaids and ships, old bugles, and rum bottles made of hand-blown green glass. Walls glow in shades of dusty pink and ivory, floors are decked with long wavy boards of yellow pine.

While the furnishings lend a certain formality to the site, manager Pat Reed makes it easy to appreciate the inherent rowdiness of daily life in Sir William's time. "I try to get everybody to imagine what it was like. No walls. Just *land*, open to the river. He might have had a hundred meetings around here at any time.

"He was a man," Reed observes with awe, "who was up till two, three, four in the morning partying every night. He may have had as many as seven hundred kids!" Of a particularly elegant bedroom she speculates, "This room was probably wall-to-wall Indians. The journals say it was not unusual to wake up and step on a sleeping Indian. They were all over the place."

The display children most enjoy, says Reed, is the Indian Room upstairs, with its homey jumble of old trade beads, arrowheads, and turtle-shell rattles. Nineteenth-century engravings of the four "kings" of the Iroquois Nation grace the walls; tattoos and nose rings aside, they look mostly like Roman emperors. And on the east lawn beside the rushing Kayderrosseras Creek, the paneled privy with the cathedral ceiling is reputedly the oldest in New York State.

If You Go: While children might not find the sight of Queen Anne highboys, gilded harps, and copper kettles particularly enthralling, they may well thrill to the Indian room and the dim display of sleighs, sleds, and model barges in the attic. Plan on spending at least an hour at Fort Johnson, and don't fail to take advantage of the cheery expertise of the caretakers and the guides. The historic home has many steps and narrow hallways, so wheelchair access is a problem.

Special Events: In mid-May Fort Johnson hosts an open house that often features a living history encampment; call for details and times.

Exploring Further: East on Route 5, and then onto Guy Park Boulevard, is the Walter Elwood Museum (see page 119), housed in a former school. West on Route 5 takes you to the hamlet of Fonda, dotted with historical markers and home to the Fonda Kateri Shrine (see page 7), which gives an excellent glimpse of Mohawk life before Johnson's time. Johnson Hall (below) was Sir William's final home in the valley.

James Thomas Flexner's *Lord of the Mohawks: A Biography of Sir William Johnson* (Syracuse University Press, 1989) is thorough background; for a swashbuckling adventure tale, read *The Firekeeper* by Robert Moss (Forge Books, 1995), which casts Sir William as the playboy/diplomat of the Mohawk Valley.

JOHNSON HALL STATE HISTORIC SITE
Hall Avenue
Johnstown NY 12095
Open: Mid-May–Oct. 31, Weds.–Sat. 10am–5pm, Sun. 1–5pm
Admission: $3 adults, $2 seniors, $1 children 6–12
518-762-8712

William Johnson bought the vast territory surrounding present-day Johnson Hall in 1752, but the outbreak of the French and Indian War delayed his plans to develop thousands of fertile acres. He served the British with distinction during that war, aided considerably by his many Mohawk friends, including Joseph Brant. In 1755 Johnson and Brant were key figures in the French defeat at the Battle of Lake George. Following that victory Johnson was made a baronet, and in 1756 he was named Superintendent of Indian Affairs for all of the territory north of the Ohio River.

Soon after the war ended Johnson turned his attention homeward, modeling this new property after an Anglo-Irish estate, with hundreds of indentured servants and dozens of black slaves living on the nearby farms. An unprecedented experiment in the northern colonies, the compound included a store for trading with the Indians, blacksmith shop, bake house, summer kitchen, and numerous outbuildings. The centerpiece was, and still is, Johnson Hall, a stately wooden mansion (with siding that actually looks like stone) built in 1763. The lady of the manor was Molly Brant, Joseph's sister and a full-blooded Mohawk, who joined Sir William following the death of his first wife.

An average day at Johnson Hall found several hundred native Americans from all tribes camped on the grounds and waiting in the cavernous hallway to meet with Johnson to conduct business, to settle disputes, and to visit, sometimes for days and nights on end. Johnson's job became increasingly complicated as thousands of white settlers encroached on Indian lands; to make matters worse, many Mohawk Valley farmers joined the Revolutionary tide, demonstrating open opposition to the Johnson family's aristocratic lifestyle.

The fiefdom ended abruptly: Sir William Johnson died in 1774, following a conference with the Shawnee. His son John inherited the title and the lands, but — as a high-profile Loyalist with no chance of evading his patriot neighbors — had to escape to Canada in 1776. Johnson Hall was confiscated by New York State in 1779, sold at auction, then acquired again by the state in 1906.

The house is beautifully proportioned in the true Georgian ideal, with four rooms down-stairs, four rooms upstairs, and a

A portrait of Sir William Johnson hangs above a fireplace at Johnson Hall. B. Folwell

winter kitchen in the basement. Settings have been restored to appropriately vivid colors and wallpapers; unfortunately, because Johnson died true to the British crown, all of his belongings were seized and auctioned off in the 1780s. Household inventories have helped modern historians fill the rooms with appropriate period furniture and reproductions, but as a result, many items look strangely shiny and new, especially the native American artifacts. Well-informed tour guides help visitors picture the place as it was 230 years ago, deftly mixing anecdotes and historical facts.

If You Go: To find Johnson Hall, follow the brown-and-white historic site signs from Route 5A. You'll drive through downtown Johnstown, past the courthouse Sir William Johnson built. The museum is in a park on the edge of a residential neighborhood.

Allow at least an hour for a visit. Start your tour in the stone building nearest to the parking lot, which provides an important overview to William Johnson's role in settling the region. A staff member will then lead you through the house. Children younger than six or so might find Johnson Hall too austere; barriers prevent visitors from entering most of the rooms. One room, though, is set up with replicas of toys, clothing, and furniture that youngsters are encouraged to play with, try on, and climb over. They can open the cowhide trunks to find a vest, tighten the ropes on the bedstead, or snuggle up in the featherbed. The interpretive building and the first floor of Johnson Hall are wheelchair accessible. There's a nice park with picnic tables next to the parking lot.

Special Events: The annual Market Fair, held on the second weekend in June, recreates eighteenth-century life around Johnson Hall, complete with Indians and soldiers in period dress and craftspeople working in authentic media. In late September, John Johnson's raid is commemorated with reenactors — some of them Canadian descendants of original Scots Loyalist settlers — in an event called "Burning of the Valleys." During the St. John's Day Holiday Open House, usually slated for the Sunday between Christmas and New Year's Day, there are traditional food and decorations, and an encampment of the Third Regiment of the Tryon County Militia, a local group of reenactors. Herb workshops are scheduled throughout the year and, from time to time, performances of eighteenth-century stories and music, and a history camp.

Exploring Further: Fort Johnson, outside Amsterdam, was William Johnson's home from 1749–1759, and is open to the public from May–October (see page 28). Mount Johnson, another home, is next to the Amtrak station in Amsterdam, but is not open to visitors. Guy Park, in Amsterdam, was built for one of Johnson's daughters; formerly a state historic site, it's now closed. Bear in mind that Johnson Hall is located on the edge of town — Johnstown, which is to say Sir William Johnson's very own town. A walking tour guide (ask for a copy at the office of Johnson Hall) shows how he planned the buildings and streets in his seat of power.

Johnson had two country retreats — Fish House and Castle Cumberland — a day's ride north in the Sacandaga River valley, near Northville. Using those homes as jumping-off spots, he frequently explored the southern Adirondacks for fishing and hunting, guided by Indian friends. When the time came to flee during the Revolution, William's son John Johnson escaped northward on snowshoes. But a spring thaw overtook the party in the central Adirondacks, and all were forced to leave their snowshoes on the shore of a large lake, which is now named Raquette Lake — after the French *raquette*, meaning snowshoe, according to local lore.

Several other historic sites in the Mohawk Valley interpret the same era: Fort Klock, near St. Johnsville (see page 33), and Herkimer Home, near Little Falls (see page 34).

Isabel Kelsay's *Joseph Brant, 1743–1807, Man of Two Worlds* (Syracuse University Press, 1984) gives a different perspective on the era and the region. Maurice Kenny's epic *Tekonwatonti/Molly Brant: Poems of War* (White Pine Press, 1992) tells her story in mesmerizing verse. *Empire of Fortune* by Francis

Jennings (Norton, 1988) is an excellent treatment of the French and Indian War; the book shows Johnson Hall on its cover. *Wilderness Empire* (Little Brown, 1969) by Allan Eckert can be found in libraries and used-book stores; it's a very engaging volume of eighteenth-century historical fiction based on fact.

FORT KLOCK HISTORIC RESTORATION
Route 5, about four miles east of St. Johnsville
St. Johnsville NY 13452
Mail: PO Box 42, St. Johnsville
Open: Memorial Day–mid-Oct., Tues.–Sun., 9am–5pm
Admission: $1 adults, 50¢ ages 10–15, under 10 free
518-568-7779

At the time of the French and Indian War and the War of Independence, uneasy settlers of the Mohawk Valley frequently took refuge in the fortified homesteads along the river — once there were two dozen of them — to sit out the threat of raids from Indians and Tories. In periods of relative peace, these strongholds also served as trading posts, taverns, and, of course, the simple farmhouses they were at heart, homey places with tall hearths and clumps of herbs hanging from the hand-hewn beams.

In Fort Klock, one of the few surviving Mohawk River forts open to the public, you get a feel for what it must have been like to hunker down in a place both this cozy and claustrophobic. The nearly two-feet-thick walls are loopholed so besieged farmers could fire their muskets from within. There was no need to go outside for water, since a spring bubbled handily in the cellar. Even the position of the fort is strategic — just above a sheltered cove along the riverbank, easy to defend.

Most of the time the Klock homestead was not a fortress but an ordinary farmhouse, with rope beds in the attic and a store downstairs, where you could buy comfrey (still can) or even a birch-bark canoe and a pelt or two (on display now, emphatically not for sale). On a summer's day, the cool dimness of the keeping room is mercifully refreshing. Wooden shoes stand on the hearth. Bird song drifts in on a breeze, and when a train rolls by along the nearby river, the hard floors laid down in 1750 by Palatine settler and fur trader Johannes Klock thrum faintly underfoot.

For almost two hundred years, until the Great Depression, the Klock family occupied this house. Since that time, a committee of local volunteers have maintained it without benefit of state or federal funds. While few of the donated furnishings are original, all are period and evocative of their time. The blacksmith shop and schoolhouse are open only by appointment, but anyone can wander into the massive murk of the Dutch barn, moved to Fort Klock post by post from an adjoining farm.

If You Go: Forty-five minutes should be enough for a leisurely exploration of both barn and fort, but you may wish to stretch it out with a picnic on the quiet, grassy grounds. The first floor of the home is handicap accessible.

Special Events: Every Memorial Day, Fort Klock invites the Third Tryon County Militia to drill, march, and camp in full colonial regalia. Local fiddlers sometimes cut loose in the old barn around July Fourth and reenactors march through the fields. On the first weekend in August, the eighteenth century is revived through demonstrations of crafts and skills that last all day. The first weekend in October marks the "Interrupted Harvest," when granaries and fields along the Mohawk Valley were burned by Tories in 1780. St. Nicholas Day, celebrated on the first Sunday in December, is a grand day for children, with homemade stollen, gingerbread, and old-time trinkets.

Exploring Further: Montgomery County is rife with great historic sites within striking distance of Fort Klock. In addition to the well-known Fort Johnson (see page 28), outside Amsterdam, there is the Canajoharie Art Gallery (518-673-2314), whose surprisingly strong collection includes works by Thomas Eakins, Winslow Homer, Albert Bierstadt, and Edward Hopper; the open-only-by-appointment Van Alstyne Homestead (a fortified colonial home like Fort Klock; call 518-673-3317); and the graceful and still-active Stone Arabia Reformed Church, legacy of the Palatine-German settlers who were granted a patent in the region in 1723. Read Walter Edmond's classic *Drums Along the Mohawk* for background on this hotly contested river valley.

HERKIMER HOME STATE HISTORIC SITE
Route 169
Little Falls NY 13365
Mail: RR 3 Box 331, Little Falls
Open: Mid-May–Oct. 30, Weds.–Sat. 10am–5pm, Sun. 1–5pm
Admission: $3 adults, $2 seniors, $1 children
315-823-0398

During colonial times, the Mohawk River was a major highway for moving farm products, furs, settlers, and armies across New York. The broad stream was navigable between Cohoes, north of Albany, and a place known as the "little falls." At the portage around this gorge, the son of a Palatine-German immigrant named Nicholas Herkimer carved a fertile farmstead from acreage given to him by his father in the 1750s. About 1764, Nicholas, by then a prosperous farmer-trader, built a brick mansion in the English Georgian style to show to valley residents and travelers alike — who passed beneath his imposing home on their way around the falls — that he had, indeed, arrived.

Sugaring-off day in early spring re-creates colonial life at Herkimer Home. Courtesy of Herkimer Home State Historic Site, Little Falls

The French and Indian War disrupted life considerably in the Mohawk Valley, leading prominent settlers to build fortified homes: Fort Klock, east of Little Falls; Johnson Hall, in Johnstown; Old Fort Johnson, near Amsterdam; and this site are a few examples. The war enabled some, like Herkimer, to profit immensely, and when the time came for Tryon County (a vast expanse of land stretching from Lake Ontario to the Mohawk River) to elect a commanding officer for the local militia, Nicholas Herkimer was named. At the Battle of Oriskany, in August 1777, he rallied some eight hundred local troops to try to stop the advance of British colonel Barry St. Leger, en route from the west toward Albany. But an ambush led by Mohawks and Loyalists — including Nicholas's brother Johan — thwarted the militia, and left General Herkimer mortally wounded. He died at his home ten days after the battle.

The hero's homestead has been a New York State Historic Site since 1913; the house was restored in the 1960s, and a large nineteenth-century barn was attractively rehabilitated as a visitor center in 1976. Of all the state-managed sites in northern New York, Herkimer Home is among the best for permanent exhibits depicting local culture and the historic personage associated with the house. An excellent slide program orients visitors, and skilled guides lead tours.

The house has beautiful proportions and elegant simplicity; a few fine pieces of Chippendale furniture belonging to Herkimer are displayed, plus several examples of eighteenth-century German folk art, from elaborate baptismal certificates to painted trunks. The garden, on a flat plain overlooking the river, contains herbs, flowers, and vegetables appropriate to the time, which are dried for arrangements or prepared in authentic recipes using the vast kitchen hearth. On most summer days costumed volunteers and staff are hard at work weaving, spinning, making fishing nets, gardening, and cooking.

If You Go: Allow one or two hours for a visit. In the barn's auditorium, be sure to see the introductory slide program about Palatine settlers and the Herkimer family, and wander around the lovely grounds. In late summer, the garden is spectacular. There's a nice picnic grove and plenty of room for kids to run.

Children six and older will probably enjoy Herkimer Home; guides make a special effort to key their presentations to the ages and tastes of visitors, explaining, for example, how young girls would spend their time learning needlework and all the skills necessary for securing a husband and running a household.

The grounds and first floor are accessible; call for details.

Special Events: Popular annual affairs add even more eighteenth-century flavor, such as a sugaring-off party in early spring, "Wool Day" in early June, the herb and garden fair in late June, and "Portage Day," which includes an apple bee, at the height of fall color.

Exploring Further: About five miles away from the homestead, on Route 5S, is a lovely stone church built by General Herkimer's father in 1767. Ask directions at the visitor center. Numerous historic sites are all along the Mohawk Valley, including Fort Stanwix (page 38), Oriskany Battlefield (page 36), Fort Klock (page 33), Johnson Hall (page 30), and Old Fort Johnson (page 28). Johnson Hall was built at approximately the same time as the Herkimer home, and shows the property of an Irish immigrant who remained a Loyalist. If you'd like to concentrate on the American Revolution, a visit to Saratoga Battlefield National Historical Park (page 41) illuminates the fateful summer of 1777, when a three-pronged British attack nearly captured New York.

ORISKANY BATTLEFIELD STATE HISTORIC SITE
Route 69, 2 miles west of the village of Oriskany
Oriskany NY 13424
Open: Memorial Day–Labor Day, Weds.–Sat. 9am–5pm, Sun. 1–5pm
Admission: Free
315-768-7224

In early August 1777, Fort Stanwix, under the command of patriot Colonel Peter Gansevoort, was surrounded by Barry St. Leger's British troops and his Indian allies. The hike eastward from Fort Dayton to Fort Stanwix was forty miles, but Brigadier General Nicholas Herkimer was determined to come to young Gansevoort's rescue. His men, a hastily assembled militia of eight hundred Tryon County irregulars, were settlers and farmers, inexperienced and ill-equipped. On August 6, the exhausted, mosquito-maddened New Yorkers reached a boggy ravine two miles west of Oriskany Creek, only three miles from Fort Stanwix.

The ambush happened there.

From three directions four hundred Iroquois, under the command of Mohawk Joseph Brant, crashed down the wooded slopes. Stunned militiamen were met with tomahawks and the bayonets of Sir John Johnson's Royal Greens. General Herkimer — his leg shattered by a musket ball — managed to improvise a headquarters in the shade of an enormous beech tree, and as the battle shifted to higher, drier ground, the patriots were able to hold firm. Iroquois and Loyalists were counting on a swift victory and easy spoils, but the resilience of the patriots was more than they had bargained for. Five hours after the initial ambush and the deaths of several chiefs, the discouraged Indians pulled back. True, they had dealt a fatal blow to Herkimer's plan to relieve Gansevoort, but the colonials, for their part, had scotched the Tory agenda as well, to get artillery and aid to the British troops around Fort Stanwix, without which St. Leger was compelled to give up the siege and go back to Canada.

Thus was the larger plan to drive a wedge between the New England and the New York continental armies effectively subverted; and thus does the historic site's literature describe the battle as a victory. In terms of the outcome of the Revolution, it was.

In strictly regional terms, however, this "victory" was anything but. During a single afternoon, many families from the Mohawk Valley lost all their menfolk; demographically, the region never quite recovered. Between losses from the battle and the ongoing threat of Iroquois attack, settlements along the Mohawk River were devastated.

Today the Oriskany Battlefield is a parklike, grassy plain scattered with picnic tables, illustrated plaques describing the clash in its many stages, and a splendid view of distant woods. To get a sense of the horror of the ambush itself, it's necessary to leave the meadowlike area and find the trail that winds down toward the ravine. Only when you're suddenly waist deep in grass and weeds, the picnic tables well out of sight, the only sound the din of peepers and crickets, can you imagine how it must have been two centuries ago. The famous creek at the base of the ravine is still, as it was then, no wider than a gutter; it takes no great feat of the imagination to picture how it could be made to run red with blood.

The monument itself was dedicated in 1884, one hundred and seven years after the battle.

If You Go: Despite its macabre history, Oriskany Battlefield happens to be a terrifically pretty place to break up a long drive with a picnic and a stretch. Guided tours are available, and group tours by appointment, but you may want to content yourself with following the plaques and studying the tomahawk-waving Iroquois on the bronze relief around the obelisk, which, incidentally, is made out of stones recovered from the dismantled Utica lock of the Erie Canal. Allow an hour or so for a visit. Wheelchair access is not good.

Special Events: On August 6 each year the Battle of Oriskany is commemorated with speeches and ceremony; if that day falls on a weekend, reenactors sometimes join in.

Exploring Further: Oriskany is only a hop, skip, and a jump from Fort Stanwix (below). See the two sites together if you can. Near Little Falls, on the banks of the Mohawk River, is the state site, Herkimer Home, where the injured General Nicholas Herkimer repaired to die soon after the battle (see page 34).

In the hamlet of Oriskany, the village museum (315-736-7529) has recently moved to new, bigger confines on Utica Street. There you'll find, among other local displays, a four-part diorama of the battle, and in Trinkaus Park, you can't miss the A-4 Skyhawk bomber, plus anchor and bell from the U.S.S. *Oriskany*, which saw action in Korea and Vietnam. The museum is open Monday, Wednesday, and Friday afternoons.

FORT STANWIX NATIONAL MONUMENT
112 East Park Street
Downtown Rome, between Black River Boulevard, Erie Boulevard, and
    N. James Street
Rome NY 13440
Open: Daily April 1–Dec. 31, 9am–5pm, except Thanksgiving and Christmas
Admission: $2 adults (17 and older)
315-336-2090

At first glimpse Fort Stanwix — in downtown Rome, flanked by parking lots, banks, service stations, and motels, sundered from pedestrian life by boulevards all around — exudes the unreality of a theme park. Against the roar of passing trucks and the silhouette of a modern skyline, student interns in continental homespun, cleaning muskets on the northwest lawn, can't help but look contrived.

But give it time to work its slow magic. Take an afternoon to venture behind the spiky palisades into the barracks, to read the labels, explore the museum, and listen to the rangers and volunteers, and you can't fail to be impressed and moved by the history and achievement of this painstakingly accurate reconstruction.

First, though, it's necessary to imagine a single route between the Atlantic Ocean and the Great Lakes, a water route, lifeline to tens of thousands of Indians, traders, soldiers, and settlers, with only *one portage*, a slim stretch across near-level ground between the Mohawk River and Wood Creek. Known to the Iroquois, Hurons, and Algonquins for centuries, the strategic Oneida Carry, as the British called it, was the colonial version of the Suez canal or the Straits of Gibraltar. Thus the reason for the building of Fort Stanwix in 1758 by the British: to protect the critical portage during the French and Indian War.

Members of the New York Third Battalion pull a cannon into place during a living-history program at Fort Stanwix. Richard Frear, for the National Park Service

When the American patriots took over the defense of the Oneida Carry in 1776, Fort Stanwix was in ruins. Under the command of twenty-eight-year-old General Peter Gansevoort, a thousand infantrymen from Massachusetts and New York rebuilt the fort, and none too soon. In 1777, a British and Tory army led by Barry St. Leger besieged the American-held Fort Stanwix and might have taken it, had not so many Iroquois deserted Loyalist ranks. Two things drove the Iroquois to quit: heavy losses in the Battle of Oriskany (see page 36) and a colonial raid on one of their encampments.

They weren't the only ones to jump ship: when St. Leger was deceived by American spies into believing that Benedict Arnold was on his way to Stanwix with a siege-busting force some three thousand strong, he withdrew his troops to Canada. The British departure meant that General John Burgoyne never got the supplies and reinforcements he needed to prevail at Saratoga, and Burgoyne's defeat is widely regarded as a turning point in the war.

So Fort Stanwix was never taken from colonial control. Still, the twenty-one-day siege took a toll. Eight hundred and fifty colonial militia were holed up in a fort built for half that number. Yellow fever broke out twice. Even before the onslaught, Indian raids were so common that women needed armed guards just to go berrying in the virgin forest outside Stanwix's walls. All this we learn from an intern who has taken on the role of the wife of a sutler, or storekeeper. Ask her anything about fort life and she'll keep her answer right in character; and, hokey as it sounds, it works: her impersonation of the beleaguered "Mary McCormack" brings the hardship and isolation of the fort to vivid life.

In 1781, George Washington decommissioned Fort Stanwix. The old palisades rotted and collapsed, and in their stead rose farmhouses, then the tenements of young Rome. Not until 1965 did a full-scale excavation of the original site begin. The dig unearthed some seventy-six thousand artifacts spanning three centuries, including glass inkwell liners, shoe buckles, stirrups, a delftware punchbowl, a Jackfield teapot, all on display in the museum. Check out the roomy officers' quarters and then the stablelike, low-ceilinged soldiers' barracks. By all means time your visit to take advantage of the twice-daily musketry demonstrations. On weekends, they blast the cannons, too.

If You Go: On North James Street, or Route 26, west of the fort, there's public parking. Save the picnic for Oriskany Battlefield, or the nearby, more bucolic Erie Canal Village. Between the visitor center and the museum, the barracks and the living history enactments, there are several hours' worth of solid sightseeing inside the fort, and plenty to keep youngsters enthralled. Take full advantage of an uncommonly well trained, helpful staff of park rangers and volunteers. Visitors in wheelchairs will have no trouble getting around this site.

Special Events: In mid-June the annual evening open house adds another dimension of the eighteenth century: candlelight, fires in the fireplaces, music, dance, and refreshments. Every Fourth of July inside the parade grounds, a state notable reads the Declaration of Independence, and three cheers are raised for the United States, George Washington, and the Continental Congress — *hip, hip, huzzah!* In late July thousands crowd the lawn to enjoy fireworks, the simultaneous firing of all the cannons, and the Syracuse Symphony Orchestra's rendition of the *1812 Overture*, among other favorites. Call for the date and time.

Exploring Further: A permanent exhibit on local history is on display at the Rome Historical Society, only two blocks north of Fort Stanwix at 200 Church Street. A few miles to the east, on Route 69, the Oriskany Battlefield (page 36) is a place to absorb the nuances of woodland warfare; plan a picnic in its shady glen. Or better still, save the al fresco lunch for Erie Canal

Village, just west of Rome on Route 49 (see page 56).

If you wish, you can follow the path of history all along the Mohawk Valley to Saratoga Battlefield, linking many of the sites in the chapter.

SARATOGA BATTLEFIELD NATIONAL HISTORICAL PARK

County Road 32
Stillwater NY 12170
Mail: RD 2, Box 33, Stillwater
Open: Visitor Center open daily except for Thanksgiving, Christmas, and New
    Year's Day, 9am–5pm; park roads open Apr.–Dec., weather permitting
Philip Schuyler House open Memorial Day–Labor Day,
    Weds.–Sun. 9:30am–4:30pm
Admission: $4 per vehicle; $2 per adult for hikers and bicyclists
518-664-9821

The plan was to have it all come together at Saratoga. In June 1777 British general John Burgoyne and his troops began a long march from Canada, following Lake Champlain and the Hudson River. They were to meet Colonel Barry St. Leger — who was advancing from Lake Ontario along the Mohawk River — at Albany, and proceed to New York City to join forces with Sir William Howe, in what they felt would be an invincible attack. Burgoyne was successful in his initial forays: he captured Crown Point in late June, and Ticonderoga fell after a four-day siege on July 6.

The outcome of two encounters in August — St. Leger's retreat from the Battle of Oriskany, near Rome, and heavy Loyalist losses at the Battle of Bennington, on the Vermont border — led Burgoyne to take dangerous risks in his southward journey. When British and German troops crossed the Hudson River at old Saratoga (now Schuylerville), on September 13, they met an American army nearly ten thousand strong under General Horatio Gates. The battles at Saratoga that ensued were a turning point in the American Revolution: not only did the colonial forces prevail, but also following the victory here at Bemis Heights, France decided to assist the American cause.

Saratoga Battlefield National Historical Park covers about twenty-eight hundred acres in the rolling hills east of Saratoga Springs. Within its boundaries, two major battles took place, involving more than eighteen thousand troops. A ten-mile loop road winds through old farm fields, woodlands, and bluffs overlooking the Hudson River, with ten interpretive stations describing important fortifications and events; audio commentaries by actors portraying a Hessian soldier, the wife of a British officer, a Loyalist farmer, a French aide to Polish general Thaddeus Kosciusko, and so forth, describe the scene from quite different perspectives. (At first, the tapes seem corny, but after a while, these different approaches create a complete and intriguing picture.) Red- or blue-topped poles mark British or American redoubts and fortifications; cannons and monuments are found throughout the park.

The visitor center contains a small museum with muskets, cannonballs, and other archaeological finds, plus dioramas and a few maps. A diagram that shows a good overview of the site is unfortunately lacking, and the introductory movie seems awkward and dated.

The park itself is an excellent destination and ideally suited for touring by bicycle. The loop road, especially in spring and fall, doesn't have a great deal of car traffic, and the hills are quite manageable on mountain bikes. Besides the main tour road, there are numerous other paths to hike, including the 4.2-mile Wilkinson National Recreation Trail. Walking along at least part of this trail gives you a good sense of scale, so you can appreciate the deep, sheltered ravines and high redoubts and hillsides, and imagine exhausted soldiers scurrying through the forests and fields.

At Saratoga Battlefield, a stone monument honors Benedict Arnold's boot. During the battle he was wounded in the leg, but because of his traitorous acts at West Point, he was deemed unworthy of a full statue. B. Folwell

If You Go: Allow at least three hours for a visit; you can easily spend an entire day here. Bring a picnic, a camera, binoculars, and field guide to the birds. (Because of the open fields and scattered stands of trees, numerous species are found here.) The park is a fine place to bring children of any age; older students will be able to envision the battles from the lookouts, and younger ones can race around in the fresh air. The park is very accessible, with paved, sloped paths to the different stations.

Special Events: Volunteers occasionally lead after-dark hikes of the fortifications; there are demonstrations of eighteenth-century crafts and skills in summer and military encampments in the fall. Lectures by military and social historians are offered year-round. Independence Day at the battlefield is a grand affair.

Exploring Further: General Philip Schuyler's home, eight miles from the visitor center, in Schuylerville, is part of this site, as is the nearby Saratoga

Monument. Built in 1777, Schuyler House underwent extensive repairs in 1994–95. It's a lovely building of stately proportions, with large airy rooms appointed with period furniture and decorative arts. The annual eighteenth-century day, in mid-August, and the candlelight tour, in mid-October, are particularly fitting ways to see the structure. For a tour of important Revolutionary War sites that relate to the summer and fall of 1777, visit Crown Point State Historic Site (page 18), Fort Ticonderoga (page 22), and Oriskany Battlefield (page 36). Fort Stanwix (page 38) and Herkimer Home (page 34) also tell part of the story of the American Revolution in the Mohawk Valley.

Numerous books cover this slice of our nation's past. The novel *Rabble in Arms* by Kenneth Roberts, detailing Burgoyne's campaign, is one of the most entertaining.

STEUBEN MEMORIAL STATE SITE

9977 Starr Hill Road
Remsen NY 13438
Open: Late May–early Sept., Weds.–Sat. 10am–5pm, Sun. 1–5pm
Admission: Free
315-831-3737 or 315-492-1756

When Benjamin Franklin was advised by his French allies to enlist Friedrich Wilhelm Augustus von Steuben as advisor to the newly formed continental army, the Prussian soldier was already a hard-boiled veteran of the Seven Years War. Luckily for the Americans, he took the job, and in the grueling winter of 1777–1778, Steuben managed, with a little help from his interpreters, to whip the hungry, demoralized American troops at Valley Forge into a fighting army worthy of its opponent.

Steuben taught the raggedy continentals how to march and how to drill. He showed them how to maintain their weapons, how to use their bayonets. His manual, *Regulations for the Order and Discipline of the Troops of the United States*, remains a keystone of military training in the United States.

After the American victory, Steuben was granted a large parcel of land in northern Oneida County. There Steuben built a solid but modest two-room cabin for summer use and his retirement, and there he and later his adopted son tried with some success to recruit other farmer-settlers to this remote frontier with the lure of cheap, abundant land. Thus were the first enclaves of Welsh immigrants drawn to the towns of Steuben and nearby Remsen; their cemeteries and churches grace the countryside even now (see page 65).

If the cozy cabin that anchors the Steuben Memorial Park is not the original, and its furnishings are not authentic, they still evoke the general's age and quiet taste. Behind the cabin, in the woods of the so-called "Sacred Grove," plaques erected by Americans of Welsh and German descent testify to the immigrant Steuben's heroism and largesse. And here, too, in a dappled glen, is Steuben's tomb, a chunky, plain monument of stone, all set about with pyramids of cannonballs.

If You Go: From downtown Remsen, head west on Steuben Road, cross Route 12 and follow the signs to the Steuben Memorial, about a half-mile past the Welsh Baptist cemetery, *Capel Isal*. The cabin sits at the end of a long meadow. The small grove and the memorial, a tiny site with limited exhibits, can easily be covered in half an hour, but bring a picnic and enjoy the peace. While the cabin is not wheelchair accessible, the rest of the site is.

Special Events: The Friends of Baron Steuben schedule a full roster of events, and visitors who'd like to plan their tour around a military encampment or a *gymaffa ganu* (a Welsh-style singalong), might want to call 315-831-2823 to see just what's in store.

Exploring Further: Several historic Remsen chapels, among them the Stone Meetinghouse, *Capel Cerrig*, on Prospect Road, and the wood-frame *Capel Enlli*, on Fairchild Road, testify to the two-hundred-year-old Welsh presence in the region. While these lovely old structures are mostly closed for worship, visitors can still scour the library in the Stone Meetinghouse for old Welsh prayer books and texts, and pick up maps of suggested self-guided tours to key Welsh sites in the area (see page 65).

Two locally available books on Steuben and the community that bears his name are *Steuben: The Baron and the Town*, published by the local historical society, and Augustus L. Richards's *Steuben, the Pioneer*.

FORT OSWEGATCHIE MARKERS
Library Park
Riverside Drive and Caroline Street
Ogdensburg NY 13669
Admission: Open and free at all times
No phone

Part of the Battlefield Trail of the North Country, Ogdensburg's Library Park honors Fort Oswegatchie (originally about a city block to the east) in a walking tour with assorted metal descriptive plaques on wooden posts scattered around a sloping, pleasant green with a view of municipal tennis courts and the shining St. Lawrence River beyond. If this sounds dull, it isn't: each plaque is full of odd news and usually pegged to some highly dramatic event or fact of early Ogdensburg life.

Today, the open and peaceable nature of U.S.–Canadian relations makes it easy to forget just how thorny and hard-disputed a border can be. The profit to be realized from contraband commerce with Canada across the river, for instance, early on spawned an enthusiastic community of smugglers in this town. Indeed, as the plaque on the lawn of the Frederic Remington Art Museum informs us, Ogdensburg's love of smuggling was so great that when the first American troops arrived to enforce the embargo of 1807, the resentful community formed its own counter-militia and hailed the army's withdrawal from the town with a cacophony of tin horns, cowbells, and cannon fire. Another plaque, "How Ogdensburg Captured Brockville," describes a little-known American raid on a Canadian prison, during which, in the dead of winter, two columns of local volunteers led by a tavernkeeper and a U.S. rifle regiment stole across the frozen St. Lawrence to the lightly guarded jail, seized muskets, rifles, ammo casks, and released a number of American prisoners of war rumored to have been badly treated. The fort itself, yet another plaque relates, was more concept than working reality. It is true that a famous local smuggler, Jacob "Potash" Brown, put up some fortifications here as a base for hit-and-run raids on military Canada around 1812. When the British overran the village a year later, however, the modest fort, "unfinished, unmanned, and undefended," went down without a peep.

It should come as no surprise to learn that the towering and wreath-bearing Winged Victory in the middle of City Park commemorates not the locally unpopular War of 1812, but local boys who perished in the Great Rebellion some fifty years anon.

If You Go: Twenty minutes should see you through a walking tour of signs in this pretty park. Combine it with a visit to the Remington Art Museum, across the street, one-time home of the land baron David Parish, one of Ogdensburg's many prominent, scrupulously neutral businessmen who continued to take high tea with British officers after the War of 1812 began.

AUGUSTUS SACKET HOUSE: URBAN CULTURAL PARK VISITOR CENTER
301 West Main Street
Sackets Harbor NY 13685
Open: July 1–Labor Day, Mon.–Sat. 10am–4pm; Labor Day–Columbus Day,
    Weds.–Sat., 10am–2pm
Admission: Free
315-646-2321/1700

As more than a few overambitious land speculators in the early eighteenth century would learn, you could buy up all the dirt-cheap upstate wilderness in the world, but without easy access to a market, your settlers would desert you and your colonies would die. New York City lawyer Augustus Sacket struck gold when he picked up a mighty swath of land on Lake Ontario at an auction in 1801. In his holdings was a naturally sheltered, deep-water port less than thirty miles from Canada. By 1804 Sacket had built a village and a

Ships at Sackets Harbor, 1814. From *A Pictorial History of the New World,* 1870

fishery. American potash and pearl ash were fetching as much as $320 a ton on the Canadian market; it would seem he had it made. But international politics got in the way when the U.S. Embargo Act outlawed trade with Britain and its Canadian possessions in 1808; Sacket, undoubtedly discouraged by this turn of events, retired his post as customs inspector, and within a year the fate of his village would fall into the firm hands of the U.S. military.

The first troops came in 1809 to enforce the embargo against Canada. Three years later the United States declared war on Great Britain, and the strategically situated Sackets Harbor became the northern headquarters for the U.S. Army and Navy both. Here Canadian warships converged on the village in 1812, and were pummeled by the American vessel *Oneida* and gun batteries on shore. The Canadians got luckier in 1813; they actually landed in the village and did a fair amount of damage, but a change in the wind — literally — left them stranded without reinforcements, and the Americans eventually prevailed.

Sackets Harbor then emerged as the nation's biggest naval port and a nucleus of shipbuilding: eleven ships were built here, and in 1815 the Madison Barracks were erected. This flush of prosperity would tide the boomtown right into the 1840s, but with new railroads providing so many other upstate towns with access to a market, Sackets Harbor lost its competitive edge. Only with a railroad spur of its own and the discovery of the Thousand Islands region as a potential resort would Sackets Harbor regain something of its old cachet.

Then, after World War II, the Navy left, the Army pulled out for new digs at Fort Drum, near Watertown, and the railroad closed the local station. For the next two decades it seemed the fate of the semi-abandoned town was sealed. But the village's rich history, combined with architectural marvels in the village core — a virtual showcase of American styles as diverse as Federal, Georgian, Greek Revival, Gothic, Queen Anne, Colonial Revival, and more — inspired loyal citizens and preservationists to undertake the first of many graceful and ambitious renovations in the 1970s.

In 1982 the historic village was adopted by the Urban Cultural Park program as one of eleven state sites, and the revival of the village, marina, and former barracks is astounding. Dixieland bands serenade summer visitors in the waterfront park; restaurants, B&Bs, antique shops, and cafes abound; self-guided walking tours dramatize the military story at the same time that they double as a primer in American architectural history.

At the very least, before you stroll around the village, treat yourself to half an hour in the Urban Cultural Park Visitor Center in Augustus Sacket's former home, a one-story neoclassical Palladian villa perched on a sweep of green with a great view of the lake. Four rooms full of pictorial and photographic panels give the history of the village, sort out the confusing origins of the War of 1812, recall the Sackets Harbor sojourn of Ulysses Grant and his wife, Julia, in the 1850s, and note the early impulses of New York City mayor-to-be Fiorello LaGuardia, who when he was five and his father was the bandleader of the 11th Infantry, pitched a rock through the window of an officer who had disassembled his toy fort. And if four rooms seem too much to handle, at least take in the thirteen-minute video in the rear room that gives it all in one fell swoop.

If You Go: This is not a village you'll want to rush. Make a visit here a major destination and plan on at least half a day, allowing time for lunch in town or perhaps dinner at the restaurants in the renovated Old Stone Row in the Madison Barracks. Come summer, Sackets Harbor hops with waterfront concerts, Canadian-American festivals and parades, polo matches, comedy acts, and the like, so plan your visit and reservations accordingly. Available at the Urban Cultural Park Center, the thirty-seven-page "Harbor Walk" booklet — a guide to architectural gems — is well worth the couple of bucks. But if a soup-to-nuts walking tour fails to appeal, sample a few key sites like the 1817 Joshua Pickering House, the 1849 Commandant's House (page 48), the Sail Loft, or the Historical Society Museum in the 1834 Bank Building (see page 50), all within strolling distance of each other. And check out Madison Barracks just to the north of town (see page 49).

Special Events: The three Sackets Harbor museums open briefly on the weekend of December 21. The best-known of the special events occurs the last weekend in June, the Can-Am reenactment of the second Battle of Sackets

Harbor, in the War of 1812. Military tattoos and fife players swell the parade. On Independence Day, the battlefield lights up with fireworks and a band concert. And if you miss the hoedown on the Fourth, you can still see a parade, fireworks, carnival, and crafts during Firemen's Field Days in late July. Lastly, on Labor Day Sunday an international festival treats the village to traditional dance music and ethnic food from all around the world.

Exploring Further: A few miles to the south is Henderson Harbor, which has two historical driving-tour brochures available; pick them up at the visitor center. North is the way to Cape Vincent (see page 127), and farther up the riverfront is Clayton, with several fine museums: the Antique Boat Museum (page 170) and the Thousand Islands Museum (page 128) most notable. Heading inland, just a short distance away is the twenty-two-room General Jacob Brown Mansion (315-782-7650), in Brownville, home to a hero of the War of 1812. In another nineteenth-century mansion, at 228 Washington Street, in downtown Watertown, is the Jefferson County Historical Society (page 149). The Northern New York Agricultural Historical Museum is in the little hamlet of Stone Mills (see page 68).

Other War of 1812 sites include Fort Oswegatchie, in Ogdensburg (page 44), and places along northern Lake Champlain. Local libraries might have a 1968 reprint of Benson Lossing's 1868 guide, *The Pictorial Field-Book of the War of 1812*, which describes dozens of sites.

COMMANDANT'S HOUSE
West Main Street
Sackets Harbor NY 13685
Open: Mid-May–mid-Oct., Weds.–Sat. 10am–5pm, Sun. 1–5pm
Admission: $3 adults, $2 seniors, $1 children
315-646-3634

From 1837 to 1840 many Canadians disaffected with British rule staged a revolt known as the Papineau Rebellion, or the Patriot's War. The uprising was suppressed, but the consequent strain on border relations between Canada and the States was grave enough to move the U.S. government to beef up the military presence at Sackets Harbor with a new naval station, which included a fine house for the commandant that faces the original site of the barracks and the fortifications.

Today, the pretty house with the picket fence and the stunning Greek Revival doorway is a museum furnished in the era of Captain Josiah Tattnall, who lived here with his wife and many children in the 1850s and 60s. Not many of the original furnishings are left; a hanging lamp aside, most of the Tattnalls' things were sold at auction long ago. Still, the guided tour has much to teach about life in an antebellum military home in upstate New York. From the formal Victorian parlors the visitor is led to an up-to-the-minute kitchen with indoor water pump and metal-lined pantry to keep out rats, and on to the attic to the stifling quarters for the maids. Also in the guided tour are such nuggets as the origin of the expression "Sleep tight!" (a reference to the tightening of a rope bed with a bed key to ensure a good night's sleep), and how winter rugs were cleaned: by covering them with snow and sweeping it all off. Nothing registers so poignantly, however, as the news that at the outbreak of the Civil War, Captain Tattnall, born in Georgia and by then married for a quarter-century, went south with his three sons to join up with the Confederates, while his Connecticut-born wife and daughters stayed north. They never met again.

Continue your tour to the Sail Loft. In the stable where the commandant once kept his teams of horses, just behind his big house on the shoreline of the lake, is a stylish, fact-packed interactive exhibit called "Life Aboard the U.S.S. *Jefferson*," named for a twenty-gun brig that was built locally and launched in 1814, sank after the war, and was never retrieved. In the 1980s underwater archaeologists studied the remains of the sunken ship, working in frigid, turbid water. What they learned about ship design, Lake Ontario trade, and the daily lives of sailors and ships' carpenters, is the backbone of this exhibit.

Sackets Harbor was home to as many as one-third of the men in the U.S. Navy during the War of 1812, and most of them were stationed at this windy end of the village. On exhibit panels made of lashed white canvas we learn not only all the parts and pieces of an eighteenth-century brig, but that sea captains were daily allotted six and a half pints of grog (rum, whiskey, and water), and that sailors preferred to eat their biscuits at night so they wouldn't see the bugs. There's a berth deck with a hammock you can crawl right into, full-weight replicas of shot and powder cartridges that let you feel what a gun crew had to lug and hoist when it was time to load the cannon, and a mock forty-two-pounder cannon with a press button you can move, aim, and fire at a painting of a masted ship that moves.

MADISON BARRACKS
85 Worth Road
Sackets Harbor NY 13685
Open: Staffed Mon.–Sat. 8am–8pm, Sun. 10am–4pm
Admission: Free
315-646-3374

From the War of 1812 to the close of World War II, the forty-acre Madison Barracks, north of the village, has been a proud player in American military history. Today part resort community, part living museum, it forms a

National Register Historic District and is undergoing extensive renovation. The oldest section is the Old Stone Row, built after the War of 1812 to secure the country's northern border. The barracks were added to yet again in 1837–1840 — the time of the Papineau, or Canadian Rebellion — with a fine old limestone hospital in the Greek Revival style. The easing of tension on the Canadian-American border led to the abandonment of the fort from 1852 until the Civil War, when Union troops came here to train. Then in 1879 a fire claimed half of Stone Row and the fort was very nearly abandoned, but thanks to the intervention of President Ulysses S. Grant, the row was rebuilt and the place restored. In the 1890s the original parade ground was joined to a polo lawn, an officers' row of brick duplexes went up, as well as a thoroughly medieval-looking Romanesque Revival mess hall and water tower that concealed a 55,000-gallon tank.

If You Go: Forty acres can be a lot of trudging. Plan a visit around a dinner at one of the barracks restaurants or a picnic on the breezy parade ground. Bicycle rentals in Sackets Harbor make it easy to stitch together a tour of Sackets Harbor village with a lazy spin around Madison Barracks.

SACKETS HARBOR HISTORICAL SOCIETY MUSEUM
Broad Street
Sackets Harbor NY 13685
Open: July–Labor Day, Weds.–Sat. 10am–4pm, Sun. 12 noon–4pm
Admission: Donation
315-646-1708/2321

What makes this museum particularly special is its location in Jefferson County's second-oldest bank building, made of limestone in 1836, and one of the first village historic structures to be restored. Today the elegant space houses a bank in the main part and the historical society's offices and exhibit space in one wing. The comprehensive, well-scripted exhibit changes from year to year: a recent subject was the historic churches of Sackets Harbor, of which there were no dearth.

If You Go: The exhibit in the historical museum is small, and you can see what there is to see in twenty minutes or less. A guided tour of the Commandant's House runs roughly half an hour. Add another thirty minutes for the self-touring Sail Loft, and don't neglect to take the measure of the twenty-eight-acre battlefield just across the lane from the commandant's front door, where ten rows of silver maples were planted in 1913 to commemorate the War of 1812 — a more than pretty place to take in a band concert on a Sunday summer afternoon. The battlefield is also where you'll find signs that mark the history of three military encampments: the Smith

Cantonment, once the scene of a tough battle; Fort Tompkins; and Fort Kentucky. The renovated Madison Barracks is an easy bike ride or short drive to the north.

PICKERING-BEACH MUSEUM
501 and 503 West Main Street
Sackets Harbor NY 13685
Open: July 1–Labor Day, Weds.–Sat., 10am–4pm; Sun. 12 noon–4pm
Admission: Donation
315-646-1529/2321

After boning up on the history of Sackets Harbor at the Urban Cultural Park Visitor Center in the Augustus Sacket house, head down West Main toward the lake and the Sackets Harbor Battlefield, now a village park. On the left is a structure made out of two houses, an 1809 gable-front cottage typical of early Sackets Harbor homes, and a big house with an impressive colonnaded porch, erected in 1817. This was the home of Massachusetts-born Joshua Pickering, whose son, Captain Augustus Pickering, appears to have rebuilt and expanded the house in the 1830s or 40s, and whose twentieth-century descendants, the Beach family, longtime summer residents of Sackets Harbor, bequeathed the pretty home to the village in 1941 after it had been in Pickering hands for 120 years.

The evolution of the house into a fully functioning and well-accoutered museum has been slow, but visitors are assured that by 1997 the Pickering-Beach Historical Museum will indeed be fully furnished in the fashion of Captain Pickering's widow, Caroline, who lived here with their five children after his death. Stay tuned.

CHAPTER THREE

Forests, Farms, and Furnaces

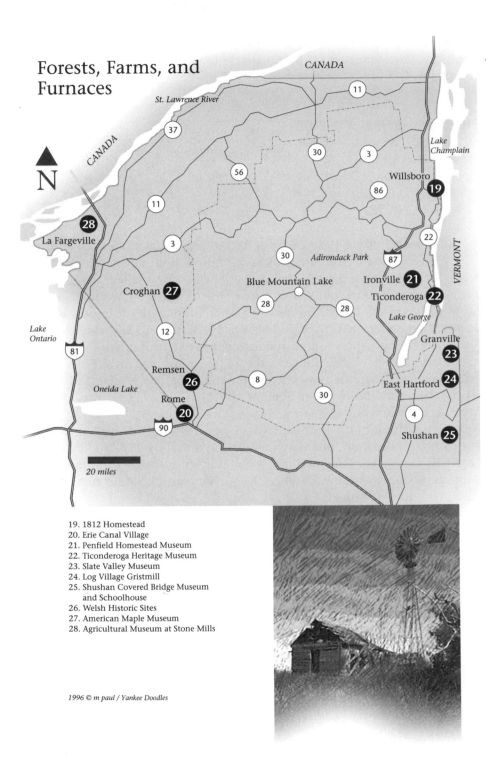

CANADA

St. Lawrence River

CANADA

N

Lake
Champlain

Willsboro **19**

28

La Fargeville

Lake
Ontario

Adirondack Park

VERMONT

Croghan **27**

Blue Mountain Lake

Ironville **21**

Ticonderoga **22**

Lake George

Granville **23**

Remsen **26**

Oneida Lake

East Hartford **24**

Rome **20**

Shushan **25**

20 miles

19. 1812 Homestead
20. Erie Canal Village
21. Penfield Homestead Museum
22. Ticonderoga Heritage Museum
23. Slate Valley Museum
24. Log Village Gristmill
25. Shushan Covered Bridge Museum
    and Schoolhouse
26. Welsh Historic Sites
27. American Maple Museum
28. Agricultural Museum at Stone Mills

1996 © m paul / Yankee Doodles

FORESTS, FARMS, AND FURNACES

■■■■■■■■■■■■■■■■■■■■■■■■■■■■■■■■■■■

Northern New York's waterways, key to native American passage through the region and to the movement of troops and supplies during three wars, were in the early years of the nineteenth century absolutely critical to settlement. Towns along Lake Champlain and the Mohawk, St. Lawrence, and Hudson rivers were thriving; from these civilized bases, would-be farmers, speculators, miners, and loggers penetrated the wild interior we now know as the Adirondacks. They followed the Schroon, the Black, the Raquette, the Oswegatchie, and smaller streams to find resources in abundance and inexpensive, well-wooded land, ready and waiting for the ax and plow.

Where settlers went, sawmills quickly followed, using waterpower to cut softwood logs into house and barn frames, rafters, joists, clapboards, and planks to build growing hamlets. Next to be developed were minerals; iron ore deposits seemed inexhaustible, especially in the eastern Adirondacks, and could be dug with hand tools right from the ground. A well-known forge was turning out good-quality iron near present-day Lake Placid by the 1820s; within two decades, several mining communities were thriving commercial centers with hundreds of workers, and even company stores and schools. The iron age in the Adirondacks lasted well into the twentieth century, with national concerns operating mines in Port Henry and Lyon Mountain as late as the 1960s. Other ores and minerals — graphite, garnet, zinc, talc, feldspar, to name a few — also added millions to the regional economy.

While the woods rang with the pounding of triphammers and smoke from charcoal kilns darkened the skies, cities all around expanded. As they grew and exhausted nearby timber, eyes turned to the North Country for lumber, especially softwoods, which could be floated to market. Early in the nineteenth century, the state legislature made sure that major rivers were available for this traffic by declaring many of them public highways. Beyond building materials, though, the vast forests held the raw materials necessary for tanning and papermaking. Hemlock trees — marginal for lumber — yielded bark that had all the right chemistry for processing leather, and dozens of communities in the central and southern Adirondacks grew up around tanneries. After the Civil War, papermaking technology developed so that wood fibers could be ground and processed into paper, and a lumbering boom ensued that lasted till the 1900s. Spruce was the most sought-after species; Glens Falls and Corinth, both on the mighty Hudson River, became centers of the paper industry.

Early garnet miners pose with the tools of their trade, North River. Courtesy of the Adirondack Museum, Blue Mountain Lake

Throughout this time, farming in the high country remained a subsistence enterprise. The season was short, barely long enough to grow grains, and the soil sandy, stony, or sparse. Folks who were serious about the business of farming took advantage of river-bottom lands near the Mohawk and St. Lawrence or barged off on the Erie Canal to find acreage with more potential. Some stayed on, realizing there was money to be made in supplying food for lumberjacks and miners and fodder for their horses and oxen.

This chapter begins with the 1812 Homestead, a living-history center near Willsboro, in the northeastern section of the region. From there, we follow a rough chronological order, to the Erie Canal Village and Penfield Homestead and other sites that depict the pioneer days.

For background on these industries, try *The Story of Adirondac* (Adirondack Museum/Syracuse University Press, 1968) by Arthur Masten; the entertaining *History of the Lumber Industry in the State of New York with an Appendix: The Role of the Pioneer Lumberman* by William Fox (reprint; Harbor Hill Books, 1985); John Todd's tale of a lonesome town, *Long Lake* (reprint; Harbor Hill Books, 1989); *Hides, Hemlocks and Adirondack History: How the Tanning Industry Influenced the Growth of the Region* by Barbara McMartin (North Country Books, 1992); *The Great Forest of the Adirondacks*, also by Barbara McMartin (North Country Books, 1994); *Guides of the Adirondacks: A History* by Charles Brumley (North Country Books, 1994). Harder to find, but available in regional libraries, are *Our North Country Heritage: Architecture Worth Saving in Clinton and Essex Counties* (Tundra Books, 1972) by Allan S. Everest, which shows vernacular architecture of backwoods settlements and prosperous towns, and *Architecture from the Adirondack Foothills: Folk and Designed Architecture of Franklin County, New York* (Franklin County Historical Society, 1988) by Robert McGowan.

1812 HOMESTEAD
Route 22
Willsboro NY 12996
Open: July 1–Oct. 15, Sat.–Sun. 1–4:30pm, and by appointment
Admission: $5 adults, $2.50 seniors and children
518-963-4071

At this early farmstead, the emphasis is on doing rather than observing: the 1812 Homestead is arguably the most kid-friendly historic site in the North Country. In the cozy cabin, youngsters can try making candles, cooking at the open hearth, squeezing apple cider, spinning wool, or making shingles, under the watchful eye of craftspeople who are happy to share their stories and skills. A pioneer post-and-beam barn, heirloom gardens, and pastures evoke the nineteenth century. Sheep, oxen, chickens, and a pig are also among the faculty here; think of the site as an informal field school rather than a prim and proper museum. Artifacts are scant, and the ones that are here are meant to be used, even in the one-room schoolhouse.

The property — part of a summer camp and outdoor education complex — also includes a self-guided nature walk along Long Pond. Call ahead for information about special seasonal activities and workshops like cheese making, blacksmithing, and furniture building.

Exploring Further: For a glimpse of another pioneer home, ask directions to see the two-hundred-year-old Adsit log cabin, on Willsboro Point. For more on Essex County settlement, see the Adirondack History Center (page 140) and the Penfield Homestead Museum (page 58).

ERIE CANAL VILLAGE
5789 New London Road
Routes 46 and 49; near Exits 32 and 33 of the New York Thruway
Rome NY 13440
Open: Daily May–Labor Day; Labor Day–Columbus Day,
    Sat.–Sun. 9:30am–5pm
Admission: $6 adults, $5 seniors, $4 children 7–17, under 7 free
315-337-3999

In the twenty-odd years since somebody hitched an 1840s-vintage boat to a pair of mules and offered rides along a grassy stretch of the old waterway, Erie Canal Village has grown to the point where it more than lives up to the promise of its name. Scattered about the site today are fifteen historic buildings representing aspects of nineteenth-century canal life, all gathered from within a fifty-mile radius of Rome and linked by pretty paths. The arrangement of the buildings is meant to suggest the homely contours of a frontier village, though only in a fantasy park of this kind would a rustic settler's cabin sit near a Victorian house or a Methodist church by a tavern. Well, never mind. Picnic tables abound, the restorations are full of fascinating things, the tavern sells fresh-squeezed lemonade, there's a New York State Cheese Museum on the premises (did you know the first cheese factory was built near Rome in 1851?), and, in the schoolhouse, pretend students can scribble on real chalkboard slates.

If children love this place, it's easy to see why. The script in the canal museum is simple and dramatic; the print is big and blocky and easy to read. You learn how locks work, clamber into a low-ceilinged model packet boat, and ogle pictures of canal mishaps — smashed boats, busted culverts, and the like. There are photographs of immigrant Italian canal workers playing cards and posters for floating canal museums and circuses complete with freaks and historical tableaux. Most engrossing is the story of the construction of the canal itself, a project "little short of madness," said a disapproving Thomas Jefferson, but this 363-mile feat of engineering changed the course of American history forever.

Construction of the canal began in Rome in 1817; seven years and eight million dollars later, the thing was done. Commerce paid off the construction cost in eleven years. Wrote an admiring engineer, "They have built the longest canal in the world in the least time, with the least experience, for the least money, and to the greatest public benefit." Hard on the heels of the Erie ditch came the phenomenon of canal-town culture: mules and drovers, stores and taverns strung along the waterway, skating parties, kids hitching illegal rides on the towlines, church groups taking Sunday excursions on barges.

After the museum comes the general store, with its bright display of cocoa tins, calico, oil lamps, and so on. Other highlights of the walking tour are a Victorian house (formerly belonging to Jacob Shull, a cattle broker) with

Wash day at Crosby House, Erie Canal Village. Courtesy of Erie Canal Village, Rome

fine and fancy dolls, a bird cage, pianoforte, sewing machine, and lovingly restored oak trim; an old schoolhouse with giant maps and definitions on the blackboard from an 1856 *McGuffey Reader*; and the cool, well-annotated Harden Museum, with long rows of vintage surreys, cutters, run-abouts, and laudelettes.

If You Go: Only minutes from the hustle of downtown Rome, Erie Canal Village seems a world apart, a site that manages to be at once relaxing, entertaining, and informative. A solid afternoon or morning is time enough to savor a mule-drawn boat ride along a short stretch of the canal and to take the village walking tour, either self-guided or with a volunteer. If time is brief, stick with the canal museum, the wonderfully restored Victorian house, the old-time schoolhouse, and the tavern for a fifty-cent glass of root beer or lemonade. Alongside the canal, there is a snack bar, too.

New in 1996 is a fourteen-minute video on the canal. All but a few of the stops are handicap accessible; wheelchairs are available for visitors.

Special Events: In July and August, the mule-drawn packet-boat rides go on in the evening, too. During Independence Day, the original digging of the Erie Canal is celebrated with speeches, games, and strawberry shortcake. Over Labor Day weekend, a harvest festival honors nineteenth-century farm life with demonstrations of horse-drawn field work, old-time children's games, corn on the cob, and fresh-pressed cider. On Halloween, a Haunted Night features hay rides, a haunted house, bonfire, and six-foot talking pumpkin. Christmas time means sleigh rides, caroling by candlelight, and Victorian gifts for sale in the general store.

Exploring Further: In downtown Rome, the restored Fort Stanwix (page 38) represents one of the most complete and accurate full-scale models of a log-and-earth fortification in existence. Built by the British during the French and Indian War, and rebuilt by American patriots to defend the Mohawk Valley against the threat of a British invasion from the north, the fort, now managed by the National Park Service, deserves a long, attentive visit. Just behind the fort is the Rome Historical Society, worth checking out for its fine special exhibits on local history and lore.

For a further bit of Americana, take a moment to pay homage to Francis Bellamy, author of the *Pledge of Allegiance*, buried in the Rome Cemetery, near Erie Canal Village.

Try Carol Sheriff's *The Artificial River* for lively background reading about the canal.

PENFIELD HOMESTEAD MUSEUM
Ironville Road
Crown Point NY 12928
Open: Daily, May 15–Oct. 15, 10am–4pm
Admission: Donation
518-597-3804

Allen Penfield moved to Crown Point from Vermont in the 1820s to mine the high-quality iron ore found abundantly throughout southern Essex County. His 1828 Federal-style clapboard home in Ironville attests to his growing family and growing fortune. Soon a whole town surrounded the heart of his empire, with white clapboard buildings (church, parsonage, company store) lining the shady country road just a short distance from the coal sheds, charcoal kilns, ore separator, and forges. Several charming buildings still stand, and the remnants of industry (circa 1845–72) can be found by following a self-guided tour through woods and fields.

The house itself is a fine artifact, with unusual painted floors upstairs and gracious proportions. It's absolutely stuffed with artifacts ranging from mining equipment (including the first magnetic separator for iron ore) to quilts, baskets, musical instruments, photographs, clothing, and toys. Labels are scarce, but the whole effect is an eye-popping aggregation, and it's easy to understand what's on display. Several rooms are arranged to reflect Penfield family history, such as the Missionary Cousin's Room. (Her influence is positively rampant: Biblical passages in gold Gothic script are painted above every doorway.) A connected shed holds blacksmith equipment, farm implements, woodworking tools, and more. There's even a birch-bark "crooked" canoe, donated by a local man who brought it back from Canada.

Beyond the main house is a small brick smokehouse and a large barn with carriages, sleighs, and an ornate horse-drawn hearse. Across the street, the church, an austere Greek Revival building, remains remarkably untouched by the twentieth century. On a bright summer day, sunlight streams through the windows to create a peaceful oasis.

If You Go: Follow signs to the Penfield Homestead from Route 74 between Ticonderoga and Paradox Lake. Allow an hour or so to tour the homestead, outbuildings, and church, and an additional hour for the walking tour. Bring a picnic lunch, fishing gear, or even a canoe for exploring Putts Pond. This is a fine place to bring children of any age; there's plenty to explore out-doors and exhibits indoors are easy to see and comprehend.

Special Events: The museum sponsors a pair of enthusiastic annual events, like Heritage Day, with old-time music, crafts demonstrations, and a chicken barbecue, in August; and the Apple Folkfest, with fresh-pressed cider, bag-pipers, apple desserts, and activities for children, on the Sunday of Colum-bus Day weekend.

Exploring Further: If you're interested in learning more about the mining industry in the Adirondacks, Port Henry is launching a new museum called the Iron Center, slated to open in 1997. Call the Moriah/Port Henry Economic Development department at 518-546-3606 for information.

Near Newcomb, on County Road 4 (the route to a major High Peaks trailhead; follow the brown-and-yellow signs), you'll find the remnants of the McIntyre ironworks, circa 1854. The first major structure is a huge stone furnace located on the east side of the road just past the drive to NL Indus-tries' former titanium mine; below the furnace near the banks of the Hudson River are the blowers that supplied compressed air to the process. A few miles farther along is a white Greek Revival-style building, which served as the of-fices for the mine. In late 1996 plans were afoot for some of this land to be acquired by the state, some by the Town of Newcomb, which may eventu-ally allow for better access and interpretation. (Note that the abandoned brown buildings are not part of the village called the Upper Works, and date instead from a private club that operated at the turn of the century.) To read about this site, try Harold Hochschild's monograph *The MacIntyre Mine — From Failure to Fortune* (Adirondack Museum, 1962), a concise history.

TICONDEROGA HERITAGE MUSEUM
Montcalm Street
Ticonderoga NY 12885
Open: Daily, July–Aug. 10am–4pm; May–June, Sept.–Oct.,
    Sat.–Sun. 10am–4pm
Admission: Free
518-585-2696

International Paper Company once used this brick building as its main office; all around the structure were mill buildings and sheds dependent on the water and power of the LaChute River. A landscaped, grassy park and a small hydro plant now occupy the site, and the former office now interprets the history of paper and pencils.

Graphite for common lead pencils (the reason those familiar yellow Dixon pencils are stamped with the word "Ticonderoga") was mined nearby, as early as 1815. American Graphite had extensive holdings south of town, although the pencils themselves were manufactured in New Jersey. Part of the exhibit space in this clean, bright building explains how pencils are made and shows photographs of the heyday of graphite mining, while displays in other rooms explain paper and wood products.

Two very well done videos are available for viewing: a ten-minute program showing the industrial and agricultural growth of the town and a sixteen-minute show on old-time and contemporary papermaking.

If You Go: Allow about thirty minutes for a visit. If it's a nice day, pick up a map for the LaChute River Interpretive Trail, which begins just outside the Heritage Museum. The quarter-mile-long walk follows the river upstream and takes about twenty minutes, with stops explaining waterpower, papermaking, geology, and ecology.

Special Events: Lots of activities for children are scheduled during the summer, ranging from morning-long workshops in arts and crafts to daylong affairs. The big tent of the Ticonderoga Festival Guild is set up in the park during July and August and offers regularly scheduled performances for adults and children. Most any time, youngsters visiting the museum can make their own paper at a special station.

Exploring Further: Drive south on Route 9N and turn west on Route 8 at Hague to drive through the Joseph Dixon Memorial Forest. Tucked back in the woods is what little remains of the graphite mines: a few tottering shacks, lots of cellar holes, and miles of tunnels — now a bat hibernaculum protected by the Adirondack Nature Conservancy. Guy Baldwin, who was granted the patent for the first wood-encased graphite pencil in 1839, is buried in the Streetroad Cemetery, just north of the village of Ticonderoga.

SLATE VALLEY MUSEUM
17 Water Street, south of West Main
Granville NY 12832
Open: Year round, Tues. and Fri. 1pm–5pm, Sat. 10am–4pm
Admission: $2 adults, children 12 and under free
518-642-1417

Even though the drive is only twenty minutes from the border of the Adirondack Park to Granville, the Slate Valley seems a world apart. All rolling farmland, cemeteries with ancient lilac bushes, Greek Revival churches, and fine clapboard homes, the region at first glimpse feels like an extension of New England. But look behind the farmhouses to the tucked-away, deserted quarries and glittering ziggurats of slate, and follow the slate mounds the twenty-four-mile length of the Slate Valley from Granville north into Vermont, and another landscape is revealed, one haunted with the lost lives of immigrants, tenements, pits, shanties, and other vestiges of an industry whose product once covered the roofs and paved the sidewalks in numberless American towns.

Stone workers of Yankee, Welsh, Irish, Polish, Italian, and Carpathian extraction all quarried slate in these deep, prolific beds, and it is their enterprising descendants we have to thank for the attractive, informative museum that honors this industrial past. Here, in an airy, slate-floored nineteenth-century post-and-beam barn, is everything you ever wanted to know about slate: how it's quarried, split, and trimmed, what were the tools, who did the work, and how the workers lived. In this corner is a slate-splitter's shanty, in that corner, an exquisite Work Project Administration mural of slate workers, and over there a thoughtful display of local ethnic artifacts — Welsh china, a Yiddish Bible, Italian needlepoint, and so on. Specially intriguing are Neil Rappaport's beautifully observed panoramic photographs of family-run slate quarry operations of the past forty years. Clearly, while slate has had its ups and downs, the culture lives, as these proud portraits of laborers and owners attest.

If You Go: It takes an hour, maybe more, to soak this up. A video that explains, among other things, how slate is split (carefully, and by hand alone) is a favorite with kids. Even though the barn is old, exhibits are wheelchair accessible throughout. A grassy area behind the museum overlooking the Battenkill River is a fine spot for a picnic.

Special Events: Lecture/slide shows on regional history and culture are sometimes scheduled. Call ahead for times.

Exploring Further: Up the street and around the corner, upstairs from the Pember Library, is the wonderful Pember Museum of Natural History (see page 158). Harder to find, but just as engrossing, are the immigrants' headstones in cemeteries for Welsh, Slavonic, and Jewish families.

Growin' Up In Middle by Ellen Hughes Qua is an affectionate reminiscence by a journalist from Middle Granville.

LOG VILLAGE GRISTMILL

County Route 30, two miles east of NYS Route 40
East Hartford NY 12832
Open: Memorial Day–Nov. 1, Sat. 10am–6pm; Sun. 12 noon–6pm
Admission: $2.50 adults, 50¢ children
518-632-5237

It's called "Log Village" because that was what the hamlet of East Hartford was named when Yankee carpenter Hezekiah Mann built a gristmill here in 1810. Mann's solid and sophisticated mill served the little community continuously until 1902. Then it fell into slow, seemingly irretrievable disrepair until 1972, when Floyd Harwood, a retired vocational-education teacher with a country boy's passion for old mills, bought the place with his wife and spent another few decades bringing the venerable old wreck up to speed.

Start early because the Log Village isn't such an easy place to find and also because once you get there it's not an easy place to leave. Like all enterprises driven by the force and vigor of a single imagination, it has qualities almost magical, as if you'd stumbled into one man's dream.

Drive through the grassy lane down a slope to the patch of lawn marked "Parking" and follow the faint path directly toward the mill on the right. In the mill, with the wooden flume poking through the walls, is a massive waterwheel, seventeen feet in diameter and six and a half feet wide, its flat paddles looking almost big enough to sit on. Climb to the top floor, and there's the chute where Harwood pours in wheat, corn, and buckwheat kernels to be ground, as well as an assortment of obsolete foot- and waterpowered machinery. On the bottom floor, under the wheel, you can see where the fine ground grain spills out. When the mill is operating — most weekends — you can buy the fresh cornmeal to take home.

An old cider mill Harwood moved here from down the road houses a tool museum and gift shop. Here's where we learn from news clippings that it cost almost thirty thousand dollars to get the silt out of the millpond, that Harwood himself was once president of the Society for the Preservation of Old Mills, and that, at seventy-eight, he believes he's got another thirty years of work before the complex is fully restored. In the barn loft is a dim, pleasant-smelling museum with things like early carpet sweepers, a 1913 wall phone, a vintage bedpan, a very long toboggan.

Past the pond are two more structures, one of them a long pole shed housing horse-drawn farm equipment, bob sleighs, grain threshers, and such. Don't miss the treadmills, one for a goat, one for a dog. Enthusiastic neighbors donated many of these things to the Harwoods, but captions are sketchy and it's up to the visitor to concoct a good story to go along with the artifacts. That's all right with children, or at least one eleven-year-old of our acquaintance, who was perfectly content to run around the "big round clunky things" in the giant barns, imagining how many kids could fit into the giant hogshead or whether we could make a treadmill for Rosie the border collie when we got home.

If You Go: If it's a nice day, bring a picnic and make an afternoon of the Log Village. Call ahead to be sure someone will be on hand to work the mill. Unfortunately this is not a wheelchair-friendly setting.

Exploring Further: The Covered Bridge Museum in Shushan (see below) is just a short drive away and gives another glimpse of agrarian traditions. The hinterland of Washington County was one of the first regions of upstate New York to be settled, mainly by Scottish immigrants and Vermont Yankees. The brick and clapboard churches and homes of these pioneers are scattered on back roads throughout the "Scotch Quarter"; a county road map is indispensable for an interesting tour. In Warrensburg, the Gristmill (518-623-3949) is a classy restaurant and a restored mill with numerous historic displays and vintage photographs; reservations are recommended for dinner, which can set you back as much as hundred dollars for two.

Floyd Harwood's eighty-page *The Log Village Gristmill* is a must for mill mavens; pick it up on site.

SHUSHAN COVERED BRIDGE MUSEUM AND SCHOOLHOUSE
Just off County Route 61, under the main bridge
Open: Memorial Day–July 4, Sat. and Sun. 1–5pm; July 4–Labor Day,
    Tues.–Sun. 1–5pm; Labor Day–Columbus Day, Sat. and Sun. 1–5pm; and
    mornings for train visits
Admission: Donation
518-677-8251 or 854-3870

The beloved Battenkill, a favorite of fly fishers from all over the Northeast, was once spanned by as many as twenty covered bridges. This is one of five that remain. Built in 1858 after a Connecticut architect's design, the eighty-ton, all-wood-trussed Shushan Covered Bridge saw continuous use for 105 years. Around the time of its construction, bustling little Shushan boasted many stores, a gristmill, ax factory, woolen factory, flax mill, two blacksmith shops, a hotel, and even an opera house. Dairy and potato farms quilted the rolling terrain and, to some degree, still do.

When a steel bridge replaced the wooden one in 1964, town worthies seized the opportunity to place the decommissioned bridge on concrete foundations and convert it into a museum that would celebrate some of Shushan's agricultural and village heritage. Donations from people from town and county fill the deep, tunnely space with odd, ingenious farm equipment long out of use, and many of the pieces are even identified, if regrettably not very well explained. Here is a grub mattock, there a flax carder, a barley fork, a

Curator Elizabeth Bentley greets visitors in Shushan's Covered Bridge Museum.
Phil Haggerty

milk sled, and the inevitable pump organ. The old-time potato-chip maker from Saratoga Springs (where the potato chip was invented, as it happens) gets a workout on Harvest Days, and people swear it makes the best-tasting crisp around. A life-size plastic horse models an antique saddle and riding gear. And at the far end is an assortment of early vehicles, from first-ever snow scrapers and cultivators to hard-used plows and sleds.

If You Go: Allow about half an hour. The bridge is accessible for wheelchairs.

Special Events: The second Saturday and Sunday in August bring Harvest Day, with pancakes, hotdogs, hamburgers, homemade pie, and a chance to see as much of the old machinery in action as possible, plus a weaver, basket maker, and a small tractor-drawn train ride for children.

Exploring Further: Whether you find Shushan by car or during the hour layover from a train ride on the Batten Kill Rambler (518-692-2191) out of Salem, there's plenty to see in addition to the Covered Bridge. Right in town, the Georgi Museum offers a startling range of medieval European portrait and landscape paintings, a nice collection of geodes and minerals, and a great riverside park for picnics (see page 165).

In Whitehall, originally Skenesboro, is a fine museum in the Urban Cultural Park Center with an enormous diorama dramatizing the birth of the American Navy (see page 106). The Old Fort House (page 109), in Fort Edward, is a small museum complex with an old-time law office, an early country tollbooth, and some choice colonial artifacts on display.

WELSH HISTORIC SITES

In and around the town of Remsen, east on Route 325
The Remsen-Steuben Historical Society
PO Box 284, Remsen NY 13438
Open: Apr.–Oct., Sat. 1–4pm
Admission: Free
315-831-5443

Few communities in upstate New York can boast such a well-informed and prideful sense of their ethnic heritage as the historic towns of Remsen and Steuben. The history begins two centuries ago, when a former military aide to General Steuben, then in charge of immigration from New York City, began to direct Welsh immigrants toward remote Oneida County, and in particular to the sixteen thousand acres that Steuben hoped to see cleared, settled, and farmed. The first significant party of immigrants sailed up the Hudson to Albany by sloop, continued to Utica by flatboat, and went on to Steuben by ox and wagon in 1795.

Open the local phone book today and you can still see many of the same Welsh names that came to the region in the early nineteenth century: Williams, Davies, Roberts, Jones. . . . Pick up a map from the Remsen-Steuben Historical Society, and you can see many of the surviving early Welsh churches, schools, and cemeteries, as well.

Capel Cerrig, the 1831 stone meetinghouse on Prospect Street, right in Remsen, is the best place to begin. Here the historical society holds meetings, concerts, and other events; here a visitor can explore the Margaret P. Davis library of five hundred Welsh documents, admire the restored church windows, and browse through Welsh hymnals, cookbooks, and coloring books. Don't forget to take a brochure to guide you to historic sites in the area, like the restored 1848 *Capel Enlli* on Fairchild Road, or the 1835 Bethel Church, on Route 12, or the almost twenty Welsh cemeteries, silent evidence of an adjacent, long-gone Welsh church, in the farm country around.

If You Go: The rolling hills of Remsen are a cyclist's delight. Two surviving Welsh cemeteries are very near to the Steuben Memorial State Historic Site (page 43).

Special Events: Ice-cream socials liven up *Capel Enlli* in July and August. In late September Remsen hosts the annual Barn Festival of the Arts, a weekend affair with more than 250 booths, ethnic cooking, and a Welsh songfest. Winter holiday concerts are not uncommon in the stone meetinghouse. Call for an up-to-date schedule.

Exploring Further: What you get out of this excursion depends mainly on what you bring to it in the way of knowledge of Welsh history and lore; Margaret Davis's *Honey Out of the Rafters* or Jay Williams's *Memory Stones* (Purple Mountain Press, 1993), both for sale in the historical society, are lively insiders' introductions to the story of Welsh sites in the area.

Northeast of Remsen is the western edge of the Adirondack Park, and the settlements of Old Forge and Thendara, home of the Adirondack Scenic Railroad (315-369-6290). Plans are underway to make Remsen a stop on the line, so cyclists could board the train in Utica and bike around the countryside. Trains also run from Thendara to Minnehaha, Carter Station, and beyond, along the scenic Moose River.

AMERICAN MAPLE MUSEUM
9756 Main Street
Route 812
Croghan NY 13327
Mail: PO Box 81
Open: Memorial Day weekend–July 1: Mon., Fri., and Sat. 11am–4pm;
    July 1–Labor Day, Mon.–Sat. 11am–4pm; Labor Day–Oct., Mon., Fri., Sat.
    11am–4pm
Admission: $4 adults; $2 children 5 to 12
315-346-1107

If the geographic bulls-eye of the North American sugar-maple country is the little town of Croghan, it's only fitting that here would be the American Maple Museum, and more apt still that the museum's home is a former grade school since everything about the place, from artifacts to their write-ups to the chalky old school smell, seems pitched perfectly to kids.

Here is not the place to come, in other words, for news of the economics of the maple industry from its peak to its imperiled status today, or to learn about subtle ethnographic differences in maple culture from Vermont to Quebec. What you will learn are things like this: most sugarhouses are built on hills to take advantage of the flow of gravity; it takes a cord of wood to produce enough energy to make twenty to thirty gallons of syrup; to make one gallon of syrup, some thirty-five to forty gallons of water must be boiled from the sap.

Artifacts are minimally annotated; mostly, things are left to speak for themselves. And things there are, by the truckload: maple-syrup buckets made from birch bark, wood, coffee cans, and plastic milk jugs; shoulder yokes and storage vats; log troughs, evaporators, maple-sugar forms, and sample taps; snapshots of sugarhouses from all over the Adirondack woods. Each former classroom is dedicated to a different aspect of the industry. Room three is the Maple Hall of Fame, with winners hailing from points as distant as Minnesota and Ontario. Don't miss the pictures of the annual Croghan Maple

Queen, and the grisly news clip about one hapless local accorded "an even chance to live" upon tumbling into a boiling vat of syrup in 1922.

One arresting exhibit is a display of wrought-iron skidding tongs, peaveys, cant hooks, toggle hooks, and horseshoes from the smithy of Jack Walsh of Lyons Falls. Walsh, son of an Irish immigrant, was renowned for the endurance and sensitivity of his handiwork. Of his horseshoes it is written that "he always designed [them] out of a profound knowledge of the anatomy of the animal's feet." Across the room a model kitchen of a lumber camp features old pie tins for dinnerware and a vintage Findlay Victrola. Connoisseurs of chain-saw technology will surely thrill to a fearsome jumble of sixteen-some gas-guzzling early models that look as ready to go as ever.

If You Go: Less than an hour is plenty of time to take in this specialized and likable museum. And don't forget to pick up some maple sugar candy and maple cream at the gift counter as you leave.

Special Events: On the second Saturday in May, the Maple Museum celebrates its opening with pancakes, the crowning of a Maple Queen, two inductions into the Maple Hall of Fame, a chicken barbecue at noon, and a parade at 1pm. All day there's a craft fair and demonstrations of maple equipment. Then there's an ice-cream social (featuring — you guessed it — maple sundaes) on the weekend of July Fourth, with music and a cakewalk. The Croghan Lumberjack Festival comes to town the weekend after Labor Day. A parade and competitive events like log rolling, ax throwing, and chainsawing follow a pancake breakfast. Evening is reserved for a greased pole climb (they use Crisco), and then another breakfast with more events on Sunday.

Exploring Further: The historic Basselin home, just down the street, has long since passed from the hands of that leading family, but you may still pause a moment to admire the handsome nineteenth-century mansion, testament to the local influence and wealth of Theodore Basselin, one of the great lumbermen and mill owners of the western Adirondack region. Nearby a wrought-iron fence surrounds the Basselin cemetery, and across the street sits a steam locomotive from the Lowville and Beaver River Railway that Basselin did so much to promote. One of the last waterpowered mills in the state is on an island in the Beaver River in Croghan; window sashes and moldings are made at Croghan Island Mill just as they were 150 years ago. The place doubles as a hardware store, so you're welcome to stop by. The town is also home to a tasty sausage called Croghan bologna, made at the butcher shop on Main Street. While you're there, pick up some sharp cheese curds from a local cheese plant.

For an overview of Lewis County history, check out the Gould Mansion (page 148), in Lyons Falls.

AGRICULTURAL MUSEUM AT STONE MILLS
Northern New York Agricultural Historical Society
Route 180, Stone Mills
Mail: Box 108, La Fargeville NY 13656
Hours: Daily June–Sept., 9am–4pm
Admission: $2 adults, $1 children 6–12
315-658-2353 or 788-2882

When the United States was founded, as much as ninety-five percent of the North American population was engaged in farming. Two hundred years later the farming population is so negligible the Census Bureau barely counts its numbers — and it's shrinking all the time. Still, agrarian ideals like self-sufficiency, thrift, and rootedness in the land continue to keep a hold on our self-image, and museums that celebrate this Jeffersonian heritage exert a poignant and deep-reaching allure.

What distinguishes the Agricultural Museum at Stone Mills from other farm museums of its type is its presentation of the old-time farming life in the context of community, not a thing detached, but integrally hitched up to church, school, mill, and home. Thus barns and displays of farm tools and machinery are just part of what's in store on a visit to Stone Mills.

The sturdy 1837 Meeting House, with tall deep-silled windows and thick-as-bunkers limestone walls, was once shared equally by Lutherans, Baptists, and Methodists, and enjoyed sufficient patronage to require a shed big enough for twenty-five teams. The great red barn behind the Meeting House is sectioned into exhibit areas on the Apiary, the Chicken Coop, the Rural Carpenter's Bench, and Washing and Laundry. Some tools are identified, some not, and few are annotated with captions. But the Sears Automatic Chicken Brooder/Super Hatcher will most likely catch any child's fancy, as will the dog treadmill that once put farm-bound Fidos to good use powering butter churns or washing machines. Model country kitchens can get to looking a dime a dozen — what with the inevitable cast-iron stove, kettle, and sauerkraut crock — but don't miss the model farmhouse bathroom with a zinc-lined pine-frame tub.

Another display shed holds the bigger machinery, nearly all of it devised before the combustion engine. Here, too, space is divvied into seasons and domains of farm life, from Cropland to Sap Bush, Ice House to Barn. Enlarged photos of rituals of farm life are livened with labels ranging from the elegiac to the bluntly graphic, like this memory from a local farmer: "A couple of guys sat on the pig and cut his jugular vein. Then he ran around screaming and he fell down. [The hired girl] always went inside and pounded on the piano until the pig stopped screaming."

What strikes one most forcefully about the long rows of farm equipment is the sheer ingenuity of nineteenth-century invention, as bean seeders, corn seeders, and twine-binding harvesters gain in elaboration and efficiency at the same time that they manage to retain some feature of fine, even elegant, design. From the humble tractor seat to the turned handle of the flail, nearly every tool has some purely aesthetic aspect, some element of organic grace.

The 1837 one-room schoolhouse that with the Meeting House brackets the museum grounds came from five miles away. On weekends the school-house is often staffed with retired teachers who once taught in one-room schoolhouses themselves. Low bookshelves are aclutter with early school-books. Portraits of George Washington, pull-down maps, and framed diplomas adorn the walls. Kids can slide into the wrought iron desks and bone up on *Essentials of Geography* and *Junior Home*. The Exhibit Hall comes to life mostly for things like quilt and flower shows, barn dances, and music festivals. Across the street from the museum complex is a turn-of-the-century cheese factory with all manner of cheese-making equipment on occasional display. Additionally, you can buy lunch and a cool drink at the snack bar in the former icehouse, and pick up locally made cheese, honey, and maple syrup on museum premises as well.

If You Go: If this is your one and only expedition to a farm museum, plan on several hours. Notwithstanding the lack of consistent captions, the artifacts are neat. And the grassy grounds ringed with corn fields make a fine place to picnic on a sunny day. Most buildings — not the church — are wheelchair accessible.

Special Events: The museum launches its springtime opening with a barn dance and dairy celebration. Later in June comes a draft-horse show and pull, and halfway into July, an old-time music festival. An annual three-day crafts fair of regional renown takes over the first weekend in August, drawing two hundred craftspeople and crowds approaching eighteen thousand. The Lions Club barbecues chicken. The fire department grills franks. The third weekend in August is the Harvest Celebration, with flower show, raffle, auction, bluegrass music, and chicken barbecue again. As always, call ahead for times and details.

Exploring Further: In nearby Watertown is the hands-on Sci-Tech Center, the rolling views from Thompson Park, and the elegantly furnished Jefferson County Historical Society (page 149). And south of Stone Mills is the historic two-century-old hamlet of Brownville, famed for its gleaming limestone structures and named after the Quaker settler turned War of 1812 general, Jacob Brown. In the depot here, a facsimile of a turn-of-the-century station interior, is a fine railroad museum and a library. Much of this town is on the National Register of Historic Places, and a walking or driving tour of Brownville might combine nicely with a visit to the museum at Stone Mills.

Notable Homes

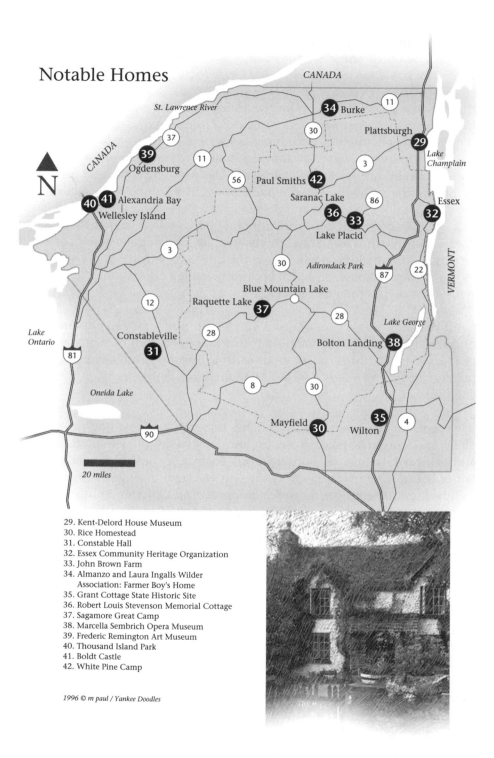

CANADA

St. Lawrence River

34 Burke

11

30

Plattsburgh

29

Lake Champlain

37

CANADA

39
Ogdensburg

11

56

Paul Smiths 42

3

40 41 Alexandria Bay
Wellesley Island

Saranac Lake

86

Essex

36 33

Lake Placid

32

N

3

30

Adirondack Park

87

22

VERMONT

Blue Mountain Lake

12

Raquette Lake 37

Lake Ontario

Constableville

28

28

Lake George

Bolton Landing 38

31

81

8

30

Oneida Lake

Mayfield

35

4

90

Wilton

30

20 miles

1996 © m paul / Yankee Doodles

CHAPTER FOUR

NOTABLE
HOMES

■■■

O ne tried-and-true method of bringing history to life is through the stories of artifacts, the possessions of people both famous and not so famous. House museums that tell these stories are common across the country, indeed the world. Sometimes the personage in question is undeniably an important figure in the grand march of global affairs and everything he or she touched takes on iconic significance. Other times, we treasure historic homes for thoroughly interpreting the stories of ordinary people who happened to leave behind furniture, toys, tools, scrapbooks, diaries, and a structure that all function for modern observers as a freestanding biography with walls, windows, and roof. Sometimes family furnishings and artifacts invoke the taste and hobbies of a single contained era — colonial or Victorian, say — and sometimes, as in the case of the Rice Homestead, in Mayfield, they showcase the changing interests and styles of a single family over many generations. Then there are historic homes like the Old Fort House, in Fort Edward, where the whole community has sent in family heirlooms, and in these cases the biography is of a hamlet more than any one dynasty or clan.

Historic homes in the Adirondacks and surrounding valleys tend to fall into the latter category, although in this chapter — in more or less chronological order — you'll find described the humble farmstead of abolitionist John Brown, the final resting place of General U.S. Grant, the studio of a grande dame of the opera, and Calvin Coolidge's summer White House. In other chapters there are house museums, too, but if they're listed elsewhere it's because they deal with more than simple family heritage or serve as a backdrop for unique collections that have meaning larger than the life of the collector.

KENT-DELORD HOUSE MUSEUM
17 Cumberland Avenue
Plattsburgh NY 12901
Open: Mar.–Dec., Tues.–Sat. 12 noon–4pm
Admission: $3 adults, $2 students and seniors
518-561-1035

Plattsburgh's Kent-Delord House was built in 1797 and is one of only a few eighteenth-century homes left along Lake Champlain's western shore. Robin Brown

Set in a strategic spot overlooking where the Saranac River empties into Lake Champlain, the Kent-Delord House seems far removed from the business and bustle of modern Plattsburgh. Its white wooden fence, manicured gardens, and handsome Federal-style facade reflect two hundred years of local history; the home was occupied by the Delord family from 1810 to 1913, after which the place became a museum.

The location was far from peaceful, though, during the War of 1812. British officers commandeered the house just prior to the Battle of Plattsburgh, which was a true test of naval power. A few artifacts in the house recall those days: an officer's mess chest, cannonballs, portraits; but the museum itself is not solely a time capsule of that era. Every couple of years the theme changes to represent different generations of the family, and furniture, decorative items, even kitchenware are replaced. In 1997–98 the house will be dedicated to the period from 1830 to 1860, when Elizabeth and William Swetland lived there; clothing, jewelry, and early photographs will be displayed.

The house itself is a lovely artifact, with wide board floors, finely crafted woodworking, and graciously proportioned rooms. There's exceptional eighteenth-century furniture (a cupboard, table, desk, and the like), including pieces made in the Champlain Valley, and paintings attributed to John Singleton Copley, Henry Inman, and other well known portraitists. Only the first floor is open to the public; offices are upstairs. Docents lead tours; feel free to ask questions about the house's residents whose life and times may not just then happen to be on display. Members of the Delord family, for instance, include Fanny Hall, who had a successful business manufacturing Fanoline, a popular salve, in the late 1800s.

If You Go: Allow about an hour for a visit, and plan extra time to walk along Cumberland Avenue to the Champlain Monument. There are benches overlooking the water; the Saranac River is also one of the few places in northern New York where you can fly fish year-round. Although the Kent-Delord House projects a formal, restrained aura, older children will probably find it interesting, especially during the holidays, when the place is decked out in ribbons, greenery, toys, and candles.

Special Events: On Friday evenings in the summer, concerts of classical and traditional music are held in the carriage barn. The museum also sponsors house and garden tours of noteworthy homes in the area in spring and summer; Christmas programs are held during the first two weeks in December.

Exploring Further: Although few War of 1812 sites remain in the region and fewer still are open to the public, the Champlain Trail Map Guide lists all kinds of historic destinations, from "Fort Blunder" (built by the U.S. on Canadian soil — oops!) to Crab Island, where casualties from the Battle of Plattsburgh are buried. To get a copy of the Trail Map Guide, call the Plattsburgh–North Country Chamber of Commerce, 518-563-1000. At Kent-Delord, ask about the current status of Fort Izard, a well-preserved earthen fortification built in 1814, which is on private land. Valcour Island, just a mile or so offshore from Peru, New York, is worth a visit by canoe or kayak, or even cross-country ski in the winter; once a year the Clinton County Historical Society (see page 137) opens up the lighthouse for guided tours. Also, the map published by the Champlain Valley Heritage Network (Route 1, Box 220, Crown Point NY 12928) shows military sites along the lake from Port Kent to Ticonderoga.

Alice T. Miner, who created a delightful museum of Americana in Chazy, was a key figure in Kent-Delord's preservation (see page 156).

RICE HOMESTEAD
328 Riceville Road
Mayfield NY 12217
Mail: Mayfield Historical Society, Box 715
Open: Early June–mid-Sept., Sat.–Sun. 12 noon–4pm
Admission: Donation only
518-661-5130

Many were the Dutch, German, and Scottish settlers in eighteenth-century Fulton County, but the group that has made the most lasting impression on the look and cultural character of the region were the land-starved Yankees from New England who surged into upstate New York hinterlands after the Revolutionary War. Some were veterans who had scoped out the territory during their military service, and one such veteran of General Washington's campaign was Oliver Rice of Connecticut. In 1789 he settled here and built the little home that twenty years later he would skid over to join with a bigger house he built across the street. This cobbled-together clapboard colonial flanked by cornfields is the Rice Homestead, bought back from private owners in recent years by the Mayfield Historical Society at twenty-five dollars a share, and lovingly restored to its colonial condition.

Most of the furnishings were donated to the homestead by Oliver Rice's descendants, and this fact gives the home a kind of cozy familial unity lacking in many other local historical collections where all too often nothing of the original inhabitants has found its way to the site. Here are footrests and an early zither, a soapstone sink, and Rice's own leather satchel and high stool he likely used when he was postmaster of the hamlet named in his honor. A blue-and-red zigzaggy stencil on the floorboards of a downstairs front room has the exotic look of a Turkish rug. Upstairs in the bedrooms are curling tongs, Royal Bay Rhum, ornate bedsteads, and two-hundred-year-old wedding slippers.

But the curatorial peak of the collection is a former bathroom converted into an exhibit area devoted to Mayfield's once-thriving glove-making industry. Ages ago there were as many as fifteen glove shops in this township. From them have come glove-cutting stamps (like giant cookie cutters); and heavy mallets to pound them down; dense, compact machines for sewing liners; and metal and wood forms for stretching and fixing gloves for all occasions.

Other display walls and cases honor Mayfield arrowhead collectors, carpenters, ballplayers, and woodworker Rusty Ruliffson, locally beloved for his folksy carvings of hounds treeing a possum or a man lugging a canoe.

If You Go: All tours are guided here — no roaming at will. Picnic tables outside make this a pleasant spot to lunch, but don't expect a country silence: Route 30 surging directly behind the homestead keeps up a steady drone. Best to combine a visit to this modest, low-key site with a tour of Johnstown, Amsterdam, or Gloversville, where historic destinations abound. Handicap access is limited to the ground floor.

Special Events: A covered-dish community picnic and flea market at the homestead the Sunday after Labor Day weekend mark the formal end of tours. Then the homestead springs to life the first Saturday and Sunday in December with an old-fashioned Christmas Open House, with hot mulled cider, homemade pies and cookies, hand-fashioned decorations, banjo playing, and fiddlers. Come mid-June, the lawn fills up with people sampling homemade strawberry shortcake. And the second Thursday in July, you can feast on ice cream and sway to the strains of the Amsterdam German Band.

Exploring Further: Fulton County is richly peppered with historic sites. Get maps, walking and driving tours, and pamphlets from the Fulton County Regional Chamber of Commerce in Gloversville (518-725-0643) and plan accordingly. Nearby sites include the Fulton County Historical Society (page 144), Johnson Hall (page 30) and Fort Johnson (page 28), and the little-known, quirky, Clark's Museum of Photography, in Broadalbin, especially if Mr. Clark is on the premises to show you around himself (see page 167).

CONSTABLE HALL
Route 26
Constableville NY 13325
Mail: PO Box 36
Open: May 30–Oct. 15, Tues.–Sat. 10am–4:30pm, Sun. 1–4:30pm
Admission: $3 adults, 50¢ children
315-397-2323

Constable Hall was built on the edge of the wilderness, beginning in 1810. B. Folwell

William Constable, an enterprising Irishman like William Johnson (page 28), invested in the North Country in 1787 as one of the partners in the Macomb Purchase, which covered more than three million acres — from the

Adirondacks to the St. Lawrence Valley. Constable began his business career as a fur buyer, expanded into the nascent China trade, and used his international contacts to sell vast tracts of woodlands to European and American land companies.

Constable never saw so much as a square inch of the celebrated purchase. In 1791 he set out to view his lands from Fort Stanwix, but illness forced him to turn back. He died two years later. In 1810, his son, William, began construction of the stone mansion — a project that lasted nearly a decade — but an injury sustained during the final stages of building resulted in a massive infection and his eventual death in 1821.

Even though William Constable never got to enjoy the estate, his widow spent forty-eight summers there, and his son, Casimir, also enjoyed many years at Constable Hall. In fact, only members of the Constable family have lived in the house. In 1948 the last inhabitant sold the estate to Mr. and Mrs. Harry Lewis and Mrs. H.D. Cornwall, who began restoration and presented the home to the Constable Hall Association one year later.

Overlooking rolling Lewis County farmland, Constable Hall is modest in size but magnificent overall. The rooms are beautifully balanced, filled with a synergistic mix of furniture and decorative arts ranging from China-trade chests, curios, and porcelain to a Duncan Phyfe sideboard, a Chippendale bed, numerous portraits, and many artifacts connected to the Bonaparte family, who were among the first eager buyers of Macomb Purchase lands in the Black River Valley. Each guided tour is very personal and entertaining, filled with dizzying details, as the narrator explains that this blue-and-gold jar belonged to Napoleon, this was Lafayette's hunting flask, this item was a gift from Alexander Hamilton. It seems positively astonishing that such a family in such a remote place could be so well acquainted with the leading citizens of the day.

Upstairs are four bedrooms, including a child's room containing cradles, dolls, and well-preserved eighteenth-century clothing, which the guide will carefully remove from the armoire so that you can admire the fine embroidery. Among the exceptional textiles is a woven coverlet circa 1849 from Jefferson County, showing a weeping willow, bull, and fence in the border.

The basement contains the kitchen and wine cellar; the garden, with appropriate perennials of the era laid out in the shape of the Cross of St. Andrew, is delightful.

If You Go: Constable Hall is on a small paved road off Route 12 about one mile from Constableville; a large sign clearly shows the entrance.

Allow at least an hour and a half for a tour. If you are interested in a particular subject — Canton china, for example — tell the guide when you arrive. Constable Hall is packed with artifacts and the barriers are minimal; although there's a great deal here for children to see, younger ones must be under control. The first floor is wheelchair accessible, but not the second floor.

The tree-shaded grounds offer plenty of places to picnic; however, be sure to bring what you need since the nearest grocery is distant.

Special Events: The annual antiques and craft show is held in mid-June; July features a candlelight concert in the hall; and three popular candlelight tours, with special seasonal decorations, are held in August, September, and October. There are also occasional workshops in quilting, lace making, china painting, and other early nineteenth-century skills.

Exploring Further: Explore the region known as Castorland, the French loyalist territory that spans from Lake Bonaparte to the towns of LeRay and Chaumont, which were within the 630,000 acres Constable sold to Pierre Chassanis in the 1790s. Also, the Constable family explored the Adirondacks extensively; on their camping expeditions they ranged as far as Raquette Lake and Blue Mountain Lake as early as the 1840s. Two books by historian Edith Pilcher give excellent background: *Castorland: French Refugees in the Western Adirondacks, 1793–1814* (Harbor Hill Books, 1985) and *The Constables: First Family of the Adirondacks* (North Country Books, 1992).

ESSEX COMMUNITY HERITAGE ORGANIZATION
Boquet Road
Essex NY 12936
518-963-7088

Essex was founded in 1765, but since William Gilliland's hamlet lay smack in the path of numerous armies roaming up and down Lake Champlain, the place was reduced to rubble on several occasions. After the Revolution, though, the town really began to thrive, thanks to stone quarries, iron mines, and tanneries; two shipyards built vessels for ferrying materials across the lake and down the Champlain Canal. By 1850 more than two thousand people lived in Essex. Then, after the Civil War, a slow fade began. Lake commerce was overshadowed by railroads, the population declined, and there was little need for new housing in town.

That loss is our gain today. Essex is a historic-preservationist's dream, a National Register community of largely intact mid-nineteenth-century brick and stone houses, churches, inns, and shops laid out in streets and alleys with prim yards and gardens. Essex Community Heritage Organization has published two self-guided tours of the town; one is a pamphlet with a map and the other — well worth the four-dollar fee — has lots more detail and photographs. Stroll around with a guide in hand and you'll happily cover about three miles.

Most buildings you'll be able to appreciate from the outside only, but by all means try the Essex Inn (circa 1810) for a meal on the capacious veranda, and check out the personable shops along Main Street. Greystone, a fine mid-nineteenth-century mansion across from the ferry dock, opened for tours in 1996; if you can plan a visit for a time when the owners are in residence, you're bound to learn quite a bit about this marvelous place (518-963-8058).

Greystone, in Essex, opened for tours in 1996. B. Folwell

If You Go: Make a day of it or even spend the night. More than a few historic homes have been recently converted to bed-and-breakfasts.

Special Events: Several non-profit groups are active locally: Essex Initiatives sponsors the Essex Maritime Festival (518-963-7504), in July, and other programs, and there are organ concerts in historic churches and performances in the old Masonic Lodge.

Exploring Further: Westport, just a twenty-minute drive away, also has numerous attractive nineteenth-century structures; for a walking tour, call the chamber of commerce (518-962-8383).

JOHN BROWN FARM
John Brown Road
Lake Placid NY 12946
Open: Late May–Oct., Weds.–Sat. 10am–5pm; Sun. 1–5pm
Admission: Free
518-523-3900

John Brown — farmer, surveyor, wool merchant, and abolitionist — moved to North Elba, near present-day Lake Placid, in 1849. The location he chose had belonged to Gerrit Smith, a wealthy upstate New Yorker and son of New York's largest land-owner, Peter Smith. Some of the land Gerrit Smith inherited he made available to freeborn blacks who wanted to homestead; Brown was supposed to assist these settlers by his own example. Some came and stayed, but rugged farming conditions in the Adirondacks kept or drove more prospective black pioneers away.

John Brown's body lies just beyond the iron gate. B. Folwell

Clearing fields, raising crops, and building barns and fences didn't hold Brown's interest as much as the call to antislavery concerns. He left his wife and children alone on the farm to travel to Kansas, Ohio, and, ultimately, Harpers Ferry, Virginia. Mary Brown's letter to her husband in May 1856 hints at the privation they endured: "We have tried to use what means we had as economical as we knew how to & tried to keep out of debt. What we have now received will pay up all of our debt and some [left] over to get leather for shoes the girls and I have not had any since we came here [in 1849]." Seven years without shoes in the frozen North!

A decade after he had moved to the Adirondacks, Brown was dead, hanged following the raid at Harpers Ferry. It was his wish to be buried in North Elba and his body was brought back in solemn procession from the Essex County seat, Elizabethtown, in December 1859. His grave and those of sons and followers is in a wrought-iron-fenced enclosure near the house. All-weather signs explain the graves, the history of the property, and how the appearance of buildings has changed over the years.

The John Brown Farm has been a New York State Historic Site since 1895. The home itself is a modest frame building with a parlor and a kitchen downstairs and loft upstairs. It's sunny and spare, nicely furnished with period pieces, including some furniture in the front room (desk, chairs, shelves) that belonged to Brown's family. Interpretive labels are minimal in the house, but they're not really necessary. One case upstairs explains the true origins of the song "John Brown's Body" — the earliest version was a vernacular tune poking fun at an Irish-born soldier in Boston. Julia Ward Howe, a friend of John Brown, based her "Battle Hymn of the Republic" on that folk song.

If You Go: John Brown Farm is off Old Military Road on the outskirts of Lake Placid, near the Horse Show Grounds. Follow the signs to the site. Allow about forty-five minutes for a visit and bring a camera: the setting is quite lovely, although the Olympic ski jumps add a jarring modern accent. There's a nature trail that's a pleasant ten-minute walk through the woods. Children seven and older can relate the site to the era of homespun lessons in school; older students connect it to the Civil War. The first floor of the house is wheelchair accessible.

Special Events: In past summers, lectures and thematic tours have been offered and a Civil War encampment in July was a very popular affair, but recent state administrative changes have made future programs at John Brown Farm uncertain. The site will remain open to the public, but call ahead for information about events.

Exploring Further: Grant Cottage (page 82), in Wilton, is preserved as a memorial to a great hero of the Civil War and offers another perspective on this period in American history. For background reading on John Brown, try Stephen Oates's highly regarded *To Purge With Blood*.

ALMANZO AND LAURA INGALLS WILDER ASSOCIATION
Farmer Boy's Home
Stacey Road
Burke NY
Mail: PO Box 283, Malone NY 12953
Open: Memorial Day weekend–Labor Day, Tues.–Sat. 11am–4pm,
    Sun. 1–4pm
Admission: Donation
518-483-1207/4516

One of the North Country's newest museums played a major role in a classic of children's literature, Laura Ingalls Wilder's *Farmer Boy*. The book, a portrait of life in northern New York in the two decades bracketing the Civil War, is the second in the Little House series. In this spot James and Angeline Wilder and their six children lived a hard-working, self-sufficient life with time left over for county fairs, church socials, and outdoor fun.

In 1987 the Almanzo and Laura Ingalls Wilder Association purchased a neglected farm with a simple Greek Revival house built about 1840 on the outskirts of Malone. The place was the boyhood home of Almanzo Wilder, the author's husband, and from his charming reminiscences she derived the book. The house itself has been carefully restored with period furnishings ranging from rag rugs to an ornate wood stove made in Malone, but only a few items actually belonged to the family, which left upstate New York in 1875.

Downstairs are a pantry, large kitchen, parlor, and tiny bedrooms; upstairs are large and small bedrooms and a loft where James Wilder made shingles. Throughout the house, copies of illustrations by Garth Williams that appeared in *Farmer Boy* are placed in appropriate spots, like atop the cobbler's bench in the dining room. Helpful, articulate volunteers explain artifacts and customs without being too precious or intrusive.

The site is a work in progress and is testament to years of volunteer effort and fund-raising. A large barn — replacing one that burned years ago — has just been completed and restoration of the property continues.

Civil War reenactors gather at Farmer Boy's Home in late July each year. B. Folwell

If You Go: This is a perfect place to break up a long car trip along the northern reaches of New York and lure ten-year-olds away from playing with their GameBoys; reread *Farmer Boy* to recall episodes when Almanzo's exuberance got him into hot water. Bring a picnic, kites to fly, and even the dog. Allow at least forty-five minutes for a visit.

Special Events: In late July, Civil War reenactors take over the fields and maple grove for a weekend of pretend fighting and camp life in tiny canvas tents. Skirmishes, complete with cannon fire, are scheduled a couple of times a day. While the affair is very popular, attracting a crowd of three hundred or more, it's hard to grasp what those Rebel soldiers are doing so close to the Canadian border; maybe it's better to suspend disbelief and get into the linsey-woolsey spirit of the moment.

Exploring Further: A few miles away, in an ornate Italianate home, is the Franklin County House of History (page 153), which shows a broad sweep of local commerce, including the days when the county produced more than a million pounds of hops a year.

GRANT COTTAGE STATE HISTORIC SITE
Mount McGregor Road
Wilton NY 12866
Mail: PO Box 2253
Open: Memorial Day–Labor Day, Weds.–Sun. 10am–4pm;
    Sept.–Columbus Day, Sat.–Sun. 10am–4pm
Admission: $2.50 adults, $2 seniors, $1 for youth 5–16
518-587-8277

Ulysses S. Grant, Civil War hero and two-term president of the United States, spent his final days at a cottage on Mount McGregor, high above the farm fields of Saratoga County. There he put the last flourishes on his memoirs; he died on July 23, 1885. His son, Fred, stopped the hands of the mantel clock at a few minutes after eight in the morning to mark his father's passing. For several days Grant's body lay in state in the cottage parlor surrounded by floral tributes from the Grand Army of the Republic and other admirers. In August his remains made a final trip to New York City and were placed in a brick vault in Riverside Park.

The cottage today has been remarkably preserved, with all the furniture and personal effects left exactly as they had been more than a century ago. Grant's monogrammed pajamas and toothbrush are in a glass-fronted case near the leather armchairs he used; the ghostly flower arrangements are still in the parlor; the mantel clock reads 8:11.

Visitors are taken through the house by articulate volunteers from Friends of Grant Cottage or a staff member, and the interpretation of the site concentrates on the former president's days on the mountain rather than his military and political career. (A National Park Service brochure available in the entry room has a simple timeline that highlights his career.)

The cottage has been operated as a historic site since 1890. Since then, numerous other buildings have been added to Mount McGregor, including a sanitorium built in 1911 by Metropolitan Life Insurance Company.

If You Go: Follow the signs to Grant Cottage from Route 9N east of Wilton. The entire Mount McGregor complex is now a state correctional facility, so visitors must enter through the prison gate and check in with the guard. It *is* a little intimidating, but persevere — the site is lovely. Be sure to visit the overlook; from the brow of the hill you can see the monument at the Saratoga battlefield. Allow forty-five minutes to an hour for a visit. The cottage is accessible; although there's a paved walkway to the overlook, the path is quite steep.

Special Events: In mid-June, the friends sponsor an afternoon affair with music, Civil War readings, and storytelling; the Grant Remembrance Day, in late July, features a dramatic reenactment of the Grant family at the cottage during the somber days of 1885. The Victorian Picnic, in late August, is a good bet for the whole family, with crafts demonstrations, music, old-fashioned games for children, and lots of people in period costume.

Exploring Further: Civil War sites in the Adirondacks are few and far between, but the Almanzo Wilder Homestead (also known as Farmer Boy's home; see page 80), near Malone, holds a weekend Civil War encampment with skirmishes and speakers in July. The John Brown Farm State Historic Site (page 78), in Lake Placid, interprets the North Country life of this leader of the antislavery movement. At the foot of Mount McGregor, you'll find the Wilton Heritage Society (page 114).

ROBERT LOUIS STEVENSON MEMORIAL COTTAGE

11 Stevenson Lane
Saranac Lake NY 12983
Open: July 1–Sept. 15, Tues.–Sun. 9:30am–12 noon, 1–4pm
Admission: $1 adults, 50¢ children
518-891-1462

In this humble farmhouse overlooking the Saranac River, writer Robert Louis Stevenson spent 1887–88, hoping to recover from tuberculosis. He was a patient of Dr. Edward Livingston Trudeau, who pioneered the fresh-air cure for the disease, but RLS's immense popularity led him to find quiet, private accommodations from a local family, the Bakers, rather than stay at Trudeau's busy sanitorium.

Stevenson did not merely lounge during his time in Saranac Lake. He wrote *The Master of Ballantrae* and several essays for *Scribner's* magazine, plus a collaborative work with Lloyd Osbourne, *The Wrong Box*. He also skated, hiked, and entertained his extended family.

The house museum opened in 1916 and remains a period tribute faithful to the writer's memory, with scores of photographs showing Stevenson at work and at play, and in the company of such notables as Queen Liliokalani of Hawaii. More pictures show his ancestral home, in Scotland, Stevenson's yacht in the South Pacific, and other glimpses of the world-famous author's globetrotting. There are cases with his notebooks, first editions, and personal effects such as his embroidered velvet cap and jacket, all carefully labeled; the living room and bedroom are furnished with antiques of the time. Note the cigarette burns on the mantel: despite his disease, RLS smoked about four packs of cigarettes a day, and he often left a smoldering one on the wooden mantelpiece. One of the cases holds a bagpipe, but between Stevenson's tuberculosis and chain smoking, he just couldn't fill it with hot air.

If You Go: Allow about forty-five minutes for a visit. Special events such as dramatic readings are occasionally scheduled; call ahead for dates and times.

Exploring Further: Look for the plaque of Stevenson by sculptor Gutzon Borglum — best known for creating Mount Rushmore — next to the front door of the Baker house. Borglum also made a life-size bronze-and-marble portrait of Dr. Trudeau sitting in a cure chair, which can be seen outdoors at Trudeau Institute, located off Algonquin Drive, in Saranac Lake. Follow the signs for the institute off Route 3 just west of town.

Stevenson Cottage is a perfect spot from which to launch a tour of other Saranac Lake buildings that date back to the village's days as a health resort. Caring for men, women, and children with tuberculosis was a major local industry that began there in the 1880s. Several sanitoriums were built in and around Saranac Lake; even individual families took in the sick. Historic Saranac Lake (518-891-0971) sponsors lectures, tours, and publications about this important industry.

SAGAMORE GREAT CAMP

Sagamore Road
Raquette Lake NY 13436
Mail: Box 146
Open: Daily July 4–Labor Day, tours at 10am and 1:30pm;
   Labor Day–Columbus Day, Sat.–Sun.
Admission: Tours $7 adults, $3 children
315-354-5311

Perched like an overgrown Swiss music box on the shore of a remote mountain lake, Sagamore is in a world all its own. The complex — with a massive log main lodge, cedar-bark-sided cottages tucked into wooded hillsides, game room, dining hall, outdoor bowling alley, and servants' homes, workshops, and barns — was a self-sufficient enclave in the midst of the wilderness, ready to meet the recreational needs of the Vanderbilt family, which ranged from entertaining high-society guests like Gary Cooper and Madame Chiang Kai-Shek to woodsy pursuits like hunting, fishing, and ice-skating. For students of Adirondack traditions and American buildings this is a must-see place, with several excellent examples of rustic architecture in good condition; if you want to experience living in a Great Camp, albeit sans maids and butlers, you can even spend the night here or take a weekend workshop in crafts, music, history, or wilderness skills.

Tours begin in the servants' area, with a narrated slide show creating a context for understanding the buildings, the family, and how the entire region was a mecca for the wealthy at the turn of the century. Interns lead the way through the blacksmith shop and barns and on to individual cottages and the main lodge; because guests are usually in residence, bedrooms and service areas are not included. Guides are equally adept at telling how the staff worked as well as how the owners and guests played, contrasting their lives as you go from the lovely, spacious dining room to the cramped quarters above the laundry. Often you'll see stonemasons or carpenters at work on restoration projects, showing the constant care a place like Sagamore needs to stay in tiptop shape.

The main lodge at Sagamore was built in 1897. Courtesy of Sagamore Great Camp, Raquette Lake

If You Go: Allow at least two hours for a tour; plan to linger a while to appreciate this beautiful spot. You may bring a picnic, and a snack bar serves coffee, soda, and sandwiches. Children are welcome, and guides will try to tailor the tour to youngsters, but there's little in the way of participatory exhibits. Definitely bring a camera for shooting building exteriors, sparkling waters, and rolling, forested peaks. Bring a mountain bike if you'd like to explore woods roads, or ask about hiking trails that circle Sagamore Lake. A walk in the woods leads you to the Sagamore sugarbush and the site of the complex's hydroelectric dam on a rushing stream.

For the most part, the historic structures at Sagamore are not wheelchair accessible.

Special Events: Sagamore celebrates its centennial in 1997, so watch for a flurry of activity. Even in ordinary years, the place has an impressive roster of conferences and educational programs, including Elderhostel several times a year. Adirondack Discovery (315-357-3598), an educational outreach program affiliated with the Adirondack Park Visitor Interpretive Centers, also sponsors occasional lectures at Sagamore.

Exploring Further: "America's Castles," a video produced by the Arts & Entertainment cable network, features Sagamore, Uncas, and Pine Knot, all Adirondack Great Camps near Raquette Lake developed by William West Durant from 1876 on. The program is an excellent introduction to rustic architecture and shows places that are not open to the public. If you'd like to see other examples of Adirondack architecture in the general vicinity, a narrated cruise aboard the *William West Durant*, on Raquette Lake (315-354-5532), brings you near Echo Camp, Pine Knot, Bluff Point, and North Point.

Other Great Camps that you can visit include Santanoni Preserve, near Newcomb, and White Pine Camp (page 93), near Paul Smiths. You'll have to hike, bike, or take a horse-drawn wagon into Santanoni, which is at the end of a five-mile woodland road; the buildings are locked up and in fair — not great — condition. Occasionally there are special tours organized by Adirondack Architectural Heritage (518-834-9328).

To understand the scope of William West Durant's empire, read Craig Gilborn's *Durant: The Fortunes and Woodland Camps of a Family in the Adirondacks* (Adirondack Museum, 1986); for a full-color regional architectural history, study *Great Camps of the Adirondacks* (Godine, 1982) by Harvey Kaiser. The *Story of Sagamore* by Howard Kirschenbaum brings the buildings and the characters into sharp focus.

MARCELLA SEMBRICH OPERA MUSEUM
Lake Shore Drive
Bolton Landing NY 12814
Mail: PO Box 417
Open: Daily June 15–Sept. 15, 10am–5:30pm
Admission: $5 adults
518-644-2492/9839

A pink stucco cottage nestled under tall, somber pines on a busy stretch of Lake George shoreline seems an unlikely spot indeed in which to find a bright gem of musical history, but this site is the former studio of diva Marcella Sembrich. Today it's hard to imagine her star quality, but the walls of this lovely little home bear witness to that fact through tributes from Gustav Mahler, Johannes Brahms, Clara Schumann, Leo Delibes, and dozens more composers and conductors of the day. Sergei Rachmaninoff wrote, "I weave daisies into the crown of Marcella Sembrich," and Franz Liszt, upon meeting the seventeen-year-old prodigy in 1875, said, "You have three pairs of wings, little one, on which to fly to fame. You can become a great pianist, a great violinist, or a great singer — but sing, sing for the world, for you have the voice of an angel."

Looking into the pines from Marcella Sembrich's Lake George cottage. B. Folwell

Marcella Kochanska (she later took her mother's family name) was born in Poland in 1858 and her father was her first musical instructor. She made her operatic debut in Athens and quickly rose to the top. She joined the Metropolitan Opera Company in 1883, its first season, then went back to Europe to reign as the premiere soprano. In 1898, she rejoined the Met and stayed on for a decade, delighting American audiences from coast to coast. She founded the vocal departments of the Juilliard School, in New York, and the Curtis Institute, in Philadelphia, but her favorite spot to work with gifted students was in her studio on Lake George.

Today, the spotless studio — open to the public for some sixty years — is lovingly cared for: cases are filled with gleaming sterling silver tributes and opera posters, vintage photographs, paintings, friezes, and prints cover the walls. Sembrich's piano reposes in a corner draped with a silk shawl. Take time to read the vignettes from her scrapbook, which include passages of music and autographs from composers who admired her, and correspondence with Samuel Clemens, presidents, and so forth. Lavish costumes and accessories are displayed, as are homey things like her gardening basket, bird books, and other aspects of her life on the lakeshore.

If You Go: Allow about forty-five minutes to visit the house. The museum's summer curator is usually a composer in residence. Ask to request to hear a recording of Sembrich if one isn't already playing. Take ten minutes to stroll around the lovely, shaded grounds. There are plenty of benches for quiet picnics, nice plantings, and changing exhibits in a former bathhouse.

Special Events: Throughout the summer, there are Wednesday afternoon lectures by music historians and recitals by voice and piano students.

Exploring Further: The Bolton Historical Museum (page 102) has material on Sembrich and other musical luminaries — Samuel Barber and Gian Carlo Menotti, to name a couple — who flocked to the area. H. Goddard Owen's *A Recollection of Marcella Sembrich* (reprinted 1995) is a handsome tribute to the diva, with numerous photographs and excerpts from letters.

FREDERIC REMINGTON ART MUSEUM
303 Washington Street
Ogdensburg NY 13669
Open: May 1–Oct. 31, Mon.–Sat. 10am–5pm, Sun. 1pm–5pm;
    Nov. 1–Apr. 30, Tues.–Sat. 10am–5pm
(Closed for renovations through July 3, 1997)
Admission: $3 adults, $2 seniors and students
315-393-2425

An art museum honoring America's best-loved sculptor and painter of frontier life, of bucking broncos and lonesome cowpokes, Indian war parties and gloomy scouts, in . . . upstate New York? Why not? Frederic Remington was not only born in nearby Canton, he also spent part of his youth in Ogdensburg and later returned to build a summer place in the Thousand Islands, fish his favorite Adirondack trout streams, pal around with favorite guides, and paint his beloved North Country lakes and woods. And if he never actually lived in David Parish's grand estate with its glossy oak staircase and fine view of the river, his wife and sister-in-law did — not for long, but enough to give the place a feeling of an actual family affair.

Of Remington's twenty-two bronze castings, an impressive fourteen are in this museum, including the exuberant *Coming Through the Rye*, the chilling *Scalp*, and *Mountain Man*, figures so familiar as to seem downright iconic. Also here is the deservedly famous engraving of the buffalo hunter spitting ammo into the barrel of his rifle while astride a pony at full gallop, the painting called *The Last March* (remember the starved, riderless horse surrounded by snarling wolves under a night sky full of stars?), and a fine array of Remington's lesser-known North Country scenes that celebrate French-Canadian guides, native American canoeists, and boating on a choppy St. Lawrence.

Collectors of personal trivia will be interested to discover that Remington — unlike the sinewy figures he so fondly immortalized in his art — tipped the scales at three hundred pounds. He also favored elk-tooth cufflinks and wrote novels. But you don't need to want to learn about Remington to stop into this lovely home. Here resided one of the great land speculators and settlers of men in the North Country, David Parish, of whose estate, which once included rows of stables, carriage barns and stone walls, only this mansion remains.

Running the Rapids *pencil sketch by Frederic Remington.* Courtesy of the Frederic Remington Art Museum, Ogdensburg

If You Go: Forewarned is forearmed: the museum will be closed for renovations beginning in fall 1996, to reopen in July 1997.

How long to stay depends mostly on your love or lack of it for Remington, though be aware the museum also houses a nice collection of regional and Adirondack paintings by other artists, too, with changing exhibits by contemporary painters. There is additionally a fine gift store with lots of posters, calendars, and cards, and special-order Remington bronzes. Handicap access will improve with planned building renovations.

Special Events: The first Saturday in December the house gussies up in Christmas finery and hosts a splashy gala. Call ahead for new hours and special events that celebrate the new space.

Exploring Further: Across the street is a block-wide city park commemorating the hapless Fort Oswegatchie — "unfinished, unmanned, and undefended" when the British landed here in 1813. The fort is long gone, but you can take a do-it-yourself walking tour and play connect-the-dots between freestanding pedestals scattered around the park, each of which describes another facet of the fort's role in the War of 1812 and explains why that war, in this corner of New York, was so popularly despised (page 44).

If you'd like to read about Remington, including his own words, these books can be found in local libraries: *Frederic Remington and the North Country* by Atwood Manley and Margaret Manley Mangum (Dutton, 1988*)*; *Frederic Remington, Selected Letters* edited by Allen and Marilyn Splete (Abbeville Press, 1988); *Artist in Residence: the North Country Art of Frederic Remington*, published as an exhibition catalog by the Adirondack Museum and the Remington Museum in 1988; Michael Shapiro and Peter Hassrick's *Frederic Remington: The Masterworks* (Abrams, 1988).

For a thorough background on the community, dating back to French settlement in 1748, Elizabeth Baxter's *Historic Ogdensburg* (1995) is available for $3.00 at the Ogdensburg City Hall.

THOUSAND ISLAND PARK
On the westerly end of County Route 100, Wellesley Island
Just across the Thousand Islands Bridge; follow signs

On the National Historic Register since 1975, the Victorian village called Thousand Island Park got its start in the 1870s as a Methodist summer camp-meeting center. The first shareholders in the still-going Thousand Island Park Corporation leased forty- by eighty-foot lots for platform-tent sites, put up a tabernacle for revival meetings, and a pavilion and a dock to accommodate guests and luggage who came from the mainland by steamboat — the only way to get here before the cowpath widened into a road. Then the platforms sprouted roofs and walls, and the makeshift camps gave way to the extraordinary array of cottages whose displays of lacy gingerbread in the Eastlake style — turned and knobby porch posts, arcing or stairstep trusses and steep-gabled peaks — make the village such a giddy pleasure after the heavy baronial ambitions of the St. Lawrence River chateaux.

If you've ever been to Cape May, New Jersey, or Oak Bluffs, Massachusetts, you have some notion how a place like this might look. The difference is that Thousand Island Park isn't particularly touristy. People really live here; indeed, most of the summer residents are descendants of original campers. Stroll down the sloping green, past the elegant library, to the beloved pavilion, and amble up shady side lanes past families snoozing in hammocks and reading newspapers on side porches. Four- and five-color paint jobs pick out the fanciful handiwork of the jigsaw. The one restaurant is the Candle-light, and that's in the one hotel, the 1903 Wellesley, a simply furnished inn with a double wraparound veranda and a one-room museum (PO Box 284, Thousand Island Park, 13692).

Despite two devastating fires (one in 1890 and a blaze in 1912 that leveled the entire downtown core), the settlement of Thousand Island Park retains a turn-of-the-century mood of Sunday languor. More than this, it captures a moment in American social history when new notions of leisure and recreation, fueled by religious revival fervor, engendered an architectural style that proudly celebrated community, diversity, and play.

If You Go: Because the village started as a religious community, history-minded churchgoers might be inclined to time a visit for a non-denominational service led by a visiting minister from the region. There is no scripted walking tour; you make your own as you go along, though the museum may soon provide a guide. The lakeside pavilion is still undergoing renovation, but in a few years it should be ready for a tour as well.

Special Events: On the Fourth of July weekend, there's a children's parade and a strawberry festival with a band at the pavilion. During summer, movies play in the tabernacle every week.

Exploring Further: For an inside-and-out look at over-the-top Gothic architecture, Boldt Castle on Heart Island is accessible by tour boat from Alexandria Bay (see below). And Alex Bay itself is home to several small museums. Greater Kingston, in Ontario, boasts nineteen museums, historic sites, and art galleries: call 613-548-4415 for information.

BOLDT CASTLE
Heart Island
Alexandria Bay NY 13607
Thousand Islands International Council
Mail: PO Box 400, Collins Landing, Alexandria Bay
Open: Mid-May–mid-Oct. 10am–6:30pm; July–Aug. 10am–7:30pm
Admission: $3.75 adults, $2 children 6–12
315-482-9724, 1-800-8-ISLAND

For a long while the Thousand Islands region in the St. Lawrence River was an Algonquin stomping ground. Then the Iroquois moved in. In 1535, the lush, densely wooded region was claimed and named by France. Toward the end of the eighteenth century, the great land speculators surged into the area, spearheaded by empire builder Alexander Macomb and his partners, who acquired millions of acres. Other owners came and went (many of them never even saw their properties), but it wasn't until the age of the steamship that the islands were deemed fit for development. Rags-to-riches millionaire magnates of the Gilded Age competed to erect ever-more elaborate and ponderous lodges, mansions, even crenelated Rhineland castles — a far cry indeed from the rusticated, artsy-woodsy look of the Adirondack Great Camps.

Best-known and certainly most poignant among these enormous

mansions is Boldt Castle on Heart Island. Born in Prussia, a one-time kitchen worker turned millionaire and owner of the Waldorf-Astoria Hotel in New York City, George C. Boldt erected this palace as a Valentine's Day present to his wife, Louise. Boldt, who pioneered the notion of concierge service on every floor of his hotels, fresh flowers in every room, daily newspapers for every guest, and, best of all, a four-star kitchen, spared no expense on his island retreat. Oak, mahogany, Italian marble, tapestries, and chandeliers were purchased; hundreds of workmen came to work on site and in the quarries of Oak Island, hewing massive blocks of reddish-gray stone and constructing the six-story edifice with 127 rooms.

Then, tragedy. When in 1904 Boldt's wife died, the devastated widower ordered all construction stopped. Never again would he return to the island of his dreams. Vandals assaulted the hulking monument; graffiti left no wall unscarred. By the time the Thousand Islands Bridge Authority bought the property in 1977, the goal was simply to restore the place to its condition the year it was abandoned, that is, enclosed, heated, plumbed, and suitable for tourists.

Today, it's this and more. Visitors explore not just the gardens and gazebo, the peristyle, hennery, and seawall, they can treat themselves to a first-rate exhibit on Gilded Age culture in the Thousand Islands, the story of the castle's rise and fall and spirited recovery, and the tale of Boldt himself, who had hoped to be a surgeon, but couldn't get into medical school — so wound up making millions instead. Two dollars and a little extra time will buy a brief boat ride to Louise Boldt's exquisite boathouse on nearby Wellesley Island, where once were docked the family's three yachts and Mrs. Boldt's ten-bedroom, double-decker houseboat, *La Duchesse*.

The quick way to get to Boldt Castle is from Alexandria Bay on one of Uncle Sam's ten-minute, $6.50 shuttles. A two-and-a-half-hour scenic boat tour of Alexandria Bay also includes a stop at Boldt Castle, complete with a narration on all the local sights.

If You Go: Between the boat ride, a visit to the Yacht House, a tour of the grounds and smaller buildings, a stroll through the museum, and a hike up and down the castle itself, this is a half-day excursion for sure. Stock up on breakfast at the pancake houses of Alex Bay or pack a picnic lunch. The first floor of the castle, Alster Tower, and the powerhouse are handicap accessible, as are the shuttle to the yacht house and the yacht house itself.

Special Events: Fireworks explode over Boldt Castle on the Fourth of July. You can watch from Alexandria Bay or perch yourself underneath them on the grassy grounds of Heart Island itself.

Exploring Further: Back on the mainland in Alex Bay, wildlife buffs can enjoy the carvings and paintings at the A. Graham Thomson Memorial

Museum (315-482-3110) on James and Market streets, or scrutinize the old photographs of boats, hotels, and river life at the Cornwall Brothers Store, also on Market Street. In Clayton is the Antique Boat Museum (page 170) and the Thousand Islands Museum, with a Decoy Hall of Fame, and one for the mighty muskie, too (page 128). Historic destinations proliferate in Cape Vincent (page 127), and Sackets Harbor (page 45).

WHITE PINE CAMP

White Pine Road
Paul Smiths NY 12970
Open: Daily July 1–Columbus Day, tours 1:30 and 2pm; off-season tours by
    appointment
Admission: $8 adults, $7 seniors, $4 children
518-327-3030

The August 1, 1926 *New York Times Magazine* sums up a pivotal episode in the history of this sylvan hideaway: "Mr. Coolidge Is Learning to Play . . . Fishing Takes Its Place Alongside Politics." For six weeks during the summer of 1926 the President and First Lady turned Archibald and Olive White's lakeshore estate into a pine-scented White House, complete with chefs, maids, manservants, Secret Service agents, and a cadre of reporters eager to file every detail of their life in the woods. But even if Cal had never shown his smiling face at Osgood Lake, White Pine Camp would be a noteworthy property.

Construction began in 1907 on the cluster of twenty-some buildings — a true Adirondack Great Camp, with five sleeping cabins, a formal dining hall, two

White Pine Camp's Japanese teahouse is set on a tiny island in Osgood Pond. B. Folwell

boathouses, two teahouses, a wonderful game room with two bowling alleys, plus numerous more practical — indeed, necessary — structures: icehouse, pumphouse, woodworking shop, laundry, garden sheds, carriage house. Two architects, William Massarene and Addison Mizner, designed the massive stone fireplaces, interestingly angled roof lines, and numerous windows framing handsome views; local contractor Benjamin Muncil, who also built Marjorie Merriweather Post's fabulous Topridge estate, on nearby Upper St. Regis Lake, supervised nearly two dozen years of construction here, and added his own architectural touches.

The spectacular site is a long ridge overlooking the water, with what seems like acres of rhododendrons beneath towering red and white pine trees. A self-guided walking tour leads you from the gatehouse to a string of buildings about a ten-minute stroll away. The cabins are cozy and nicely filled with antique rustic, Old Hickory, Mission, or Arts-and-Crafts furniture; each room has a clipboard or two explaining the architectural flourishes and choice of furniture, since little information has surfaced that describes just how places were decorated. All along the way are benches and overlooks, adding to the serenity of the spot.

Architectural highlights include the "Bachelor's Cabin," with its asymmetrical floorplan, and the charming Japanese teahouse, set on a tiny island reached by a long footbridge and an arched stone bridge. Each building, though, is interesting; some even have full-size trees growing through porch roofs that have been shaped to allow them to thrive. The whole place is worth looking at as a composition, a planned community. If Sagamore strikes you as a robber baron's hotel, White Pine Camp is accessible yet private, just the kind of Adirondack retreat that would arise in the reserved, quiet years of the early twentieth century.

If You Go: Allow two hours or more for a visit; you could easily spend most of a day here. Start your tour with a short video in the gatehouse. There are more than two miles of trails to walk, and the woods are lovely. Picnicking is encouraged. Youngsters will probably enjoy this place; beside the rampant chipmunks and blueberries, the buildings are not at all stuffy. One cabin is set up with children's furniture and toys.

Although the main path is paved, most of the connecting paths between buildings are dirt, and there are many sets of stairs, a real problem for the mobility impaired. Special arrangements can be made to drive visitors close to the buildings.

Special Events: White Pine Camp opened in 1995 and remains a work in progress. A permanent exhibit space on Adirondack Great Camps is under construction and research continues on how best to interpret the site. Plans are in the works to rent some of the cabins to guests, and eventually the dining room will open for meals. Call ahead for information about special guided tours.

Exploring Further: If you're intrigued by Great Camp architecture, visit Sagamore (page 84) and Santanoni, near Newcomb, which is accessible only by foot, bike, or horse and wagon. Sagamore sponsors a couple of Great Camps Weekends, which explore several landmarks; Adirondack Architectural Heritage, in Keeseville (518-834-9328), hosts tours of selected rustic gems in the summer and fall.

To read about summers on the nearby St. Regis Lakes, *Camp Chronicles* (Adirondack Museum) by Mildred Phelps Stokes Hooker is a charming depiction of the days when families arrived with train cars full of china, silver, bedding, fancy-dress clothing — plus, of course, an army of servants and teams of horses. *Great Camps of the Adirondacks* (David R. Godine, 1982) by Harvey Kaiser describes rustic architectural gems in full color.

Town Treasures

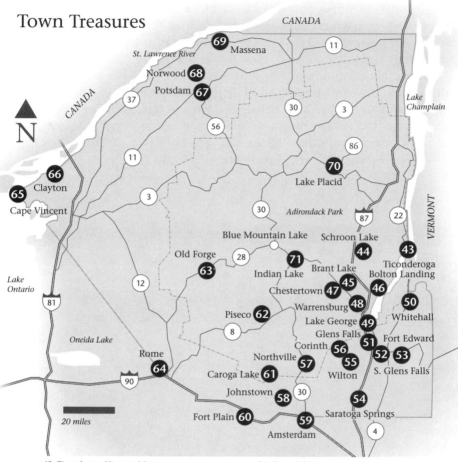

CANADA

St. Lawrence River

69 Massena

11

Norwood 68

Potsdam 67

37

CANADA

30

3

Lake Champlain

56

N

11

66 Clayton

65

Cape Vincent

3

30

Adirondack Park

86

70

Lake Placid

87

22

VERMONT

Lake Ontario

81

Old Forge

63

28

Blue Mountain Lake

71

Indian Lake

Schroon Lake

44

Brant Lake

Chestertown 47 45

Warrensburg 48

43

Ticonderoga
Bolton Landing

46

12

Piseco 62

8

Lake George 49

Glens Falls

Corinth 56

Northville

57

Caroga Lake 61

Johnstown

58

Fort Plain 60

59

Amsterdam

Rome

64

90

50

Whitehall

51 Fort Edward

52 53

55

Wilton

S. Glens Falls

54

Saratoga Springs

4

Oneida Lake

Lake Ontario

20 miles

43. Ticonderoga Historical Society
44. Schroon–North Hudson Historical
    Society Museum
45. Horicon Museum
46. Bolton Historical Museum
47. Museum of Local History, Town of
    Chester Historical Society
48. Museum of Local History, Warrensburg
49. Lake George Historical Society
50. Skenesborough Museum and Urban
    Cultural Park
51. Chapman Historical Museum
52. Historical Society of Moreau and
    South Glens Falls - Parks-Bentley Place
53. Old Fort House
54. Historical Society of Saratoga Springs
55. Wilton Heritage Society

56. Corinth Museum
57. Nellie Tyrell Edinburg Museum and
    Rural Museum
58. Johnstown Historical Society
59. Walter Elwood Museum
60. Fort Plain Museum
61. Caroga Historical Association and Museum
62. Piseco Lake Historical Society
63. Town of Webb Historical Association
64. Rome Historical Society
65. Cape Vincent Historical Museum
66. Thousand Islands Museum of Clayton
67. Potsdam Public Museum
68. Norwood Historical Museum
69. Massena Museum
70. Lake Placid–North Elba Historical
    Society Museum
71. Indian Lake Museum

1996 © m paul / Yankee Doodles

CHAPTER FIVE

TOWN
TREASURES

■■■

When it comes to defining the word *museum* Webster's New World Dictionary is straightforward: "An institution, building or room for preserving and exhibiting artistic, historical or scientific objects." Many places in this chapter fit that to a 'I'; the emphasis is on saving certain pieces of the local past to present to future generations, but the interpretation of those items is a more fluid thing. It's up to us to guess the importance of sadirons, corset stays, and whiffletrees in the larger context of progress and to decipher hand-written cards thumbtacked to fading photographs.

In small towns everywhere the museum is the community attic where things end up because they're old and in the way; they're too valuable to pitch, but not so much that someone else would pay good money for them; they belonged to a beloved resident and give us lasting physical proof of him or her; they tell a weird little story that's now a cherished piece of local folklore; or perhaps the board couldn't figure out how to politely say no when the item was proudly offered. The thread stitching artifacts together in a particular place is that these things came from *our people* — a pride of place and location that makes residents feel included at the same time that it can also, on the other hand, make outsiders feel left out. Sometimes it's nearly impossible to get around that feeling, but the best way is to ask questions if the answers aren't obvious: why did folks come to this particular place? How is it different from ten miles down the road? What do you want me, a total stranger, to know about your town?

Most of the time the answer to the last question is "Look how things have changed." In the "old days," roles and relationships were simply un-

Museums across the North Country show bygone businesses in their prime, like this well-stocked dry-goods store in Madrid. Courtesy of the Adirondack Museum, Blue Mountain Lake

derstood: there was a blacksmith, milliner, wheelwright, and if you wanted something done you had to keep up your end of the bargain. In the heart of the Adirondacks, the sheer weight of accumulated agricultural artifacts — in a region where coyotes are now more common than cows — points to the lost self-sufficiency of an age when settlers could provide their own daily necessities. We're not interdependent anymore, within the boundaries of a rural setting, and we have countless destinations and endless choices for the simplest purchase. Times are vastly different, what with paved highways, school buses, shopping malls, and supermarkets. Add telephones and televisions: cigar-box fiddles, melodeons, and harps tell of days when music was only live and enjoyed in the company of others.

That kind of change has been gradual; others were catastrophic. In a land where most civic, commercial, and residential structures were and are wood, fire has been a major player in altering the physical face of a place. Photographs show grand hotels, stately homes, general stores, all gone.

The emphasis at these museums is plainly on towns and settlers, make no mistake. Laborers who came to work in lumber camps, mines, mills, and factories and then moved away when the job was done enjoy nowhere near the attention of the ones who stayed. Usually, where local industry is celebrated, what is honored is the entrepreneurial spirit of the owners. Nothing wrong with this. The driving personalities behind a local graphite mine, horseshoe-nail factory, or tannery were models of ingenuity, persistence, and considerable civic spirit. But let's not forget the contributions of French-Canadian loggers, Irish factory hands, river drivers, Jewish peddlers, African-American miners, Italian railway crews. These too were Adirondackers, and where local museums fail to include their stories, they short-shrift the richness of their past.

Many of these sites are staffed solely by volunteers and depend on a tiny annual allocation from the town, plus donations and income from bake sales and the like. As a result, you'll see varying levels of care for artifacts; occasionally you'll find items that have been destroyed by years of sitting in the sun or otherwise careless display. Preservation — saving an item from ending up in the local dump — is not always linked with conservation, unfortunately.

In this chapter you'll find notes on dozens of local museums, arranged in rough geographical order starting in the east, in Ticonderoga. From there we proceed south, west, and finally north. Not every museum has a complete listing; some are mentioned in "Exploring Further" sections here or in Chapter Six, beneath the appropriate county museum. Generally these small museums are worth a stop if you're in the neighborhood, researching a particular subject, or interested in an annual event. Do call ahead to confirm hours since many of these organizations depend on volunteers. If you have special needs for access, always check first.

TICONDEROGA HISTORICAL SOCIETY
Montcalm Street
Ticonderoga NY 12885
Open: July–Aug., Mon.–Sat. 10am–4pm; Sept.–July, Weds.–Sat. 10am–4pm
Admission: Free
518-585-7868

John Hancock's house in Boston was torn down during the Civil War, but in 1926, Horace Moses, founder of Strathmore Paper Company and a Ticonderoga native, built an exact replica in his home town, just opposite the village's Revolutionary War monument. This fine building served for a time as the headquarters of the New York State Historical Association and is now home to the local historical society.

This historical society contains considerably more than curios gleaned from small-town life. There's a well-cared-for collection of eighteenth- and nineteenth-century furniture, including Chippendale and Duncan Phyfe pieces, some colonial-era bedroom furniture, a small ladder-back chair that belonged to a young Emily Dickinson and an ornate grandfather clock that was Diamond Jim Brady's. (Try to time your visit so you can hear the clock chime the hours, say eleven or twelve, with deep, resonant notes.) Mahogany gleams, labels are informative but not overwhelming, lighting is good.

An exact replica of John Hancock's house in Boston is the home of the Ticonderoga Historical Society. B. Folwell

The first floor contains a research library (open by appointment) with collections pertaining to Lake George and Lake Champlain history plus genealogical resources. The second floor and basement exhibit the work of local artists, with shows changing regularly. Twentieth-century local history displays highlight involvement in World War II (and the U.S.S. *Ticonderoga*) and vanished entertainment, like the annual Indian pageant and movie houses.

The top floor has a barn loom, fancy sleigh, old-time toys, and a large room devoted to the Defiance Hose Company, a local volunteer fire department founded in 1880. The group functioned much like a fraternal order and owned a lavishly decorated building filled with ornate furniture, portraits of former members, framed ribbons from competitions, monogrammed china, and a fancy embroidered banner that the marching firemen carried in parades. The whole display is quite remarkable because it's hard for us today to imagine a typical volunteer fire department having the money and time to devote to such pursuits.

If You Go: Allow about forty-five minutes to an hour for a visit. Youngsters might find some displays a bit too formal, but would probably enjoy seeing the Indian pageant diorama and the old toys. Access is a problem for the upper floors, which are the most interesting parts of this museum.

Special Events: Historical lectures and slide programs are held year-round; call for a schedule.

Exploring Further: Ticonderoga has plenty to offer the historically minded traveler, from Fort Ticonderoga (see page 22) to the Ticonderoga Heritage Museum (page 59). There's a walking tour of the town that makes the local paper industry come alive; get a map at the historical society and lead yourself on an entertaining hour-long stroll down residential lanes and commercial streets. The *History of Ticonderoga* is available in the gift shop here.

SCHROON–NORTH HUDSON HISTORICAL SOCIETY MUSEUM

Route 9
Schroon Lake NY 12870
Open: July 1–Labor Day, Thurs.–Sun. 12:30–4:30pm
Admission: Donation
No phone

A small white clapboard house at the north end of Schroon Lake's business district contains material on town history, from the ephemera of grand hotels and steamboats to records of local men who fought in wars from 1812 to Viet Nam. Glass cases hold antique clothing, cameras, china, and such; on the walls are postcards, maps, old photographs, and posters for popular long-gone events like Aqua Nite, which featured floating tableaux of famous events put together by local businesses and children from the many local summer camps. Schroon Lake and nearby Paradox Lake were once ringed with popular camps and resorts; most of them, like the Schroon Lake Camp, founded by a New York City rabbi, or the fabulous Catskills-style Scaroon Manor (where *Marjorie Morningstar* was filmed), are long gone. If the typed or handwritten labels don't answer your questions, chances are the historical society volunteers can fill you in. A new annex building covers Adirondack mining and local industry.

Previous knowledge of Essex County history and geography is helpful here. Allow about thirty minutes for a visit. If you're curious about the rise of the resort world in Schroon Lake, try Ann Breen Emerson's fine little book, *The Leland House: An Adirondack Originator.*

HORICON MUSEUM

Route 8
Brant Lake NY 12813
Open: June, Sat. 1–4pm; July 1–Labor Day, Tues., Thurs., Sat. 1–4pm
Admission: Free, but donations appreciated
518-494-7286

Neat as a pin, this peaceful homestead is clearly a source of community pride. Everything displayed — from farm implements to antique quilts — is clean and well-cared for. Rooms upstairs and down underscore pioneer home life and schools; in a second-floor case, right at child level, is a collection of dolls representing different countries that might captivate youngsters. In this room, check out a rare quilt made from screen-printed pictorial scarves that commemorated America's centennial. From all the rooms and displays a picture of the town emerges, so that visitors learn how early settlers arrived and made a living. A handwritten poster with information gleaned from 1860s census records shows that sheep nearly outnumbered people and that the community supported several stores, shoemakers, and even a milliner or two. A library space upstairs includes stacks of old photo albums and pages of newspaper articles in wall racks that you can flip through on your own. A carriage house is filled with horse-drawn equipment, boats, and large tools.

Annual events include a fiddlers' jamboree in July, historical slide shows, and a fund-raising bazaar. Allow about forty-five minutes for a visit; do bring the children.

BOLTON HISTORICAL MUSEUM
Route 9N
Bolton Landing NY 12814
Open: July and Aug., Mon.–Fri. 11am–4pm, 7–9pm;
    Sat. and Sun. 10am–3pm
Admission: Donation
518-644-9960/9620

Bolton Landing's community collection, located in a hundred-year-old church, contains what you'd expect to see at a resort town's historical society: bits and pieces of the town's past, from photographs of old hotels to farm implements and assorted kitchen items, clothing, Indian artifacts, medical equipment, and other oddments. What sets this place apart are small displays devoted to the town's most notable residents: doctors Abraham and Mary Jacobi, the founders of American pediatrics; sculptor David Smith; painter Dorothy Dehner (Smith's ex-wife); and opera singers Louise Homer and Marcella Sembrich. A thick scrapbook is packed with clippings about Smith; Dehner gave the museum a set of prints from her series of egg tempera paintings, *My Life on the Farm*, which show the couple and friends stacking wood, tending livestock, and swimming in the lake.

If You Go: Allow about half an hour for a visit. Although the space offers plenty to look at, younger children will have to be lifted so that they can see into cases. The museum is adjacent to a nice town park and beach. Lots of stairs make wheelchair access a problem.

Exploring Further: Also in Bolton Landing is the Marcella Sembrich Opera Museum (see page 86). Many of Smith's sculptures are still located at the farm, on a hill overlooking the lake, but the place is rarely open to the public. To get a glimpse of a few pieces through a tall fence, ask for directions at the museum.

The Great and the Gracious on Millionaires' Row by Kathryn O'Brien (North Country Books, 1978) gives a great introduction to the Gilded Age in Bolton Landing and Lake George.

MUSEUM OF LOCAL HISTORY, TOWN OF CHESTER HISTORICAL SOCIETY

Route 9, Main Street
Chestertown NY 12817
Open: Late June–Aug., Tues.–Fri. 10am–3pm
Admission: Donation
518-494-2711

Chestertown is a handsome community with prim-looking Greek Revival homes and vintage storefronts along the main street, and on the second floor of a bright yellow former schoolhouse is the town museum. Large, bright, clean rooms display hundreds of artifacts from the days when the local farm and forest economy was thriving; other items — doctor's kits, souvenirs from old hotels and the like — show how life changed in the twentieth century. All along one wall in an old classroom are looseleaf binders with dates or subjects written on the spine; these contain thousands of black-and-white photographs by Itsuzo Sumy, a Japanese immigrant who came to town in the 1930s and photographed people, places, and events. The pictures are a remarkable resource and give a detailed glimpse of the community and its shared values right up to the late sixties.

Itsuzo Sumy's marvelous photographs of old-time parades, competitions, and special events are preserved in Chestertown's museum. Town of Chester Historical Society

If You Go: Allow at least thirty minutes for a visit, and do bring the whole family.

Special Events: The society sponsors lectures and special exhibits from time to time, and the town historian's office has files of local and regional materials beyond the usual genealogical records, available by appointment year-round.

Exploring Further: After a tour, reward the kids with a visit to the Main Street Ice Cream Parlor, about two blocks away, which has antiques galore, including the telephone switchboard that once served every home from Chestertown to Long Lake, and delicious sundaes, too. Fans of William Butler Yeats may wish to visit the grave of his father, John Butler Yeats, which is in the Chestertown Cemetery, on Route 9. Look for the Irish flags. J.B. Yeats ended up here thanks to his friendship with poet, editor, and renowned beauty Jeanne Robert Foster, who grew up in abject poverty in nearby Johnsburg. For the story of her fascinating life and her own essays and poems about North Country neighbors, read *Adirondack Portraits: A Piece of Time* (Syracuse University Press, 1986).

MUSEUM OF LOCAL HISTORY
47 Main Street
Warrensburg NY 12885
Open: July 3–Labor Day, Tues.–Sat. 1–4pm
Admission: Donation
518-623-2928

For all the frustrations of this one-room town museum in the first floor of a present-day VFW hall — the parsimony of the captions, the scrambled layout — there are quiet gems for those who like to sift and poke. The trouble is, if you arrive and don't already know why some local figure, business, or building matters, you're not likely to discover all the reasons here. Consider the thriving mills of Warrensburg at the turn of the century. Photographs are plentiful, but where's the text that could tell us how they evolved or why they disappeared? Author John Sanford, a summer visitor, is dutifully represented with a handful of books on the bottom shelf of a display case, but nowhere is it noted that Sanford, born Julian Shapiro, was in his day an influential and highly regarded experimental writer, who came to town in the 1930s with his friend Nathanael West, who wrote portions of *Miss Lonelyhearts* during a Warrensburg stay. Similarly, while the hero of the museum, Floyd Bennett, is proudly honored with paintings of his log-cabin birthplace, nowhere is it properly explained just what he did or why it mattered. True, the guide is there to tell you if you ask, and she'll impart that Bennett was the pilot for Richard Byrd's North Pole expedition.

Well, never mind. The many fine photos (stagecoaches, Adirondack lean-tos, and shirt-factory interiors) of early Warrensburg and nearby towns are appealing and worth a look.

If You Go: Twenty to thirty minutes ought to do it. Let yourself get caught up browsing through the scrapbooks and your stay could take up an hour or more.

Exploring Further: There's a nice town museum at Bolton Landing (page 102), about a twenty-minute drive away, and south of that, the Lake George Historical Association (page 105).

LAKE GEORGE HISTORICAL ASSOCIATION
Canada Street
Lake George NY 12845
Open: Memorial Day–June 30, Mon.–Fri. 10am–4pm, Sat. 1–5pm;
  July 1–Labor Day, Mon.–Fri. 10am–5pm, Sat.–Sun. 1–5pm;
  call for winter hours
Admission: $3 adults, $1 children 10 and under
518-668-5044

A handsome former court-house on the edge of a shady village park is the setting for Lake George's village museum. The brick and stone structure was completed in 1845, expanded in 1878 and restored in 1963; in the basement (a highlight with children) are old-time jail cells. The craft of one prisoner is prominently displayed: a church carved by one George Ouellet in 1881. He was convicted of murder and sentenced to die, but, with plenty of time on his hands, he created the intricate model, sold it, hired a new attorney and got off scot-free. The little building — a fine example of local folk art — has become known as "the church that cheated the hangman."

A former county courthouse — complete with antique jail — is Lake George's village museum today. B. Folwell

Three spacious levels house exhibits dealing with the lake and surrounding territory, including a dugout canoe and other native American pieces; displays on ice harvesting, steamboats, and hotels; memorabilia from the Japanese Bazaar, a souvenir shop run by the Kurosaka family for more than half a century. Another example of the woodworker's art is "George," cobbled together by a summer resident at the north end of the lake as an elaborate sea-monster hoax.

If You Go: Allow about forty-five minutes, more if you get involved with a light-up map showing historic sites along the lake. Youngsters are welcome; while there's not much in the way of hands-on, they'll certainly find plenty to inspire projects back home — like building their own personal sea monster. A gift shop contains a good selection of books and materials on area history.

The building is on the National Register of Historic Places and contains several sets of stairs, making wheelchair access difficult.

Exploring Further: Saunter down Canada Street to the Steel Pier and Million Dollar Beach, where it's fun to watch the tour boats come and go, especially the *Minne-Ha-Ha* and the *Mohican*, a pair of old-time paddlewheelers. Narrated cruises are scheduled throughout the day. Across the street from the beach is Lake George Battlefield Park, with statues and monuments honoring the French and Indian War, and a nice place to picnic. Fort William Henry (page 24) is also a short distance away.

SKENESBOROUGH MUSEUM AND URBAN CULTURAL PARK
Skenesborough Drive
Whitehall NY 12887
Mail: Box 238, Whitehall
Open: June 15–Labor Day, Mon.–Sat. 10am–4pm, Sun. 12 noon–4pm;
   Labor Day–mid-Oct., Sat. 10am–3pm, Sun. 12 noon–3pm
Admission: Donation
518-499-0716/499-1155

Why is the museum named Skenesborough when it's in the town of Whitehall? When the land was more or less secured for the British empire after the French and Indian War, British veteran fighter Sir Philip Skene bought a huge swath of land in the "Northern Wilderness" and moved up with dreams of building a fiefdom complete with imported tenants and slaves from the West Indies. But come the Revolution, Skene, a Loyalist, backed the wrong side, and while abroad was stripped of all his holdings. Perhaps the best remembered of these confiscated properties was Skene's naval yard at the southern end of Lake Champlain. Here the patriots, under Benedict Arnold, built the fledgling American Navy — hastily assembled gundalows and galleys that went down in the defeat at the Battle of Valcour, but stalled the advance of British forces just long enough to give the Yanks time to turn things around at Saratoga.

That's the thumbnail sketch. For a more detailed account of the shipyard, the boatwrights who flocked here to build a fleet in record time, and, of course, the battle itself, step into this fine, bigger-than-usual town museum and turn right. Panels and a crisp script tell the poignant story of the rise and fall of one of the late, great, empire builders of upstate New York. And while Adirondack dioramas are as commonplace as arrowheads, this big one — of Skene's shipyard, boats, sawmill, bloomery, blockhouse, and all —

features push-button explanations that tell you what you're looking at and why you ought to care.

In the nineteenth century the coming of the Champlain Canal and the D&H Railroad helped turn Whitehall into a prosperous and lively mill town, with discrete ethnic neighborhoods and churches to minister unto every group. At one point, fully a third of the spun silk in the nation was produced in Whitehall's mills. Then the industry moved east and finally south, and with it went the jobs. But in the other front portion of the museum the portrait of downtown Whitehall in its nineteenth-century industrial heyday is rich and quite absorbing. Indeed, just looking at the pictures of endless columns of machinery in workrooms is enough to make your ears ring with the imagined din.

If You Go: Plan to spend an hour here, at least.

Special Events: Around the Fourth of July, the town's summer party is in the park by the museum, with crafts, music, barbecue by the "French" church. On Independence Day at noon reenactors known as Arnold's Marines honor the thirteen colonies with a salute from antique cannon and a dramatic reading of the Declaration of Independence.

Exploring Further: Eighteen miles southeast of Whitehall is Granville, with many slate quarries and a bright new museum to honor them (page 60).

CHAPMAN HISTORICAL MUSEUM
348 Glen Street
Glens Falls NY 12801
Open: Year-round, Tues.–Sat. 10am–5pm; July–Aug. Sun. 12 noon–4pm
Admission: $2 adults, $1 seniors and students, under 12 free
518-793-2826

The DeLong House, which belonged to a prosperous hardware store owner, is the heart of this local history museum, with five period rooms appealingly restored to the tastes of 1860–1910. There are sparkling chandeliers, the obligatory horsehair sofa, a Victorian floral arrangement made of human hair, an array of colorful songbirds in a bell jar, and sentimental portraits. Volunteers guide visitors around, casually picking up obscure artifacts to explain them: a watch fob made of tatted hair, a ruffling iron, a wooden board for lacing corsets (so the laces don't pinch as the corset gets cranked tight). A room casually set up with assorted kitchen items is a favorite spot with children.

Chapman deserves its good reputation for well-researched, original, and highly professional changing exhibits. In 1996 the focus was on the long-gone world of the dude ranch culture in Lake Luzerne. In 1997 outdoor

Victorian furniture in the parlor of the Delong House. Courtesy of the Chapman Historical Museum, Glens Falls

themes predominate, such as "A Walk on the Wild Side: Victorian America and the Natural World." Photographs by Seneca Ray Stoddard, a Glens Falls native who was a highly acclaimed nineteenth-century photographer, are prominently featured in a pleasant new space. The museum owns a vast resource of Stoddard scenes — more than seven thousand images in all, from Ausable Chasm to Lake Placid to Lake George.

The adjacent carriage house was renovated and moved to accommodate another gallery that is used for exhibitions and lectures.

If You Go: The Chapman Historical Museum is on Glen Street across from Glens Falls Insurance, the tallest high-rise building you will see. Allow about forty minutes for a visit. All tours are guided by museum volunteers, many of whom also lead school groups so they know which aspects of the museum appeal to youngsters. All of the first floor public spaces are accessible.

Special Events: The museum sponsors frequent lectures on the history of local businesses, ethnic groups, and community organizations, in the evening and at lunch time. Occasionally Magic Lantern shows using hand-colored scenes from the collection and slides owned by private collectors are scheduled. Special summer programs for children include a day camp highlighting old-time games and toys. Programs are announced in a quarterly newsletter, *The Echo*, and listed in Glens Falls newspapers. The Holiday Open House, held Thanksgiving weekend, is a favorite annual affair.

Exploring Further: Glens Falls is also home to the Hyde Collection, a lovely home with an exceptional collection of paintings, textiles, and decorative arts (see page 162). If you'd like to check out the town's industrial past and present, the Feeder Canal (information and map: 518-792-5363) makes an excellent canoe trip or hike.

To learn more about this rich, diverse community read *Bridging the Years*, collectively authored by the Glens Falls–Queensbury Historical Association. The Chapman Museum has also reprinted Seneca Ray Stoddard's 1870s guidebook *Adirondacks Illustrated*.

HISTORICAL SOCIETY OF MOREAU AND SOUTH GLENS FALLS

Parks-Bentley Place
53 Ferry Boulevard
South Glens Falls NY 12803
Open: Thurs. and Fri. afternoons, and by appointment
Admission: Free
518-745-7741

A handsome Federal-style brick building in a well-kept village park, the Parks-Bentley Place — included in the National Register of Historic Places in August 1994 — is an unexpected sight in a neighborhood of suburban-looking 1950s homes. The house's name commemorates Daniel Parks, who settled on this spot in 1773 and built a sawmill, gristmill, and brickyard, and Cornelius Bentley, whose family lived here through the 1930s. The Historical Society of Moreau and South Glens Falls has occupied the house since 1983 and operates it more as base for research and meetings than a typical house museum, although rooms upstairs and down are furnished with appropriate nineteenth-century furnishings.

The Moreau Muster, held on the weekend after Labor Day each year, is the society's major annual event, with a full Revolutionary War encampment featuring scores of costumed troops, artisans, camp followers, musicians, and even ox-cart rides. The society also opens the house to school guides for guided tours and has a small library for research in genealogy and local history. Marvelous antique postcards mapping the battles around Lake George and Saratoga are yours for a dollar.

OLD FORT HOUSE

22 Broadway (Route 4), less than a mile south of intersection with
    Route 197
Fort Edward NY 12828
Open: Mid-June–Labor Day, daily 1–5pm; weekends through Oct.
Admission: $1 adults, free under 18 (accompanied by adult)
518-747-9600

The "Fort" was Fort Edward of the French and Indian War that lent its abandoned timbers to the construction of this venerable frame house in 1772. During the American Revolution, some who enjoyed the local hospitality at this one-time inn and tavern were Benedict Arnold, generals John Stark and John Burgoyne, and Colonel Henry Knox. After the war, George Washington dined here too.

In the 1830s one notable tenant of the Old Fort House was the African-American laborer Solomon Northup, who was duped and eventually sold into slavery by flimflam men he met in Saratoga Springs, and who after his release wrote about his hard times in the extraordinary slave and plantation narrative, *Twelve Years A Slave*.

But the Old Fort House, a museum now, and only recently reopened after a three-year hiatus, is not a place to learn about regional or even local colonial history. Read up on that in advance: History with a capital H is not the point here. Rather, the place is set up to get across a rough sense of the daily domestic lives of ordinary people over the two-hundred-year-old span of a rural outpost in upstate New York. To that end, local folks have donated nearly all the artifacts in the museum (none of them from this structure, incidentally), which have been organized into displays that invoke typical rooms at different times.

This can make for a bumpy ride as the docent leads you from a cozy 1930s kitchen (donut maker, sink, vintage spice tins), to a 1770s dining room with its lean long trestle table and fine period chairs, and from there to the Victorian age in the parlor called "The Lodge" upstairs. Here the ponderous elegance of that era makes itself felt through heavy, ornate furniture, gilded landscapes, a glorious old phonograph, and an elaborate stove from Troy. Particularly arresting is a lurid folk painting of the capture of Daniel Boone's daughter. At the head of the fine tiger-maple stairway is a small room full of toys, dolls with pinched porcelain faces, a fancy lithograph of General Tom Thumb, a wooden hobbyhorse, and a clown. Look for an upstairs room that the curator plans to fix up to suggest what living conditions were like when Northup boarded here before his move to Saratoga and abduction to the South.

Downstairs, on the way out, check out the fine, unmarked collection of early lusterware on the secretary, and the framed photograph showing what the Old Fort House looked like in 1929, with a wide front piazza, big bay window, and cupola — all gone. Then, mosey over to "A.D. Wait's Law Office," one of several outbuildings that are part of the museum complex, and still looking as it did when it was a working operation near where Scott Paper is today. In here, under the original pressed-tin ceiling, are towering glass-fronted bookcases heavy with law books, a swivel desk chair, and a hefty Seneca oil stove.

Other structures include the John P. Burke Historical Research Center, across the street, home to seventy thousand identified photographs and genealogical records where historians hunker down to delve into the lives of early Scottish settlers and the story of Fort Edward's famous stoneware (not on display in the Fort House yet, but this will change as space permits).

Behind the law office is a recent, welcome addition to the complex, a one-room schoolhouse from Saratoga County. A steep-roofed 1840s tollhouse from a plank road between Fort Edward and South Glens Falls looks like something from *Babes in Toyland*. Last, not least, is the Baldwin Barn, opposite the tollhouse, which houses a walk-around diorama of the original star-shaped Fort Edward, lots of portraits, and news on the saga of colonial martyr Jane McCrea (a young woman from the county's Scottish community who was murdered on her wedding day by Indians), and loads of small artifacts unearthed from around the fort by archaeologist David Starbuck. A gift shop here is full of books for sale on local history, including the paperback of Northup's *Twelve Years A Slave* (Louisiana State University Press reprint, 1968).

If You Go: The guided tour (and you will be guided, like it or not), takes about forty-five minutes. Leave another ten for the bookstore/gift shop at the end. Youngsters will enjoy the diorama, the funny tollhouse, and the dolls. Handicap access exists for the first floor of the museum only.

Special Events: Come July, the annual antiques auction and flea market brings browsers and buyers to the wide lawns of the Old Fort House. The weekend of or just before Halloween, the Old Fort House turns haunted (at least for a few hours). Christmas means a flurry of activities, from the annual Customs of Christmas Past exhibits to Candlelight Evenings in the Old Fort House. For all of these events, call ahead for times.

Exploring Further: Maps will show the way to the historic Wing-Northup House (page 142), and Rogers Island, where archaeologist David Starbuck has turned up evidence of Robert Rogers's Rangers' huts and the foundations of an early military smallpox hospital. Keep heading south on Route 4 and you'll pass the site of long-gone Fort Miller, hardly perceptible today. This highway follows the route of bookseller-turned-patriot Henry Knox, who, with a small crew in the dead of winter, dragged cannons from Ticonderoga to Boston, where George Washington would so usefully deploy the ordnance to scare the British right out of town. "The Mohican Trail," published by the Adirondack Regional Chambers of Commerce (136 Warren St., Glens Falls NY 12801; 518-798-1761) sketches many eighteenth-century sites in the area.

HISTORICAL SOCIETY OF SARATOGA SPRINGS
Canfield Casino, Congress Park
Saratoga Springs NY 12866
Open: Summer, Mon.–Sat. 10am–4pm, Sun. 1–4pm; remainder of year,
    Weds.–Sat. 10am–4pm, Sun. 1–4pm
Admission: $3 adults, $2 seniors and students, under 12 free
518-584-6920

Built as a casino in 1870, this handsome building is now the Historical Society of Saratoga Springs. Michael L. Noonan, photographer, from the George S. Bolster Collection of the Historical Society of Saratoga Springs

Perched in a lovely setting in Congress Park, and taking up three floors of one of Saratoga's best-known buildings — Canfield Casino — the city's historical society is a fine local museum. What was once just a couple of rooms full of oddments now incorporates some interesting galleries with well-conceived interpretation. A recent exhibit on the second floor, for instance, was "Honorable Work: African-Americans in the Resort Community of Saratoga Springs, 1870–1970." The spas, hotels, and track employed numerous blacks, who supported a full range of community activities from churches and organizations to nightclubs like the Tally Ho, Jack's Harlem Club, and the Golden Grill. There are plenty of period photos, lithographs, maps, and artifacts, and a good narrative to make an compelling story. A temporary exhibit through April 1997 covered local Jewish history, with the help of images from the outstanding collection of town photographer George Bolster.

Part of the museum interprets the casino itself, which opened in 1870. Even though gambling was illegal in New York State, that minor administrative detail didn't appear to deter countless poker, faro, and roulette players. Public tables were on the first floor, but an upstairs room with chandeliers, marble fireplaces, and Oriental rugs shows a typical high-stakes-game room. The casino closed in 1907; gambling then moved out to Saratoga Lake. (Interestingly, no mention is made here of historic mobsters like Dutch Schultz,

Lucky Luciano, and Legs Diamond, who added a certain flair to town when bootlegging was going strong.)

There's also a large exhibition space devoted to displaying Victorian rococo Belter furniture — elaborately carved tables and chairs, a sideboard and a settee, with a gaggle of mannequins flaunting period garb.

The third floor is the Walworth Memorial Museum, memorializing Reuben Hyde Walworth, the first and last Chancellor of the state, who was in office from 1828–1848. (The Chancellor was the supreme justice for all equity cases; Daniel Webster and Henry Clay argued cases before Walworth.) Six rooms with furnishings from Pine Grove, the Walworth home, on Broadway, show the trappings of a wealthy upstate family. There are display cases full of shells, fossils, minerals, baskets, and foreign curios; a parlor, dining room, bedroom, and the courtroom. The Walworth family history includes enough juicy details for a potboiler: the marriage of stepbrother and sister, patricide, political radicalism, and a smattering of insanity.

If You Go: Allow about an hour for a visit. Children ten and older should be able to read labels for themselves; younger ones will need an alert adult to point out and explain artifacts. The first floor features changing exhibits by local artists and craftspeople; it's wheelchair accessible, as is the second floor, via an elevator.

Special Events: Workshops for children and adults are offered regularly, covering everything from seasonal flower arrangements to recording family history. The annual antiques show is held in August. Planned for summer 1997 is a show highlighting public sculpture, "Monumental Saratoga."

Exploring Further: Stroll around Congress Park, with its fountains, gazebos, artwork, and springs. Across busy Broadway is the Saratoga Visitor Center (518-587-3241), which offers information on the National Urban Cultural Park and all the offerings in town. Several different walking-tour brochures can be picked up here; there's a map showing the way to more than a dozen public springs, where — if you dare — you can sample some very peculiar-smelling waters once touted for their health-giving qualities. Additionally, several ingenious, largely photographic displays introduce the newcomer to the history of spa-going and bottling.

Not surprisingly, Saratoga is the subject of several fine histories: *Saratoga, Queen of Spas* by Grace Swanner (North Country Books, 1988); *George S. Bolster's Saratoga Springs* (Donning, 1990), a marvelous documentary of vintage images by the town's best-known commercial photographer edited by Chris Carola, Beverly Mastrianni, and Michael Noonan; and the recent, lively *They're Off! Horse Racing at Saratoga* by Edward Hotaling (Syracuse University Press, 1995).

WILTON HERITAGE SOCIETY
Parkhurst Road
Wilton NY 12831
Mail: Box 2417
Open: Memorial Day weekend–Labor Day, Fri.–Sun. 1–4pm
Admission: Donation
No phone

Wilton's reputation as a bedroom suburb of Saratoga Springs and Glens Falls and magnet for sprawling megastores has so eclipsed its small-town origins that the discovery of its early rural history in a modest one-room museum comes as something of a shock.

First called Palmertown, the settlement was founded by veterans of the French and Indian War in 1764, Scotch-Irish Loyalists who later fled the area during the Revolution, then afterward returned to claim their land. The heritage society pays homage to the pioneers with a small-scale log cabin diorama and assorted artifacts (note the peat-moss packer!), early irons, lots of fine quilts, toys, a Victorian mini-parlor, and a corner dedicated to Wilton's many one-room schools. As is the case with many underfunded local historical groups just getting by on volunteer help, the displays seem somewhat scattershot, and captions about artifacts often have more to tell us about their donors than their social context.

Do note, however, the display on nearby Mount McGregor, and the institutions that have made the hill their home over the last century. After the narrow-gauge railway pushed through from Saratoga to Mount McGregor in 1882–83, a terminally ill Ulysses S. Grant (page 82) moved into Drexel Cottage to wrap up his memoirs. In 1911 Metropolitan Life Company built a sanatorium for workers with tuberculosis. New York State converted that facility into a veteran's rest home in 1945 and later into a country place for the Rome School for the Retarded. Then the Mount McGregor Correctional Facility moved in, whose razor-wire fences are visible from Grant Cottage. From logging to recreation to recuperation to corrections, the uses to which this forested ridge has been put represent a typical succession of classic North Country industries.

If You Go: This is by no means a primary destination, but it can't hurt to tag it onto a visit to Grant Cottage State Historic Site. Allow a half hour here.

Special Events: The third Saturday in June there's an old-fashioned strawberry social; in autumn, there's apple pie with cheddar cheese. Call 518-584-2839 for dates and times.

Exploring Further: Saratoga and Glens Falls are close at hand, and packed with interesting collections.

CORINTH MUSEUM
600 Palmer Avenue
Corinth NY 12822
Open: July and Aug., Sat. 1pm–3pm
Admission: Donation
518-654-6620

Half in and half out of the southeastern corner of the Adirondack Park, the papermaking town of Corinth — with its longstanding and sometimes fractious dependence on International Paper — could supply a certain kind of museum with a pretty lively narrative. But this is another kind of museum: small, cautious, artifact- not story-oriented, and doggedly celebrational, with little in it (unless you happen to know what to ask for) to hint at the strikes and showdowns, layoffs and negotiations that ruled local headlines for some years.

Lengths of clothesline separate the visitor from the exhibits, which feature an old GE fridge, early insecticide sprayers, hats, parasols, a Victorian wreath of human hair, fancy Valentines, and tarnished basketball trophies. On one wall hang various military uniforms and wasp-waisted dresses. Another corner, pulled together by curator Rachel Clothier's teenage daughter, Anne, spotlights early schools, with appropriate artifacts and group pictures of class groups — country kids shoeless, town kids with their shoes and socks pulled proudly high. There are also photographs of Corinth's former hotels, bridges, and the interiors of some better-known, long-gone stores, like Woodcock's Hardware, and a case of artifacts from Corinth's long-lived mills. But to really get a feel for the old days, ask the curator for some of the scrapbooks on the pulp- and papermakers' strikes of 1910 and 1921. The black-and-white pictures of mounted state militia filing into Corinth speak volumes about a vivid chapter in local history that has yet to come to light.

If You Go: Drive to the back of town hall and go into the rear entrance; the museum is downstairs in a former town boxing ring. It can be seen and savored in less than half an hour.

Special Events: Call ahead to find the exact day and time of October History Day, which features outdoor demonstrations of wood-stove cooking, butter churning, tractor pulls, and the like.

Exploring Further: Three historical sites await the ambitious traveler bound for nearby Lake Luzerne: a pulp-mill museum, the Kinnear Museum of Local History, and a historic one-room schoolhouse. Southwest from Corinth leads to U.S. Grant Cottage, on Mount McGregor (see page 82), and farther south still is the summery resort town of Saratoga Springs, home to the lovely thoroughbred race track, the Saratoga Performing Arts Center, with a plethora of historic homes, parks, neighborhoods, walking tours, and museums too numerous to mention here.

NELLIE TYRELL EDINBURG MUSEUM AND RURAL MUSEUM
Saratoga County Route 4
Edinburg NY
Mail: PO Box 801, Northville NY 12134
Open: Memorial Day–Columbus Day Sat.– Sun. 1pm–5pm; other times
  by appointment
Admission: Free
No phone

Where Great Sacandaga Lake thins to a gooseneck is the little hamlet of Edinburg in the town of the same name, home to two small historical museums and to the only remaining covered bridge in Saratoga County.

The more venerable of the two museums is the former Beecher's Hollow School and town hall for thirty years, the Nellie Tyrell Edinburg Museum, named after a longtime local schoolteacher and town historian. In this one-room clapboard building is an array of rural North Country artifacts and photographs all hinting at a past way of life, especially poignant in this setting because of the deliberation of its destruction: this, after all, was where in 1930 the State of New York turned the wild Sacandaga River into one of the biggest lakes in the North Country, forcing the abandonment of half a dozen rural communities, parts of Edinburg among them. The purpose was to put an end to the devastating annual spring and summer floods along the Hudson, and this the dam achieved, but it also sank some very old and handsome little hamlets, and a sense of loss abides.

The pictures and testimony on the ghost towns of the Sacandaga Valley are only one reason to drop into this unassuming museum. There's an exhibit on "Women's Work," and a moving exhibit on the one-room schoolhouse, the best part of which isn't the artifacts (old-time desk, early schoolbooks, a sixth grader's dismal report card from 1938, and a metal lunch pail like a toy bucket) but typed-out quotes from local schoolteachers ("I've known children that brought nothing more than cold pancakes in their lunch pail"; "We used to read the Bible in the morning and say the Lord's Prayer, until the law put a stop to that"; "Some of the desks were just great boards. Later, they had desks that were manufactured. . . ."). The walls are lined with enlarged, blurry photographs of rural scenes of the general store, men chopping river ice, a cartload full of farm rakes, and the like. Local arrowheads fill one glass case, and in another are shards and relics from an early glass factory at Mount Pleasant that turned out deep-green bottles for the mineral waters of nearby Saratoga Springs.

Batchellorville, the hamlet directly across the river (when it *was* a river) from this part of Edinburg, was half a century past its prime when the dam flooded it in 1930, but the destruction of this pioneer hive of American manufacturing is no less affecting for that. More than a thousand people were displaced by the dam. Graves and headstones had to be moved, and buildings too. Here's a picture of the Batchellorville Presbyterian Church, hauled to nearby Northville. On display, too, are products from the original woodenware factories: rakes, a washboard, a cart.

Just a hop south on Route 4 is the Rural Museum, housed in a big cool barn with a cement floor. Each of the cordoned-off display areas in the barn is devoted to a theme: a "Victorian Parlor" has the requisite pump organ, heavy gilt-framed portraits, a Bijou Graphapone, and a grumpy-looking stuffed owl in a case. The "Country Kitchen" features a cast-iron Model Acorn wood-burning stove and the usual assortment of corn and muffin tins, canning jars, carpet beater, and the like. Fresh wood shavings underneath a workbench evince recent signs of life in the "Workshop Exhibit." "Early Logging" is a red-painted sleigh laden with logs, and some photographs of Tennantville, one of the largest lumber camps in the area. Explication is nominal. Bring your imagination, and put it to work.

If You Go: Don't make a special trip, but if by chance you're passing through Edinburg of a summer afternoon, stop in for a look at some of the more intriguing items on display in these prototypical country museums. The Rural Museum can be covered just about as fast as you can stroll it; the Nellie Tyrell Museum easily compassed in half an hour.

Special Events: The last Saturday in June is when the town hosts Historic Edinburg Day. There's a car wash, a strawberry shortcake festival at the Methodist Church, craft demonstrations, and a bake sale.

Exploring Further: Pick up a copy of the "Edinburg Walk-About," a walking tour of Beecher's Hollow, the name for the part of Edinburg that survived the flooding of the dam. This tour may be the best way to get a feel for how the community once looked and how it lived. Highlights are Barker's store, now a sometime antique shop, the Arad Copeland House, the Beecher House, the old Methodist Parsonage, and the Copeland covered bridge, built by Nellie Tyrell's great-grandfather to get his cows to pasture across Beecher's Creek after the ramshackle footbridges kept washing out. Northville, a bustling resort hamlet on Route 30, has a couple of museums that are currently undergoing restoration.

JOHNSTOWN HISTORICAL SOCIETY
17 North William Street
Johnstown NY 12095
Open: May 1–Oct. 31, Sat.–Sun. 1–4pm; call for added weekday hours
Admission: Donation
518-762-7076

The museum of the Johnstown Historical Society takes up most of the first floor of a modest Victorian home on a main street downtown, just a half block from the historic courthouse and jail, and catercorner from the historic Drumm House, built by Sir William Johnson for the schoolmaster of his tenants' children.

This is a small collection organized around a very shrewd idea: single out seventeen or so influential personalities that each exemplify a different moment in Johnstown's 250-year-old history, hang their pictures and tell their stories in clear, comprehensive captions, and surround picture and story with lots of artifacts that illustrate their life and times.

Inevitably, of course, the eighteenth century belongs to the omnipresent, charismatic, ambitious Sir William Johnson: colonizer of this region; military leader; Superintendent of Indian Affairs for the crown of England, treaty maker with the Six Nations of the Iroquois; land baron who recruited emigrants from Ireland, England, Scotland, Wales, and Germany; founder of the first nonsectarian church in New York State; and one of the biggest landowners in the colonies. Here are his Hepplewhite chairs, coat-of-arms, map of his Tory son John Johnson's Adirondack escape route to Canada, and a fragment of an old lilac bush that grew on his estate. Other local heroes of this time include patriot and guide Nick Stoner, commodore-turned-New York legislator Silas Talbot who occupied Johnson Hall after the Johnson family fled, and Molly Brant, bilingual sister of the brilliant Iroquois warrior Joseph Brant, and Sir William's beloved common-law wife. A display case on the Battle of Johnstown, fought six days *after* the British surrender at Yorktown, suggests how unimaginably poky were lines of communication two centuries ago.

In the next room, artifacts from the Ireland Brothers Glove Factory clue us into the leather industry in Johnstown. Here are tiny gloves no bigger than a man's thumb used by salesmen as samples, wooden hand-shaped forms to keep new-made gloves from wrinkling, business cards stamped on kid, and early sewing machines for every kind of stitch. Another exhibit celebrates the local Cady family, whose patriarch, Judge Daniel Cady, was "said to be the most profound jurist in New York," and whose daughter Elizabeth Cady Stanton reportedly took up the cause of women's suffrage after observing her father's "helplessness when women came to him for legal help."

Three rare and happy qualities distinguish this historical museum from others of its kind. First, most artifacts are clearly labeled and many are even explained. Second, as has been noted, exhibits tend to focus on a person —

a welcome shift from the typically indiscriminate, anonymous scramble of pitchforks and fine china that do so little to fix a collection in a time and place. Finally, some of these local heroes — four of the designated seventeen — are women. In addition to Brant and Stanton, there is a section on businesswoman Rose Knox, who against counsel and convention took over the Knox Gelatin Company on her husband's death and transformed it into a food-industry giant. And a small exhibit honors the work of small-town author Grace Livingston Hill, whose hundred romantic novels include titles like *Pansies for Thoughts*, *Big Blue Soldier*, and *A Girl to Come Home To*.

If You Go: To get the full picture, make a walking tour of the historic quadrangle of Johnstown. Start with the four explanatory plaques in Sir William Johnson Park, in the center of town (his grave is just beyond the last plaque), stroll over to the graceful and imposing St. John's Episcopal Church behind the plaques, and then, with a nod to the plaque that notes Elizabeth Cady Stanton's birthplace across the street, cross the park to the Fulton County Courthouse, on William Street, erected by Sir William in 1772 and said by some to be the oldest colonial courthouse in the country. Learn a little of its illustrious history (Aaron Burr pleaded a case here in 1812) from an excellent brochure written by the county historian. Then head the few doors down to the historical society; after this, down the same street and across to the 1763 Drumm House, one of six that Sir William built for his staff, this one for Edward Wall, schoolmaster of the first free school (open Wednesday, Saturday, and Sunday, 1:30pm–5pm, or by appointment). In the Drumm House are a number of attractive colonial artifacts, only some of them identified. Headstones in the Old Colonial Cemetery next door include heroes of the Revolutionary War, along with Washington Irving's sister, Ann Irving Dodge.

Exploring Further: On Hall Avenue in Johnstown is Johnson Hall, Sir William's Georgian manor and the heart of his 1763 estate (see page 30), and if that's not enough Sir William for you, try his other home, Fort Johnson, outside Amsterdam (see page 28). Also in Amsterdam is Guy Park, which used to be a museum but is no longer. A small outdoor museum cluster of buildings explores farming and the early tanning and lumber industry at the Caroga Museum (see page 122), a pleasant drive to the north.

WALTER ELWOOD MUSEUM
300 Guy Park Avenue
Amsterdam NY 12010-2228
Open: Sept.–June, Mon.–Fri. 8:30am–4pm;
   July–Aug., Mon.–Thurs. 8:30am–3:30pm, Fri. 8:30am–1pm
Admission: Donation
518-843-5151

The Walter Elwood Museum, billed by its curator as the "only school-owned museum in New York State," is housed in a boxy, turn-of-the-century, red-brick schoolhouse on a residential boulevard lined with Victorian mill mansions and roomy lawns. The school is older than the children's museum it now houses, but the museum, which moved into this building thirty years ago, seems as old as the nation itself. Forget about up-to-the-minute interactive exhibits with press-button, surround-sound, holographic displays: this repository is of the old-fashioned variety, and the awkwardly rendered murals, the giant politically incorrect stuffed walrus head (second largest in the United States!), the model pioneer hearth and old-time drugstore made out of corrugated cardboard are all part of its appeal.

Two gallery spaces for changing art displays aside, the focus of the museum is on the social and natural history of the Mohawk Valley. Artifacts that suggest the pursuits and hobbies of daily life are showcased in pleasingly jumbled, period-bound stations — like a pioneer corner with obligatory butter churn, a Victorian-era bedroom with a chamber pot not quite hidden beneath a tiger-maple bed, or a Gilded Age parlor with pump organ, framed Lincoln portrait, and wax fruit under glass. Faux Main Street storefronts invite a peek into a typical drugstore or a toy shop with a magic lantern and vintage Noah's Ark.

Weakest of the exhibits is the Amsterdam Room, which short-shrifts this mill city's dramatic social and labor history for uninspired displays of artifacts from once-leading local industries like Wilton Weave and Mohawk Rugs. Fortunately, the museum art gallery frequently hosts special exhibits on subjects such as local Hispanic culture or Ellis Island that give some needed hint of Amsterdam's vibrantly diverse social profile today.

Then there is the Wildlife Room, beneficiary of private collector and world traveler Robert Frothingham, from Johnstown. "Everybody's in there," says museum director Mary Margaret Gage with pride, and she's right. Before the Endangered Species Act, when exotic-game hunting was all the rage, natural-history museums abounded with the likes of elephants'-foot umbrella stands, carved cowries, speckled birds' eggs, stuffed anteaters ("Its mouth is no wider than the head of a thumbtack!" the label boasts), and mounted hawks and rare toucans in a fabulously ornate wood-and-cardboard aviary modeled after one that once graced the Waldorf-Astoria. But if the Wildlife Room represents a curatorial throwback, its uses are more than sentimental. The collection testifies to a kind of sensibility, an attitude about collecting, now as imperiled (mercifully) as some of the booty it contains.

If You Go: An hour should be ample for a tour of the Elwood Museum's main exhibits, more if you're a fanatic for peering at captions, old postcards, and the hometown art that's often on display.

Special Events: On the third Wednesday in July, the museum hosts an ice-cream social in the evening.

Exploring Further: A few miles to the west on Route 5 is Fort Johnson, third home of celebrated colonial trader and Superintendent of Indian Affairs Sir William Johnson, and a lovely building in its own right (page 28). From the nearby Port Jackson neighborhood of Amsterdam, visitors can explore Yankee Hill Lock (of the Erie Canal) and Schoharie Crossing State Historic Site's Visitor Center along a new 7.5-mile bicycle path that ends at a public boat launch west of Schoharie Crossing.

FORT PLAIN MUSEUM
Three miles west of New York Thruway, Exit 29, on Route 5S
Upper Canal Street
Fort Plain NY 13339
Open: May–Sept., Tues.–Sun. 10am–4pm
Admission: Donation
518-993-2527/3419

Don't be misled by the name: German Palatine settler David Lipe's attractive 1848 Greek Revival homestead was never a fort. The original fortress was dismantled shortly after the Revolutionary War, and the blockhouse out in back of the house is a replica of the original one built on George Washington's orders.

But that shouldn't deter visitors from sampling this small, folksy museum. In it are a good many artifacts recovered from excavations of where Fort Plain once stood, and what they show about daily life in a colonial fort and in the prehistoric native American villages around and under it is quite revealing.

Consider, for instance, what was found in the Mohawk firepits near the stronghold: Dutch ice skates, iron hoes, and spoons, all evidence of considerable trading between the tribe and settlers and soldiers. Unearthed from the fort site itself are buttons, buckles, powder ladles, cannonballs, and half a bushel of grapeshot. Bead enthusiasts will admire the exquisite native beadwork on display, and pottery hounds will thrill to the early English ceramics unearthed from the Fort Plain home where, in 1783, General Washington stayed on a post-Yorktown tour of the Mohawk Valley troops.

Perhaps the liveliest, most evocative exhibits concern Fort Plain's nineteenth-century prime as a waterfront town, when the Erie Canal flowed right down Main Street. A revolving postcard machine (actually an automated Timex watch-display case), shows assorted townscapes, from elm-lined Main Street to old hotels and an opera house. A marvelously detailed model of the old-time Fineour General Store, whose front door opened right onto the canal, anchors the Canal Room, along with homely dioramas of canal days and the requisite prints and maps. Farm life gets its due as well, with a choice display of tools from butter workers to hop forks, once so common in these fertile parts.

Not everything in this small museum is equally reliable. A horrific mural of an Indian raid, apparently derived — and none too ably — from *The Rape of the Sabines*, reveals more about 1940s attitudes toward native Americans than it does about anything else. But all of Fort Plain Museum is worth a glimpse, with a word of gratitude to the unpaid volunteers who keep such repositories of local culture alive.

If You Go: Unless you have a special interest in colonial artifacts or pot-sherds, plan on forty minutes in the museum and another twenty for the walking trail that leads to the hilltop site of the fort and the military trails around. This is a museum to savor less for any sustained introduction to co-lonial or military history than for the odd, delightful artifact that happens to catch your eye.

Special Events: In early June the museum sponsors a barbecue at the Fort Plain Reformed Church. On the first weekend in December, the museum opens for a Victorian Christmas party. All the dolls get a change of clothes, the tree is decorated with antique ornaments, and Victorian finery — hair wreaths and the like — deck the halls.

Exploring Further: Southwest on Route 80 from Fort Plain village is the way to Cooperstown, home of the Baseball Hall of Fame, the Farmers' Mu-seum, and the Fenimore House Museum, with exhibits of American folk art, fine art, and native American art and artifacts showcased in the Thaw Col-lection. Farther west on 5S takes you to the historic Indian Castle Church, and across the bridge at Fort Plain returns you to Route 5, along which his-torical sites — the Kateri Shrine (page 7) to the east and Fort Klock (page 33) to the west — abound.

CAROGA HISTORICAL ASSOCIATION AND MUSEUM
London Bridge Road
Caroga Lake NY 12032
Mail: Box 434
Open: July–Aug., Weds.–Sun. 1–4pm
Admission: Free
518-835-4400

The Bicentennial spawned numerous historical projects across the coun-try, among them the Caroga museum. A modest white home — that once housed tannery workers — contains several rooms with furniture and decorative arts of the 1880s, including a nicely put-together parlor and a bedroom with a few fine local quilts. A display that gives this place a particular flavor is the one of wildlife sketches and prints lining the walls in the dining room, by noted book and magazine illustrator, resident Paul Bransom. A large barn (circa 1860) contains assorted farm implements, a birch-bark canoe, a guideboat, and some sad-looking taxidermy specimens (including, inexplicably, a huge capybara, a sheep-size rodent from South America); worth checking out is an informative display on the local tanning industry with maps, diagrams, and photographs. Also part of the complex is an outbuilding set up like an old-time general store, with shelves and cases full of antique tins, high-button shoes, and the like.

If You Go: Allow about thirty minutes for a visit. The barn is wheelchair accessible, but other buildings pose problems.

Special Events: The museum really comes alive in a series of workshops for children and adults, teaching everything from papermaking to basketry. Guided hikes take participants to remote lakes and historic spots; lectures, concerts, and storytelling programs are held in the barn almost every week in the summer.

Exploring Further: About a mile away, on Caroga Lake's grassy shore, is a true gem: Sherman's Amusement Park. There's a fine antique carousel with carved horses, elephants, camels, and giraffes (be sure to pick a creature that goes up and down) and a small Ferris wheel, reportedly the only one in the state that goes clockwise and counterclockwise. During the Bicentennial, the town of Caroga published a comprehensive local history by Barbara McMartin, *Caroga, The Town Recalls its Past*; it is expected to be reprinted in 1997.

PISECO LAKE HISTORICAL SOCIETY
Old Piseco Road
Piseco NY 12139
Open: July–Aug., Fri.–Sun. 1–4pm
Admission: Donation
No phone

Before the Civil War, the area near Piseco Lake was thriving, home to tanneries, sawmills, and small farms that fed the workers and their teams; a modern visitor would be hard pressed to find much evidence of these industries. Two buildings on Old Piseco Road date back to the days of the Silver Lake Tannery, and since 1986 they've been home to the Piseco Lake Historical Society.

The nicely restored Riley House (named for a former occupant) contains display cases full of everything from celluloid collars to cock-fighting spurs to coins that melted together in a hotel fire (plus photographs, ledgers, furniture, and the like). A well-thumbed penny-dreadful paperback, *Lucretia: Lost in the Adirondacks—A Tale of Love at Piseco* by ex-Sheriff Ephraim Phillips, warrants reading someday, we're certain.

Inside Riley's Tavern, at the Piseco Lake Historical Society. B. Folwell

Look closely, too, because some artifacts and pictures have surprising stories to tell: a scattering of color snapshots of carved carousel animals leads from an old amusement park to the Shelburne Museum, in Vermont. The carousel — now regarded as one of the finest in the nation and displayed at that museum — was on a Piseco beach during the Great Depression and tourists and locals alike flocked to it on a summer's night. You'll also learn about a peculiar local industry, spruce-gum gathering, which earned woodsmen a very decent living before chicle was discovered. There are sections on local hotels, charts on local families, material from long-gone schools. Everything is spotlessly clean and well preserved, and volunteers are eager to answer questions.

The best artifact is Riley's Tavern itself, an intact mid-nineteenth-century saloon that still has the bar, brass rail, cider barrel, back room (set for a card game, complete with a dazed-looking mannequin in barfly attire). The beds crowded together upstairs give a graphic picture of overnight accommodations of the time: lumpy mattresses, worn quilts, chamberpots; it doesn't take much to imagine bedbugs, snoring lumberjacks, and the wind whistling through the rafters.

If You Go: Allow at least half an hour for a visit; bring a camera with flash so you can take pictures of the kids in the tavern. Both buildings have a step or two, so wheelchair access is a problem.

Exploring Further: Barbara McMartin's *Hides, Hemlocks and Adirondack History* (North Country Books, 1992) can help you locate the ruins of other tanneries across the region.

TOWN OF WEBB HISTORICAL ASSOCIATION
Main Street
Old Forge NY 13420
Open: Year-round, Tues. 9am–2pm, Weds. and Fri. 4–9pm
Admission: Free
315-369-3838

In summer 1996 the Town of Webb Historical Association moved into the former Goodsell home, across the street from the post office. For many years the museum had occupied the second floor of the Old Forge library; this new location gives the organization better visibility and more room to display collections. Exhibit spaces are coming together gradually, so that the first floor of the house will contain general background about the town and upstairs will have displays on hunting (there's a gargantuan pack basket that must be three feet tall), fishing (including a display of deer-hair Tuttle Bugs, locally made bass lures that resemble mice and frogs), and Dr. Goodsell's former medical office. The barn will house guideboats from the Parson brothers' shop in Old Forge and large outdoor-recreation artifacts. The association hopes to have everything in place by late summer 1997.

This is one local museum that not only has an intriguing assortment gleaned from nearby barns and basements but also offers a decent overview of the town's origins, beginning with the years following the Revolutionary War. The town of Webb was once part of John Brown's Tract (as in Brown University, not the abolitionist); at the close of the eighteenth century the Rhode Island merchant intended to develop far-flung settlements, with tidy farmsteads carved from deep wilderness. He surveyed the huge region — more than 210,000 acres — and named the various parcels Sobriety, Frugality, Industry, Regularity, and for other virtues he hoped his enterprise would inspire. A small iron mine (not far from the Adirondack Scenic Railroad's depot, in Thendara) gave the hamlet its present name — Old Forge — but like so many Adirondack sagas, this spot was doomed by its isolation and unforgiving climate. By 1820, all was in ruins.

After the Civil War, tourists found their way north to the interlinked lakes, trout-filled streams, and bountiful woods. The resort business really took off with the arrival of the New York Central's Adirondack line, in 1892. Vintage maps and photographs, plus mementos from old hotels (brass luggage tags, menus, china) represent this era well.

If You Go: Allow about half an hour for a visit. Children are welcome, but at present there's little hands-on material. The first floor is accessible.

Special Events: Occasional slide shows and lectures are scheduled; call ahead.

Exploring Further: To get a glimpse of old-time Old Forge transportation systems, try the Adirondack Scenic Railroad (315-369-6290) or the Old Forge Lake Cruises (315-369-6473); while not always a hundred percent historically accurate, these trips are amusing for youngsters and pleasant for people who don't wish to hike or canoe. A few miles from downtown Old Forge on Route 28 is the Forest Industries Exhibit Hall (315-369-3078), which depicts Northeastern logging in dioramas, diagrams, and photographs; dozens of different kinds of native woods make up the floors, walls, ceilings and trim.

The scholarly book *John Brown's Tract* (Phoenix Publishing, 1988) by Henry A.L. Brown and Richard J. Walton is a moving account of one of the North Country's most spectacular failures in land settlement.

ROME HISTORICAL SOCIETY
200 Church Street
Rome NY 13440
Open: Mon.–Fri. 9am–4pm
Admission: Donation
315-336-5870

With a recent state grant, the Rome Historical Society is in a great position to spruce up its permanent exhibit, "There's No Place Like Rome," to the extent this venerable old city's rich and varied history deserves. Right now, the display is short on artifacts and long on hard-to-read and awkwardly positioned labels. A push-button light-up topographical map helps make sense of the rash of colonial forts that preceded the formidable Fort Stanwix, and there's an interesting section on the impact of canals and railroads on Rome's precipitous growth as an industrial center, but the best of this promising exhibit has yet to be installed.

More engaging at this point are the temporary exhibits, all fully furnished with good artifacts and strong informative captions. "A Community Realignment" sensitively explores the painful impact on the local community of the closing of nearby Griffis Air Force Base — one-time employer of some 5,600 people, five percent of the local work force, with a combined payroll of $240 million. "A Woman's Place is in the Home . . . The Workplace . . . The Community" employs artifacts from pioneer times to the industrial heyday of the mills to dramatize the lives of Roman women hard at work. Particularly intriguing is a display of exquisitely tied McHara fishing flies, all done by female factory workers from Rome.

If You Go: The Rome Historical Society gives an introduction to the history of Rome, but at this time, anyway, the more engrossing account of Rome's history, both colonial and nineteenth century, resides in the exhibits of Fort

Stanwix across the street. Even so, the always-changing, sharply focused, special exhibits of the historical society make it worth a try.

Exploring Further: Beside Fort Stanwix (see page 38), a great place to while away an afternoon in Rome is the Erie Canal Village (see page 56), a scattering of historic buildings and exhibits in a bucolic, picnic-ready setting alongside the historic canal at the edge of town. Northwest of Rome is the way to Remsen — hilly, long-settled, dairy country, and an early upstate bailiwick of Welsh settlers (see page 65). Southeast is the one-of-a-kind Musical Museum, in Deansboro (see page 164).

CAPE VINCENT HISTORICAL MUSEUM
Lower James Street, near the International Ferry Crossing
Cape Vincent NY 13618
Open: June, Fri.–Sat. 10am–4pm, Sun. 1–3pm; July–Aug.,
    Mon.–Sat., 10am–4pm, Sun. 1–3pm
Admission: Donation
315-654-4400

Here's a clean, well-lighted place to linger during the long wait for the only remaining car ferry on the St. Lawrence River. It used to be a barracks in the War of 1812. Then it was a foundry that made ironware and cookstoves for sailing vessels, and a municipal garage. In 1993, the village museum took over the building, and the newness of the move still shows in the relative freshness of the exhibits. While many artifacts might benefit from more and better captions, they do suggest the Gallic heritage of this village adopted by French émigrés at the turn of the last century, and the heyday of the railroad, when Cape Vincent boasted as many as five hotels, three meat markets, five doctors, two undertakers, two general stores, and a steamer that made three trips a day across the river. Here are the elaborate hotel menus, the monogrammed china, the pictures of the aproned staff. French names are prominent among the list of early families, and many of the pictured homes are made of the luminously pale limestone quarried in these parts.

Also here are metal sculptures by the late local folk artist Richard Merchant, who painstakingly assembled his doll-size scenes (cowboys, buffalo, a sow with piglets, horses hauling logs) out of baling wire, tailpipes, ball bearings, tractor fenders, and other scraps from around the farm. Then there are various groupings of things that illustrate the details of daily life in a rural place — an old post-office box, greeting cards still in the slots; an elaborate wicker baby carriage; old yearbooks, team pictures, and some wonderful photographs of the kitchen staff in the high school, when milk still came in thick glass pint bottles, and the ladies who ladled you the gravy on your mashed potatoes were your best friends for life.

If You Go: Next door to the museum is the chamber of commerce. Pick up brochures and maps, and ask the way to where the St. Lawrence River and Lake Ontario meet up and the 1827 Tibbetts Point Lighthouse casts its pearly beacon.

Special Events: The weekend after the Fourth of July, Cape Vincent throws a party called the French Festival with crafters, fiddlers, Canadian bands, brioche, and French pastries, and a parade lead by Napoleon. And never you mind if the pastries come from New York City on a truck that gets here before dawn.

Exploring Further: Due east is the Agricultural Museum at Stone Mills (page 68), and northeast along 12E is Clayton, home to several fine museums. For more about the Bonaparte clan in the North Country, visit Constable Hall (page 75) and read *Castorland: French Refugees in the Western Adirondacks, 1793–1814* by Edith Pilcher (Harbor Hill Books, 1985).

THOUSAND ISLANDS MUSEUM OF CLAYTON
403 Riverside Drive
Clayton NY 13624
Open: Daily June–Sept., 10am–4pm
Admission: $1 adults
315-686-5794

In downtown Clayton, a former shipbuilding and lumbering port on the St. Lawrence River, a former opera house now serves as the Thousand Islands Museum — really three museums in one. In the center of the building, the hall that once seated seven hundred and offered entertainment that ranged from vaudeville to chicken plucking is lined with facsimiles of Clayton businesses and storefronts. As organizing strategies go, this is a shrewd one: we not only learn about old hats, for instance, we learn about the milliner who sewed them, and when we peek into William Reese's law office, we wonder about the accident that made him have to use such elegant-looking crutches, or the crude Dictaphone that once represented state-of-the-art office technology. With its crowded heaps of old trunks and leather hatboxes, the model of the local baggage room for the New York Central Railroad gives a feeling as no narration ever could of the hustle-bustle of Clayton when eleven passenger trains came and went each day. Note the *original* bottle of green beans, canned in 1923 and now a muddy olive drab, above the Stewarts Wood Stove in the Old Country Kitchen, and the photographs in the mock Clayton Fire Department of all the grand old wood-frame hotels, like the Frontenac, the Hubbard, and Calumet Castle, that succumbed to flames.

Toward the front of the museum are the duck-decoy and muskie exhibits. Many decoys were carved by folks from the St. Lawrence River region, including elegant and highly prized specimens by Clayton resident Sam Denny, who died "bitterly poor." The replica of the seventy-pound World Record Muskie on the wall is as chubby as a first grader. There is also a glittering display of fancy fluted trolling spoons and a disquisition on Thousand Island salad dressing, which was invented by Sophie La Londe, wife of a fishing guide, deeply admired by hotelier George Boldt (page 92), introduced in the dining rooms of the Waldorf-Astoria, and which even now retains the distinction of being "the only salad dressing in the U.S.A. named after a region."

If You Go: This museum is plenty of fun, but leave time for the Antique Boat Museum, just a few blocks away (see page 170). Also in Clayton is the Thousand Islands Craft School and Textile Museum, which has a vast collection of antique looms and related tools and offers courses in spinning and weaving. This historic building has lots of stairs, so wheelchair access is poor.

Special Events: The third weekend in July belongs to the Decoy and Wildlife Art Show, featuring carvers from around the hemisphere. Performances are held in the opera house on weekend nights throughout the summer. In fact, Clayton fairly hums with various events; call the chamber of commerce for dates (1-800-252-9806).

Exploring Further: Across the St. Lawrence River from Clayton in Ontario, just south of the international bridge, is the historic village of Gananoque: lots of Victorian cottages, a museum, plenty of shopping, antiques, theater, even a House of Haunts. A paved bike path runs along the Thousand Island Parkway that follows the river for twenty-five miles from Gananoque to Brockville. Along the river's southern shore, Sackets Harbor is a mecca for museum mavens (see page 45). Or head back into the farmlands of Jefferson County on Route 180 for the Agricultural Museum at Stone Mills (see page 68).

Anglers might want to peruse the *Skinner Spoon Fishing Lure* pamphlet at the museum. The forty-page *Clayton on the St. Lawrence: 1872–1972* will fill in the historical blanks as you poke around town.

POTSDAM PUBLIC MUSEUM
Park Street
Potsdam NY 13676
Open: Year-round Tues.–Sat. 2–5pm; call for additional summer hours
Admission: Free
315-265-6910

Grand entrance to the Potsdam Public Museum.
B. Folwell

The Potsdam Museum is easy to spot when you come into town; it's a handsome red sandstone structure with tall white columns that's part of the civic center. Town and village history take center stage here in changing exhibits such as the 1996 installation on the Clarkson family's impact on local industry and education and a 1997 temporary exhibit on the post office.

Permanent displays include the Burnap Collection of English Ceramics, several examples of fine Sheraton furniture that belonged to the Knowles family and informative sections on the town's two colleges, agriculture, quarrying, and so forth. The Burnap Collection — some two hundred pieces mainly from the early 1800s — is great fun: a lusterware jug showing a lion tamer and lions; Staffordshire animals and miniatures; pitchers with political cartoons; chargers, plaques, and pots in gaudy colors and peculiar shapes. Throughout the museum, labels are instructive and amusing; for example, the modern milk bottle and waxed-paper milk carton were both invented by a Potsdam druggist. There's a wall-size timeline that compares international events (Ireland's potato famine) with local affairs (the Raquette River declared a public highway). Well-produced brochures add to captions and labels, too.

If You Go: Allow about forty-five minutes for a visit. Youngsters might well find this an interesting spot, especially if you point out the doll-size tea sets and china tigers in the Burnap cases. While the front entrance to the museum contains a daunting number of stairs, there is a ramped entrance for wheelchairs; call ahead so you can find your way through the building.

Special Events: In May the Potsdam Museum usually sponsors a traditional crafts day for local students at Potsdam College, with glassblowers, rope makers, weavers, and others. Lectures, workshops, and special tours are also scheduled to coincide with exhibits.

Exploring Further: Pick up a copy of Potsdam's excellent architectural walking tour and spend a couple of hours wandering past Federal, Greek Revival, Gothic Revival, Queen Anne, and Italianate houses, churches, and shops. The town has numerous lovely homes and a fine-looking commercial district with wall-to-wall nineteenth-century buildings. Twenty-minute drives put you at the doorsteps of the Silas Wright House, in Canton (page 151); the Norwood Museum (below); or the Parishville Museum (315-265-7619), which has some intriguing folk-art carvings and is open weekday afternoons in July and August.

NORWOOD HISTORICAL MUSEUM

39 N. Main Street
Norwood NY 13668
Open: Mid-May–late Oct. Tues.–Thurs. 2–4pm
Admission: Donation
315-353-2167 (curator's home)

Originally known as Potsdam Junction, Norwood dates to the 1850s, when the railroads came to town. The community — set in rolling, fertile dairy country — prospered, with numerous hotels and a thriving business district; a former doctor's home is now the local historical repository. Curator Pat Veraldo keeps an eye on the place, changing exhibits now and then, and making sure that local youngsters get a good grounding in the days of yore. Rooms are filled with railroad lanterns on loan from a local collector, an appealing patent model of a hay rake devised by a town inventor, a small pen-and-ink sketch of two very tired horses signed by Frederic Remington, plus military artifacts, a fine old map of the county, a vintage kitchen, handsome Victorian furniture and clocks, and lots of material from bygone school days.

Fred Morgan's musical mailbox at the Norwood Historical Museum. B. Folwell

Even if you don't know anything about the surrounding area or its inhabitants, the Norwood Museum is fun. On the second floor, Fred Morgan's mailbox — made out of a tuba — is a marvelous piece of folk art; open the door and Dixieland jazz fills the air, courtesy of a cassette tape deck. On top is a sign reading "Notes Come and Go," and there's a little figure inside playing a tuba, in commemoration of Morgan's years with the Norwood fire department's brass band. If you've got kids in tow, head for the room with the Frederick Permanent Wave Machine and have them guess what it was used for, and be sure to ask about the wreck of the Ringling Brothers Circus train.

If You Go: Plan on forty-five minutes or thereabouts. Bring the youngsters.

Exploring Further: For an out-of-the-way place, Norwood has a surprising number of older homes with towers, proof of a well-established business and professional community. Ask for a copy of the Norwood Village Tour, a brochure and map that leads you past three dozen historic structures. Music has long played a major role in town, beginning with banjo and cornet groups in the early 1900s. The tradition lives on in the Norwood Brass Firemen, who played at the opening ceremonies of the 1984 Winter Olympics, in Sarajevo, and the Norwood Village Green Concert series, featuring classical, jazz, and traditional music in the summer. Just up the road in Norfolk (say "Norfork") is another town museum; call the Norfolk historian (315-384-3136) for information on hours. The Massena Museum (see below) is about fifteen miles away, the Potsdam Public Museum (page 129) is even closer. If you'd like to see more folk-art figures made by Fred Morgan, visit the gallery operated by Traditional Arts of Upstate New York (315-386-4289), in Canton.

MASSENA MUSEUM
200 East Orvis Street
Massena NY 13662
Mail: PO Box 387
Open: Mon.–Fri. 10am–12 noon, 1–4pm
Admission: Donation
315-769-8571

Deer, moose, and other mammals were the first to savor the oddly flavored mineral springs of Massena. And where game collected, American Indian hunters followed, and after them the French guides and explorers, and sundry European settlers in their wake. The town itself was named after a marshal in Napoleon's army who never saw the place and likely never even knew the fact it bore his name.

But the founders and developers of Massena itself were not French; they were Yankee pioneers and farmers who wasted little time in developing the spa for health-seeking tourists. At one time, as many as fifty hotels thrived in the village on the banks of the St. Lawrence, Grass, and Raquette rivers. Thousands of invalids and spa-goers thronged the boardwalks and soaked in slate-lined tubs. Mineral water from Massena was bottled and marketed all over. By this century's turn, however, failure to modernize the aging facilities and the decline of spa-going in general spelled the end of an era.

Massena rallied fast. The opening of a canal between the St. Lawrence and Grass rivers in 1903 spurred industrial development; specifically, the factories and plants that would become Alcoa. At its height, this thriving industry employed as many as six thousand workers, Hungarian, French Canadian, Polish, Italian, and Irish immigrants among them. Today, the company employs about a fifth of that and no particular industry has moved to take its place. Still, Massena continues to trumpet its pioneer, Victorian, and industrial heritage in this museum, which will join ranks with the Alcoa Aluminum Museum sometime soon.

As with many small upstate museums whose collections are comprised almost wholly of donations, artifacts come first and don't necessarily bind together to suggest a unifying script. Here's a school and toy corner with an early Mother Goose, a Boy Scout sash, and a classroom globe. Painted lamps and fancy furniture alert us to the obligatory Victorian section. Three sepia photographs show Alcoa boardinghouses under construction. A glass case full of business orders, receipts, and bills recalls a busy Main Street. Two glass-sided horse-drawn hearses (one on sleigh runners) invoke the pomp and gravity of the American funeral. Of certain interest to admirers of folk art is a scale model, all in wood and complete with pews, stained-glass windows, and marble pulpit, of the local Sacred Heart Church, made by a retired lawnmower dealer for his grandchildren.

Downstairs, farm and kitchen tools line pegboard walls, and also implements for cutting ice, like fat-toothed saws and hand drills as tall as a ten-year-old boy. A copper still, the director notes hastily, is not from Massena, but nearby Norfolk. Annotation is sparse at best, though many items are identified, if not explained.

If You Go: This is a small museum, but there's a lot to see. You could be in and out in fifteen minutes, or if something grabs you, like the antique fire hose with its poignantly puny nozzle, you may find you linger considerably longer.

Exploring Further: If you'd like to trek around town, *Massena Historic Sites* by Theresa Sharp and Marian O'Keefe describes scores of interesting buildings; ask the museum guide to lend a copy since the first printing has sold out.

About a half hour's drive southwest from Massena is the college town of Canton, home to St. Lawrence University and the Silas Wright House (see page 151). Route 37 south along the St. Lawrence Seaway is rich with historic sites, the John C. Moore Museum, on Main Street in Waddington, among them (315-388-5967), and at the end of Main, a number of fine old clapboard and brick historic homes, along with a marker commemorating the Battle of Chrysler's Farm, of the War of 1812. More military markers pertaining to this war dot the town park across from the Frederic Remington Art Museum in Ogdensburg, farther west on Route 37 (see page 88).

LAKE PLACID–NORTH ELBA HISTORICAL SOCIETY MUSEUM
Averyville Road
Lake Placid NY 12946
Open: June–Sept. 12 noon–4pm, closed Mon.
Admission: Free
518-523-1608

The handsomely restored Lake Placid train station (circa 1903) now serves as the village attic, packed with artifacts, photographs, souvenirs, and ephemera relating to two centuries of local life. It's a time capsule of a place, with equal billing given to the marvelous and the mundane.

In the waiting room is a diverse assortment of material from the Lake Placid Club, the world wars, the 1932 Olympics, and Adirondack hermit Noah John Rondeau, plus farm implements, skis, and ice-harvesting tools. The D&H Railroad Company commissioned a terrific panorama photo of the town taken in 1890 by William Henry Jackson. Labels are few, so if you're not sure what an item is, ask the volunteer on duty.

In the ticket booth, original train equipment evokes seventy years of railroading in town, and a former office just off the waiting room contains mementos of beloved summer residents Victor Herbert and Kate Smith, along with a pump organ and other instruments, in keeping with that musical theme. The baggage room depicts commerce in town and includes a counter from a general store, a section of a dry-goods shop, and a post-office window.

The Adirondack room, at the far end of the building, has cases of North Country minerals, native American items unearthed at an old farm, two guideboats, numerous mounted animals — including a panther shot sometime before the turn of the century — and several pieces of locally made rustic furniture. Information on these artifacts is sketchy; in some instances it's easier to learn who donated an item than what the thing actually is.

If You Go: Allow about forty-five minutes for a visit. The museum is wheelchair accessible. The historical society's Getman Collection of Adirondack publications is located at the Lake Placid Library (518-523-3200) and available to researchers by appointment year-round.

Special Events: The Lake Placid Sinfonietta holds an annual train station concert during the summer. Watch for news about the revitalization of the Adirondack Railroad, which could run again between Saranac Lake and Lake Placid within the not-too-distant future.

Exploring Further: The 1932 and 1980 Winter Olympic Museum (page 177), in the Olympic Center, less than a mile away, is worth a stop if you're in the neighborhood, as is John Brown Farm State Historic Site (page 78). Kate Smith is buried in a pink mausoleum in Lake Placid's Catholic cemetery, not far from John Brown Farm.

INDIAN LAKE MUSEUM
Main Street
Indian Lake NY 12842
Open: Mid-June–Oct., Tues., Thurs. 1–4pm, Fri. 7–9pm
Admission: Donation
No phone

Visit the Indian Lake Museum and you'll find dozens of aboriginal projectile points discovered by the townspeople along nearby lakes and rivers, and, while you wander among the farm tools, old hats, clothing, and oddities (shoes for walking on sand and a pith helmet that belonged to a local man who worked for an oil company in the faraway desert, a tree trunk with a meat grinder imbedded in it, a fireless cooker that at first glance looks suspiciously like a commode), you're bound to hear about two native Americans who figured into the place's early history. Sabael Benedict, born in Maine and a member of the Penobscot tribe, was the first permanent settler in the area, arriving about 1762. He lived by the shore of what came to be known as Indian Lake, and the hamlet of Sabael is named for him. The woeful tale of his granddaughter Emma Jane Camp is only hinted at in her three portraits; to hear the whole story — her scoundrel husband, a child who died at the age of three, kidnapping, a forced stay at the Utica Insane Asylum, annulment, pay-off, remarriage, divorce — you'll have to ask.

In rooms upstairs and down, the Civil War–vintage house is packed with charcoal pictures of long-dead men and women; scrapbooks and displays on schools, hotels, and such; cases full of artifacts belonging to town doctors. Like most community museums, this place has more meaning if you're familiar with the names — if not the faces — but it's worth a detour if you're in the vicinity.

If You Go: Allow about thirty minutes.

Exploring Further: Indian Lake has survived a couple of major conflagrations, so many of the old hotels and landmarks in the photographs are long gone. One site that dates back to the last century is the huge dam that holds back the waters of Indian Lake; ask directions at the museum to find it.

County Museums

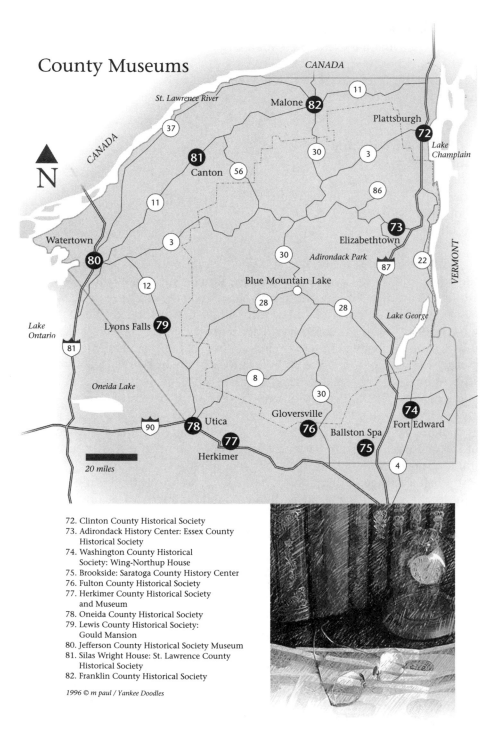

CANADA

St. Lawrence River

Malone (82)

11

Plattsburgh (72)

Lake Champlain

37

(81)

Canton   56

30

3

N

CANADA

86

11

(73)

Watertown

3

Elizabethtown

Adirondack Park

30

(80)

87   22

VERMONT

12

Blue Mountain Lake

Lake
Ontario

Lyons Falls (79)

28

28

Lake George

81

8

Oneida Lake

30

(90) (78) Utica

Gloversville

(74)

(76)   Ballston Spa   Fort Edward

(77)

(75)

Herkimer

4

20 miles

72. Clinton County Historical Society
73. Adirondack History Center: Essex County
    Historical Society
74. Washington County Historical
    Society: Wing-Northup House
75. Brookside: Saratoga County History Center
76. Fulton County Historical Society
77. Herkimer County Historical Society
    and Museum
78. Oneida County Historical Society
79. Lewis County Historical Society:
    Gould Mansion
80. Jefferson County Historical Society Museum
81. Silas Wright House: St. Lawrence County
    Historical Society
82. Franklin County Historical Society

1996 © m paul / Yankee Doodles

CHAPTER SIX

COUNTY MUSEUMS: COMMUNITIES IN CONTEXT

∎∎

Counties museums have a larger mission than local historical institutions: to build an umbrella that shelters all the different stories of all the different towns. The best ones pull together a bigger picture still and place the county in context with the rest of the state and nation. They often feature changing exhibits that highlight social history and trends that make us re-examine old notions; they reach out rather than look within. Many county museums publish original research on local industries, noteworthy personages, and unique places in monographs and newsletters; most act as a resource to guide smaller local historical groups in collections care and documentation.

Not every county in the state has a full-blown museum with a permanent collection; some county historical societies offer only library services and educational events. Every county, however, has a publicly appointed historian to keep track of vital records. To contact county historians, begin your search with a call to the county clerk's office.

For a tour of county museums, this chapter begins in the northeastern corner of New York and proceeds clockwise.

CLINTON COUNTY HISTORICAL SOCIETY

48 Court Street
Plattsburgh NY 12901
Open: Tues.–Fri. 12 noon–4pm, Sat. 1pm–4pm; closed holidays
Admission: $2 adults, $1.50 seniors, $1 students
518-561-0340

It's not surprising that the downstairs galleries in the Clinton County Historical Society, full of delicately tinted early maps, watercolors, fine Staffordshire china, and heavy oil portraits of town fathers, should exude the calm austerity of colonial museums in New England. Yankee pioneers from Massachusetts, Connecticut, and Vermont seeded most of the settlements of the North Country. Here are pictures of the Quaker Keeses, who brought their simple style of life and peaceable influence to the settlement called the Quaker Union, near Peru, and here a looming portrait of Levi Platt, with his gristmill showing proudly through the painted window at his broad back.

This is not the kind of museum that aims to walk the visitor through the key events in Clinton County history in any comprehensive fashion. The crucial story of the Clinton County iron industry, for example, remains untold, as does the saga of the French-Canadian migrations into the region over the last two hundred years, and the importance of the corrections industry in Dannemora. But it is a pleasantly compact, manageable, and informative museum for all it misses, and there is much it doesn't miss at all. A typed transcript is the visitor's guide to the battles of Valcour and Plattsburgh, here described exquisitely in a massive, glassed-in diorama (tiny sailors the size of matchsticks drowning in blue plastic waves, cotton fluffs for smoke puffs, and listing ships the size of salt shakers).

Cigar store Indian, circa 1886, from Levy's cigar shop in downtown Plattsburgh. Courtesy of the Clinton County Historical Association

Incidentally, don't let the diorama deceive you into supposing the two battles it contains were contemporaneous. Valcour is where the young American fleet, hastily assembled at Skenesboro by Benedict Arnold, took on the British Navy in 1776. Victory belonged to England, but the skirmish still managed to stall the British enough to give the patriots needed lead time to shore up for the Battle at Saratoga — a fateful encounter that would turn the tide of the war in the patriots' final favor.

The Battle of Plattsburgh, on the other hand, belonged to another war. In 1814, still disputing the American claim to the border, fourteen thousand British soldiers marched down from Canada to Plattsburgh and were met by a hastily mustered American army of four thousand seven hundred. This time the battle was won by the Americans, and the British army beat a ragged retreat, leaving two thousand wounded to American losses of two hundred.

More artifacts related to the Battle of Plattsburgh crowd display cases in the foyer, from pistols and powder horns to historical renderings in crayon by local fourth graders. Also in the foyer — lovers of fine glass, take note! — are fifty-four pieces of sea-green, rare, and highly prized Redford glass, hurricane lanterns, elegant pitchers, and an immense cloche among them. The Saranac River valley hamlet of Redford now looks to Plattsburgh for its economic base, but the legacy of the fabled glassworks that lured skilled craftsmen from Scotland, England, and New Jersey lives on in the fine collection assembled here.

A little-known slice of late-nineteenth-century social history is revealed in the full-size cigar store Indian from the Levy Cigar Store, on Margaret Street. At the time of the Civil War, German Jewish immigrants came to Plattsburgh from New York City and set up small cigar-making factories, a trade that prospered until the 1930s when cigarettes put so many cigar makers out of business. An array of vintage cigar boxes in the business gallery next door suggests the one-time widespread popularity of these locally rolled smokes.

If You Go: An hour is probably enough for this small but choice collection. Upstairs is a reading room and historical library. Books by local authors on historical subjects are for sale in the gift shop, as are back issues of the scholarly county historical journal, *The Antiquarian*, whose articles sometimes expand most helpfully on subjects merely alluded to in the displays. The museum is handicap accessible.

Special Events: Every spring the Clinton County Historical Society hosts a vintage car meet and antiques show; lectures and slide programs are scheduled during the year. A highlight of the summer is the annual open house at the lighthouse on Valcour Island, which includes a boat ride and a guided tour. Call for dates and times.

Exploring Further: A few blocks away is the Kent-Delord House, one of Plattsburgh's oldest structures, circa 1797 (page 72). For road trips, ask at the historical society about where to find ruins of several War of 1812 forts and if the early barracks at the Air Force base are open to visitors. Check out Quaker cemeteries at the Quaker Union near Peru: note the use of Roman numerals instead of named months on the small, modest headstones, reflecting the Quaker discomfort with words derived from the names of pagan gods. Tour sites are also outlined in the Champlain Trail Map Guide (518-563-1000).

For background reading on Clinton County glass, pick up Helen Allan's *Reflections: The Story of Redford Glass* (in the historical society's gift shop); for military background, try Russell Bellico's *Sails and Steam in the Mountains* (Purple Mountain Press, 1992).

ADIRONDACK HISTORY CENTER
Essex County Historical Society
Court Street
Elizabethtown NY 12932
Open: Mid May–mid Oct., Mon.–Sat. 9am–5pm; Sun. 1–5pm
Admission: $3 adults, $1 children
518-873-6466

Elizabethtown's old schoolhouse has been put to good use as the home of the Adirondack History Center (formerly known as the Adirondack Center Museum). Essex County's days as a center for logging, farming, and mining are featured in classrooms showing everything from objects of frontier life (loom, spinning wheel, cast-iron kettles, and such) to items from village industries that followed, like an old-time printing press that still works. Different areas reflect themes of county settlement in a cohesive way so a stranger feels welcomed into the heritage of hill towns, river settlements, and remote farmsteads; you don't have to be related to key players to enjoy the story.

Summerhouse in the Colonial Garden at the Adirondack History Center, Elizabethtown.
B. Folwell

There's a nicely restored stagecoach, an Olympic bobsled, a canvas boat that converts into a tent, and even a fire tower plucked off a mountain — you can get to it conveniently, sweat-free, from the building's second floor. In the basement, a sound-and-light show explains the Champlain Valley's role in battles beginning with the French and Indian War and ending with the War of 1812; the thirty-minute program does an excellent job summarizing complicated events.

If You Go: The Adirondack History Center is just beyond the county courthouse in Elizabethtown, near the flashing light on Route 9. Allow about an hour for a visit; take time to stroll through the Colonial Garden, which is at its height of color in late June. A short nature trail continues past the garden toward a lovely old cemetery. Youngsters will find plenty to stay amused here, and some exhibits have activity sheets with puzzles to solve or games to play.

The Brewster Library, on the second floor of the museum, is open by appointment year-round for research. The collection includes photographs, maps, ephemera, census records, newspapers, company ledgers, and other rare materials.

Special Events: The Forest, Field, and Stream Day, held in the fall, features traditional crafts, music, food, and even demonstrations of skills like hewing beams or firing muzzleloaders. Temporary exhibits highlight local artists, and special lectures on folklore, industry, and social history are scheduled from time to time.

Exploring Further: Elizabethtown — the county seat — has some fine architecture dating back to the early 1800s. About a block from the Adirondack History Center, on Route 9N, is the Deer's Head Inn, which opened in 1807 and reputedly was commandeered as a hospital during the War of 1812; across the street from the inn is the courthouse, an impressive Greek Revival edifice where John Brown's body lay in state after his death at Harpers Ferry in 1859. Farther east on 9N, past the blinking light, is a pair of stately Greek Revival structures, the largest of which was the home of Supreme Court Justice Learned Hand. In Boquet, a few miles from Elizabethtown on Route 22, the octagonal stone Boquet Schoolhouse (circa 1820) is under painstaking restoration; ask at the museum for hours.

In Olmstedville, off Route 28N, the Minerva Historical Society (518-251-2229) occupies a former Methodist church and is open summer afternoons. Winslow Homer painted *Leaping Trout*, *Mink Pond*, and other watercolors at the nearby North Woods Club, and the small museum contains prints and explanations of these locally inspired masterpieces. Irishtown, just a couple miles away on tree-shaded back roads, has a lovely 1840s church and cemetery; ask directions to this site and a very early pioneer graveyard near Loch Muller. Aiden Lair, north of Minerva on Route 28N, where Teddy Roosevelt stopped on his wild midnight ride to the North Creek depot when McKinley was shot, is the focus of new volunteer efforts to rebuild the ramshackle old lodge.

For military history of the Champlain Valley, see Crown Point State Historic Site (page 18) and Fort Ticonderoga (page 22). For a closer look at the

Essex County iron industry, visit the Penfield Homestead Museum (page 58). For a homespun foray with the family, try the 1812 Homestead (page 55).

WASHINGTON COUNTY HISTORICAL SOCIETY
Wing-Northup House
167 Broadway
Fort Edward NY 12828
518-747-9108

The gray stone Wing-Northup House stands as a testament to Fort Edward's more prosperous days as a manufacturing and shipping center on the Hudson River, and the immaculate condition of the building (circa 1815) is a tribute to the historical society's dedication. The group opens the house two afternoons a week for local history and genealogy research, but there are currently no collections or exhibits for the casual visitor to see. Call to make an appointment.

The society holds an open house during the town's Heritage Days in July, sponsors workshops, talks, and special events, and publishes a newsletter describing historical sites throughout the county. You can pick up here an excellent architectural guidebook for Greenwich, a longtime agricultural center nearby with scores of early nineteenth-century Federal-style homes in its historic district.

BROOKSIDE
Saratoga County History Center
6 Charlton Street
Ballston Spa NY 12020
Open: Year-round Tues.–Sat.; Tues. 12 noon–8pm, Weds.–Fri. 10am–4pm,
    Sat. 12 noon–4pm
Admission: $2 adults
518-885-4000

During an 1804 visit to Aldridge's Hotel in Ballston Spa, Washington Irving had rather a dim view of his stay: "The springs are intollerably Stupid, owing to the miserable deficiency of female company. I took a warm bath this Morning and drank the waters which however did not agree with me. . . ." Today, the stately 1792 inn — now called Brookside — is the Saratoga County History Center, with changing local history exhibits on the first floor and a permanent installation depicting county history on the second floor. The second floor also has a dandy hands-on room for kids, with try-on clothing and lots of mechanical folk toys made by Chris Morley, a local woodworker.

Temporary exhibits have focused on dairying, local amusement parks, and prominent industries. Artifacts are cleverly combined with information on a touch-screen computer, so that, for example, visitors could hear bits of oral history from the developer of a local theme park and see old photographs and postcards of long-gone places.

If You Go: Brookside is across from the Old Iron Spring and only a few blocks from downtown Ballston. Follow the signs from Route 50. Allow about thirty minutes for a visit.

The Saratoga County History Center, in Ballston Spa, is housed in a handsome 1792 inn called Brookside. B. Folwell

Special Events: Monthly programs include informal "History on the Menu" lectures and "Saratoga County Memories," which feature oral histories on various topics, from farms to restaurants. Photographs and objects from the collection get the discussion rolling, and sessions are taped for Brookside's library. Classes in traditional crafts are offered regularly, and school programs include "Native New York," with an Abenaki storyteller, and "Shuttles, Spindles, and Sheep," all about making cloth.

Exploring Further: For a look into one of the region's early industries, visit the National Bottle Museum, just a few minutes away (page 175). If you're interested in the history of springs and spas, visit the Saratoga Historical Society (page 111) or take a self-guided walking tour of Saratoga Springs, courtesy of the Urban Cultural Park (518-587-3241).

FULTON COUNTY HISTORICAL SOCIETY
237 Kingsboro Avenue
Gloversville NY 12078
Old Kingsboro Avenue School
Open: May–June, Tues.–Sat. 12 noon–4pm; July–Aug. Tues.–Sat., 10am–4pm;
    Sun. 12 noon–4pm; Sept.–Nov., Tues.–Sat., 12 noon–4pm
Admission: Donation
518-725-2230

For all the historical sites in the Adirondack region that celebrate great regional industries like farming, logging, or mining, there are surprisingly few exhibits on perhaps the most demographically influential industry of them all: tanning. Similarly, few exhibits celebrate Fulton County's highly skilled leather workers beyond a few artifacts and captions in a couple of small museums. Yet this manufacturing heritage put Fulton County on the map. And much more than logging camps or mining hamlets, tannery towns evolved into the enduring settlements of the Adirondack region today.

That's why the full-fledged displays on leather work, glove making, and tanning at the Fulton County Historical Society Museum are so welcome. Here is a three-room exhibit scripted by Adirondack scholar Barbara McMartin that details the tannery industry from soup to nuts. A giant world map shows all the places Gloversville got its hides from: dog skins from China, reindeer from Alaska, chamois from North Africa, and so on. Pictures of the tannery ghost town of Griffin, along with blown-up illustrations from Frederic Remington's 1878 Fulton County sketches for *Harper's Magazine*, and displays of little-seen tanning tools like spuds (for stripping slabs of hemlock bark off trees), beaming knifes (for scraping hair off hides), or steam-powered grinders (for pulverizing bark) all help flesh out our picture of the days when Fulton County teemed with tanneries and huge piles of hemlock bark might stretch as far as a mile.

Other exhibits focus on native American encampments (a model seventeenth-century Iroquois bark house is a particular favorite with kids), a one-room schoolhouse (also a good pick for children), a Victorian parlor with models of impossibly shaped gowns of taffeta and satin, and a weaving room with a particularly prized blue-and-white coverlet from the loom of A.J. Irvin. Another fine exhibit describes the one-time "Coney Island of the North," Sacandaga Park, a revival camp turned amusement park that had its own miniature railroad, rides, vintage merry-go-round, water toboggans, and taffy shops — and here's the taffy-pull hook itself, big enough to hang a slab of beef on, and the machine that made the ribbon candy, and lots of pictures of couples courting in the old canoes. Today, most of what was left of the grand old place is under Sacandaga Reservoir, but people still remember it with wistfulness and love.

The pride and joy of the museum, however, are two collections: the first an enormous, racked display of numbered photographs of mostly downtown Gloversville in the first half of this century, and the second an exhibit called the Glove Room, which traces the evolution of Fulton County's leather-making industries from the time of Sir William Johnson, who brought tanners here from Europe, to its nineteenth-century rise and twentieth-century decline. The first exhibit is woefully short on captioned information, but long on atmospheric appeal (check out Picture No. 20, a man in a derby plucking a harp in the middle of a bustling street, or the elephants on North Main threading between the telegraph poles and streetcars on Circus Day). But the Glove Room is as fully informative as it is visually compelling. And, says the curator, there's no other exhibit quite like it in the country.

The glove-makers' cutting table was, as it happens, no workplace for the unskilled or transient laborer. To be a great glove maker — to have the eyes and imagination, that is, to eke as many pieces of a glove out of a single scrap of cured hide as possible — took years of training, and in the blown-up photographs of a cutting room, the experience plainly shows in the careworn, focused faces of the aproned, middle-aged glove makers. Also in evidence, and reasonably well captioned, are the scores of tools peculiar to this trade: rolling pins for flattening gloves, metal and wood glove models, cutting dies, stamps, button presses, and so on. What is missing — and this is regrettable — is any meaningful discussion of the role of the European immigrant in the development of this industry, or in the growth of Gloversville overall. In fact, few cities in the North Country were as ethnically diverse as Gloversville, a town that inspired one history called *Shtetl of the Adirondacks*, by Herbert Engel (Purple Mountain Press, 1991), and sent one of the first Jewish legislators, the glove magnate Lucius Littauer, to the state senate.

If You Go: At first glimpse, this museum may look as fusty and severe as the schoolhouse it once was, but when you get into the exhibits (all in former classrooms), the displays turn out to be compelling after all. Plan for an hour at least; the director recommends two. The museum sits on a particularly prosperous, tree-lined, residential street, only a block or two from a small park with a statue of the founder of Yale College, and a colonial cemetery just beyond with some of the most venerable headstones in town.

Exploring Further: So blessed is Fulton County with historic sites, it behooves the visitor to stop into the Fulton County Regional Chamber of Commerce at 18 Cayadutta Street, in downtown Gloversville, and stock up on the driving maps and brochures. To learn about the impact of tanneries, read *Hides, Hemlocks and Adirondack History* by Barbara McMartin (North Country Books, 1992).

HERKIMER COUNTY HISTORICAL SOCIETY AND MUSEUM
400 N. Main Street
Herkimer NY 13350
Open: Mon.–Fri. 10am–4pm
Admission: Donation, plus $1 fees for special areas
315-866-6413

Since 1938 the Herkimer County Historical Society has made its headquarters a Queen Anne brick home in downtown Herkimer. The slow-to-change exhibits put the emphasis squarely on rural and industrial county history, with plenty of artifacts and explanatory panels. "All in a Day's Work: Working People, Working Lives" features logging gear and a model camp (tiny bunks, dining table, funky kitchen) and goods that traveled on canal boats, like chicken crates, a canal lantern, a captain's leather trunk, and furs. The room on agriculture honors the cheese factories of the county, once as many as 101, now down to a sole example. From the docks of Little Falls (the only city in the county), the renowned Herkimer cheddar — said to be the best in the U.S. — was shipped across the nation and to England. Here the price of cheddar was established for the whole country. Note along with the display of wooden cheese boxes, knives, and model wheels, the kosher milk carton from a Mannheim farm, signaling the presence of an immigrant community in numbers enough to form a synagogue. Also in the farm room is a wooden, ox-drawn Palatine plow fashioned in the old Rhinelander style, one of a handful left in New York.

The room devoted to industry shows Herkimer County to be a hotbed of early invention. Here Linus Yale from Newport, New York, devised the Yale lock in 1840, and in 1871 H.M. Quackenbush concocted the nutcracker (as well as manufacturing air rifles, pokers, lid lifters, bikes, and machine-gun casings) in a plant still going strong. In 1893 the Diamond Match Company bought the fifty-year-old Gates Match Factory, in Frankfort. Then there was Daniel Green's slipper factory, in Dolgeville (you can buy those felt softies on the home shopping channels even now), and woodenware factories like Standard Furniture, maker of library bureaus, card files, desks, and cabinets. Of course, the pride and joy of Herkimer industry is Remington Arms, Eliphalet Remington's humble 1816 forge-turned-manufacturing giant, leading county employer, and producer not just of famous rifles, but sewing machines and typewriters as well. Also worth a peek is a local doctor's library, with fainting couch, tile fireplace, patient charts, and tomes of Twain.

Linked to the museum by a handicap-accessible walkway is the 1870 Eckler Building, home these days to a fifteen-panel exhibit on local boy Francis Elias Spinner, who went from county sheriff to Congressman and eventually to Treasurer of the United States. Spinner was among the first federal officials to hire women for government jobs — in this case, cutting fat sheaves of paper money.

Remember the tale of Chester Gillette and Grace Brown in Theodore Dreiser's *An American Tragedy*? That was a Herkimer County story, and you can get the lowdown on the case on a tour of the 1834 limestone three-story jail, diagonally across from the museum building. More gruesome still, you'll learn about the 1884 hanging of a famously unremorseful housewife who not only shot her husband but also, with her children's help, chopped him and burned him in the parlor stove! There are nine cells, two for solitary confinement, a cell block, and a dumbwaiter. Or skip the whole sordid business and head upstairs to Joyce Keller's sweet collection of seven doll houses and eighteen doll-size "room boxes" — a quilt shop, a loom loft, flower shop, a boy's bedroom with a working miniature train set, and a girl's bedroom with a tiny Monopoly board and a petite TV.

If You Go: Three separate buildings, each packed with stuff, add up to the better part of a morning. With guided tours, you're in for three hours for sure.

Special Events: The historical society picks a private historic home to gussy up with Victorian finery and fill with food and crafts over a weekend in early September. House tours in other county towns are often scheduled; call for times.

Exploring Further: In Ilion, the county's last surviving cheese factory, Original Herkimer County Cheese Company, offers samples of their products, from beet cheese to port wine, and of course, white cheddar. In Salisbury, there's an 1870 covered bridge, and in Middleville, the Herkimer Diamond Mines, where you can dig your own quartz crystals. A museum right at the Remington Arms Factory features early guns, bicycles, typewriters, and sewing machines. To learn about the county's namesake, Nicholas Herkimer, see page 34.

ONEIDA COUNTY HISTORICAL SOCIETY
1608 Genesee Street
Utica NY 13502-5425
Open: Tues.–Fri. 10am–4:30pm; closed Jan.
Admission: Donation
315-735-3642

In an imposing former Christian Science church on the corner of Genesee and Avery streets in downtown Utica are the offices, library, and museum of the Historical Society of Oneida County. The museum, a great hall on the first floor, is largely given over to a single in-depth exhibit whose contents change every year. In 1996 the subject was "Utica in the Fifties," a shrewd analysis of the city's remarkable decade-long recovery during the fabled "Loom To Boom" period that followed World War II. The exhibit starts with an account of the demise of Utica's long-dominant textile factories and explores the rise of other industries, from electronics to fishing tackle. Particularly intriguing are oblique references to Utica's one-time reputation as "Sin City" and, as *Newsweek* put it in 1958, "headquarters . . . for big-time mobster operations in most of the Eastern half of the nation with strings reaching all the way to Cuba." The exhibit also addresses, with greater zest, the welcome arrival of new colleges, the impact of the Great Migration of African-American laborers who moved to the area after the war, and the devastation wrought by the automobile on the physical fabric of downtown neighborhoods and stores.

If "Utica in the Fifties" is gone by the time you get there, it nonetheless suggests that future exhibitions will partake of the same thoughtfulness and ambition. Call ahead to learn what's up.

If You Go: An hour or less is ample time to take the measure of this history hall. The smaller permanent exhibit at the rear of the room includes downtown landscapes by local painters and a "Guess What?" case of mysterious artifacts, including an early ballot box and a cherry pitter.

Exploring Further: The block-big, three-story Children's Museum in Utica is a great place to take a restless youngster on a drizzly afternoon (see page 178). Then there are the art and concert galleries at the Munson-Williams-Proctor Institute, just a block or two down Genesee (see page 169), and the "Munstitute's" historic house, Fountain Elms.

LEWIS COUNTY HISTORICAL SOCIETY
Gould Mansion
High Street
Lyons Falls NY 13368
Open: Mid-May–mid-Oct., Tues.–Sat. 10am–4pm
Admission: $1 adults
315-348-8089

G.H.P. Gould built his Richardsonian Romanesque home between 1899 and 1902 so that he could look out over his thriving paper mill just across the street. Now the turreted mansion serves as the headquarters of the Lewis County Historical Society as well as a typical house museum of the period. The public spaces downstairs, such as the living room, dining room, and hallway, feature much of the Gould family's own Victorian furniture. Upstairs exhibits include a room devoted to nineteenth-century resorts such as Brantingham Lake and Lowville Mineral Springs; a room on Franklin B. Hough, an eminent regional historian and one of the first forestry scientists in America; a period bedroom; and a space for changing shows on local industries, bygone events, traditional foods, and ethnic groups (Lewis County had a large Hungarian immigrant population). In the stairwell is a very unusual display: a fabulously embroidered Turkish prayer rug set in a glass frame bordered by a butterfly collection, assembled and donated by a   local resident.

Restoration of the period rooms is ongoing. The society is also assembling a research library to serve visiting scholars.

Special Events: The historical society sponsors historical lectures and tours on a regular basis which are publicized through its newsletter.

If You Go: To find the Gould Mansion, enter Lyons Falls on Route 12. Stay on Main Street until you see the main yard of the Lyons Falls paper mill, then turn left on High Street and park by the museum's carriage house.

Allow a half hour for a visit. The first floor is wheelchair accessible.

Exploring Further: Just north of Lyons Falls on Route 12 are the ruins of a lock from the Black River Canal, which allowed boats to travel from Rome to Carthage. There's a highway pull-out with a large map of the canal. In nearby Lyonsdale is Agers Falls State Historic Site, commemorating an early sawmill and paper mill on the Moose River. Pick up an interpretive brochure on the archaeological site at the historical society; the site is not staffed.

JEFFERSON COUNTY HISTORICAL SOCIETY MUSEUM
228 Washington Street
Watertown NY 13601
Open: Apr.–Dec., Tues.–Fri. 10am–5pm, Sat. 12 noon–5pm;
    Dec.–Mar., Tues.–Fri. 10am–5pm
Admission: Donation
315-782-3491

The museum of the Jefferson County Historical Society takes up three floors of a modified Tuscan villa, downtown home of the Paddocks, a Watertown banking family who lived here from 1876, when the house was built, until 1924. Victorian furnishings and some fine Asian antiques, many from the Paddock family collection, are featured in the two-room parlor. The main gallery houses three-month-long exhibits like, for instance, the paintings of French-trained local impressionist Minerva Chapman (spring 1997), or a special bicentennial display on St. Lawrence County (summer 1997). Room exhibits on the second floor introduce typical North Country subjects such as the Iroquois, pioneers, Civil War (look for the lottery barrel that was used in the 1860s draft, and the surgical instruments from a Union sawbones), more Victoriana, and the bedroom with the Tyler coverlet. Textile buffs will distinguish the 1840s coverlets of Jefferson County weaver Harry Tyler by their signature lions and borders of fences and trees.

Take restless children to the lower level and set them loose in the Please Touch Kitchen, half pioneer-era, half Victorian, while you poke into the weaving room with its spinning wheels and loom, and then explore what is surely the museum's most unusual display, the recently renovated Clarence Kinne Water Turbine Collection, which takes up two-thirds of an entire floor. Kinne, who was born in 1869 and collected waterwheels as a hobby, got most of these turbines from Watertown mills or the river towns around, back when the local waterpowered paper industry played such a key role in Jefferson County's economic growth. A ten-minute video of a Beaver River sawmill turbine shows how the great things worked.

In the Paddock barn behind the museum are farm tools, an immense lathe used for shaping the mighty columns that front Watertown's many beautiful old homes, and a collection of odd and rarely sighted vehicles, like an World War I ambulance, a locally made 1910 Babcock automobile designed to resemble the carriages that were its inventor's specialty, a couple of early surreys, and a cutter for dashing through the deep, deep snow.

If You Go: This is the biggest turbine collection north of Delaware. Start with what is surely the most unique facet of the museum's holdings, and work up. Between the barn and the main museum a tour could last an hour and a half.

Special Events: The first weekend in March is the occasion of the annual "Society In Bloom" show, when the museum spruces up with interpretive displays of artifacts and flowers. A Victorian fair and gala brightens the house in November and, in July, the museum caps an annual five-house garden tour with an ice-cream social in its own Victorian garden in back.

Exploring Further: To the west of the city is the historic village of Sackets Harbor. And also within fifteen minutes is the Northern New York Agricultural Historical Museum at Stone Mills (see page 68). In Watertown itself the Sci-Tech Center of Northern New York at 154 Stone Street (315-788-1340) is open year-round with forty-some hands-on science exhibits, many of them interactive. In Brownville, a suburb of Watertown, the General Brown Weekend takes place the weekend after Memorial Day, with a historic house walking tour, Saturday parade, vintage fashion show, and a soap-box derby. (Jacob Brown was a War of 1812 general and hero.)

To learn more about the French speculators who tried, with only limited success, to settle Jefferson County two hundred years ago, the museum director recommends *Penet's Square* by Thomas Powell.

SILAS WRIGHT HOUSE
St. Lawrence County Historical Association
3 East Main Street
Canton NY 13617
Open: Year-round 10am–4pm Tues.–Fri.
Admission: Donation
315-386-8133

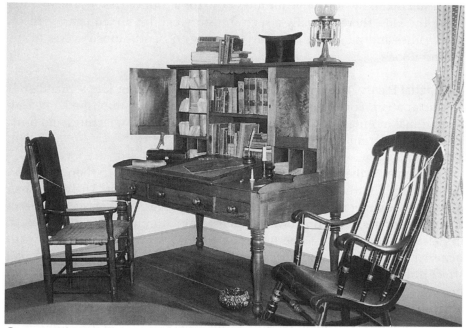

Governor Silas Wright's desk, at the St. Lawrence County Historical Association, Canton. B. Folwell

Across from Canton's lovely village park is a museum with three distinct entities: a historic house, a county historical society with changing exhibits on social and economic trends, and a bustling resource center with rare books, maps, ephemera, and records. The centerpiece of the museum is the first floor, with rooms pertaining to Silas Wright, who arrived in Canton in 1819 and was Martin Van Buren's astute political protégé. Wright was elected to the state senate in 1823; won a seat in Congress in 1827; was appointed state comptroller in 1829; then went on to the U.S. Senate and later chairmanship of the Senate finance committee; and eventually was elected governor of New York. Tour his home and you get a glimpse of his character: modest, forthright, thoughtful, as expressed in simple, elegant furnishings.

Changing exhibits are on the second floor. In recent years, as the museum has been cataloging its artifacts and photographs, galleries have showcased materials from private collections. An entertaining recent show featured antique sewing machines, with excellent descriptive captions about how these modern contraptions changed rural life. A quote from a local collector named Carl Stickney — who owns something like three hundred chairs, four hundred oil lamps, forty-two buggies and sleighs, and numerous sewing machines — introduced the exhibit: "I just collect what I like and just ignore what everybody else is doing. Sometimes I see something that nobody likes and I'll feel sorry for it and think that maybe it needs a home."

If You Go: Allow forty-five minutes or so for a tour of the entire museum. Bring the kids: there's usually a special history exhibit aimed just for them, with games and hands-on activities. There is no handicapped access to the second floor.

Special Events: The annual antiques show and sale, in late September, is a popular affair. For the past few years the museum has published an excellent annual monograph about an important local person; lectures and tours are scheduled from time to time.

Exploring Further: St. Lawrence County is huge — more than a million acres — and it fairly abounds with small museums. Many of them are open only in the summer months and even then just a couple of hours a week. Here's a sampling of places to pop in when you're passing through the neighborhood: in Helena, on Route 37C, is the Town of Brasher Museum (315-389-5717), with material on local iron mining, among other things; in Colton, across the street from the town offices, is the Colton Historical Society (315-262-2524), home to the Jackson M. Newton Cultural Collection and open Saturday afternoons July–September; the Town of DeKalb Historical Association (Box 111, DeKalb Junction NY 13630) recently formed a group that sponsors building-restoration workshops; the Gouverneur Museum (315-287-0570), open Wednesdays in summer, is an 1880s parsonage with rooms full of wondrous artifacts plus displays on talc mining and marble cutting; the Parishville Historical Association, on Route 72 (315-265-7619), has several outbuildings including a blacksmith shop; the Pierrepont Museum, Route 68 (315-386-8311), is open Saturdays; the Red Barn Museum, River Road (315-375-6390), Morristown, open summer weekends, will expand in the next few years to accommodate a display of fine antique cars; the John Moore Museum (315-388-5967), in Waddington, open Tuesday–Thursday afternoons May 1–September 1, includes Indian artifacts found by the St. Lawrence River; material from local banks, schools, and factories; a diorama of the town before the Seaway Power Project; memorabilia from Isaac Johnson, a freed slave who became a master stonemason, and background on inventor James Ricalton, who helped Thomas Edison produce the first light bulb.

FRANKLIN COUNTY HISTORICAL SOCIETY
51 Milwaukee Street
Malone NY 12953
Open: June 1–early Sept., Tues.–Sat. 1–4pm; Sat. only remainder of year
Admission: $2 for tour
518-483-2750

Franklin County's "House of History" is a marvelous Italianate building with high ceilings, lovely woodwork, a fine formal staircase, and marble fireplaces that demonstrate Malone's proud past as a center of commerce and transportation. The village isn't quite so prosperous now as it was in the days when two railroad lines came to town, but photographs, prints, and displays here help remind visitors of that time.

Visitors enter through a generic old-time kitchen, with lots of hand-cranked tools, and proceed eventually to a room set up with heavy Empire-style furniture that belonged to native son William A. Wheeler, who served as vice president under Rutherford B. Hayes. Upstairs rooms are equipped with spinning wheels, looms, and broom-making devices, emblematic of pioneer industries and now used mainly for school programs — the house is on practically every county school's fourth-grade field-trip list. Volunteers lead tours, so if a particular aspect of North Country history is of interest, like Malone's preeminence as a hop-growing center — be sure to ask.

If You Go: Allow about half an hour for a visit. Children are welcome, and some guides may encourage them to try weaving on a floor loom. The first floor is accessible, but not the second.

Special Events: Lectures and demonstrations are scheduled from time to time; call ahead.

Exploring Further: Malone abounds in impressive old homes, but presently there's no formal walking tour available. Ask about some nearby streets to explore. About six miles away is the Almanzo Wilder Homestead (see page 80), which was the site of Laura Ingalls Wilder's book *Farmer Boy*.

The historical society publishes an annual of well-researched articles, the *Franklin Historical Review*, and maintains an extensive library for the genealogically inclined. Call for an appointment.

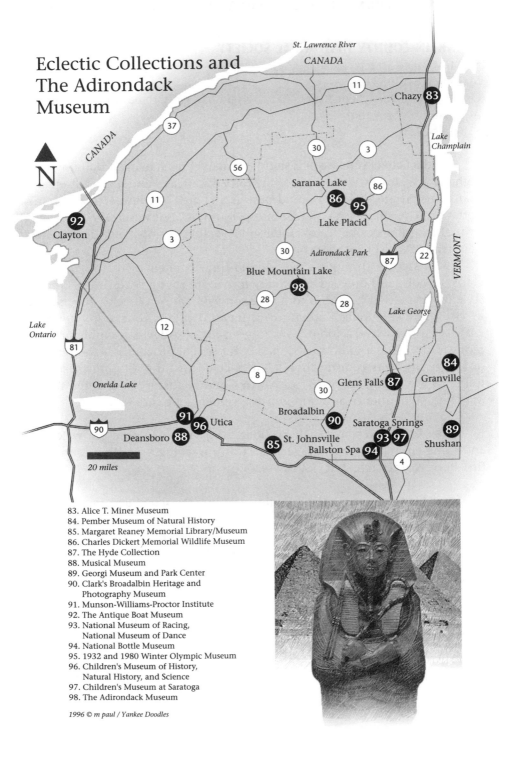

Eclectic Collections and The Adirondack Museum

N

St. Lawrence River
CANADA

Chazy **83**

Lake Champlain

37

11

30

3

56

Saranac Lake

86 **95**

86

Lake Placid

92
Clayton

3

30

Adirondack Park

87

22

VERMONT

Blue Mountain Lake

98

28

28

Lake George

Lake Ontario

12

81

84

8

Glens Falls **87**

Granville

Oneida Lake

30

90

Broadalbin

90

Saratoga Springs

89

Shushan

91
96 Utica

93 **97**

Deansboro **88**

85 St. Johnsville

94

Ballston Spa

4

20 miles

83. Alice T. Miner Museum
84. Pember Museum of Natural History
85. Margaret Reaney Memorial Library/Museum
86. Charles Dickert Memorial Wildlife Museum
87. The Hyde Collection
88. Musical Museum
89. Georgi Museum and Park Center
90. Clark's Broadalbin Heritage and
    Photography Museum
91. Munson-Williams-Proctor Institute
92. The Antique Boat Museum
93. National Museum of Racing,
    National Museum of Dance
94. National Bottle Museum
95. 1932 and 1980 Winter Olympic Museum
96. Children's Museum of History,
    Natural History, and Science
97. Children's Museum at Saratoga
98. The Adirondack Museum

1996 © m paul / Yankee Doodles

CHAPTER SEVEN

ECLECTIC COLLECTIONS

■■■■■■■■■■■■■■■■■■■■■■■■■■■■■■■■■■

T
hink back over your own past: didn't you collect *something* at some point — coins, rocks, sea shells, stamps, Barbies? For today's youth, it's Pogs, trolls, and magic cards. Items not yet invented are waiting to be eagerly gathered en masse and hoarded, coveted, and traded.

Once humans achieved basic levels of comfort and leisure in their daily lives, accumulating useless stuff became a worthy pastime — within particular cultures, anyway. The Victorians raised the notion of collecting to a passionate obsession, but objects were selected not just because they were interesting to look at, but because they could be perceived as educational — and proof positive of the collector's own worldliness.

Precisely what was appreciated — to be displayed in glass cases, hung on the walls, or put on the floor — was sharply divided between the sexes. Men pursued living, breathing creatures from Africa, the Arctic, South America, and the American West, bringing home exotic taxidermy trophies of lions, tigers, bears, elephants, antelopes, walruses. Men garnered tribal shields, mummies, totem poles, and monumental ethnographic pieces from the uncivilized world that emphasized masculine attributes of conquest and discovery. Women were introspective, handicraft and detail oriented, searching out domestic items: china, glass, dolls, textiles, and fine art, and looking to Europe and colonial America for inspiration. They also focused on bits of genteel nature found close to home: ferns, flowers, butterflies. Male and female collectors corresponded with others of like interests, exchanging specimens with all the enthusiasm of boys swapping baseball cards today.

Most of these men and women lived in towns of a size where even private collections were public knowledge, and it was no huge leap to share these treasures with others. Some collectors were moved to share as soon as they began acquiring — perhaps to boast, but also to fulfill a sincere wish to expose the less traveled, less cultured, and less fortunate to rare artifacts and prizes. Thus rural, seemingly provincial places like Chazy and St. Johnsville might gain a reputation for worldliness, where you could see for yourself a bird of paradise, a mummy, or a Degas. Alice T. Miner and her husband embodied that ideal; the couple's *noblesse oblige* was felt beyond the stone walls of their museum, in civic contributions like the luxurious public school built with Miner money and free electricity supplied to their townspeople.

From the realms of late-nineteenth- and early twentieth-century collectors like Miner, Franklin Pember, and their modern equivalents, this chapter proceeds to museums organized around a single theme, like classical dance and thoroughbred racing, and to a new notion in institutions, children's museums.

ALICE T. MINER MUSEUM
9618 Main Street
Chazy NY 12921
Open: Feb. 1–Dec. 23, Tues.–Sat. 10am–4pm
Admission: $3 adults, $2 seniors, $1 students
518-846-7336

In 1924, a year before the American Wing of the Metropolitan Museum opened, Alice Miner's "colonial collection" made its debut in a custom-designed stone mansion in downtown Chazy. The institution was part of a grand plan to better life within the community; already Alice and her husband, William, had paid for a peerless public school, erected the state-of-the-art hospital in Plattsburgh, and established an eighteen-thousand-acre farm that was a showplace of modern agriculture. The couple's generosity didn't end there: people in Chazy enjoyed free electric power right up to 1940.

William Miner's ties to Chazy began in the 1870s, when he was orphaned and sent to live on his aunt and uncle's farm. He later went west to seek his fortune and along the way became interested in engineering. Before he was thirty he had invented a coupling device for railroad cars; manufacturing it made him a multimillionaire. In Chicago he met Alice, who was a waitress, married her, and reportedly sent her off to finishing school. In 1903 they moved to Chazy.

Alice began collecting in 1911 and by 1917 had gathered together a wonderful assortment of Redford glass, Canton ware, Majolica, and other pieces. Next she pursued Americana: samplers, silhouettes, Windsor chairs, military pieces from the American Revolution and War of 1812, and portraits of Lincoln and Washington — including one particularly pained-looking George made of leather.

Although the Alice Miner Museum looks like a historic Champlain Valley home, it was built specifically as a museum. Robin Brown

Today these myriad items are in lovely rooms on three floors of the house (always a museum, never a private home); many artifacts still perch in the same spot where Alice herself had put them. Curator Frederic Smith, a former college administrator, leads tours through the rooms and is quick to pick up on visitors' interests. He opens drawers, wooden boxes, and cupboards to pull out elaborate tortoise-shell combs, minute porcelain cosmetic boxes, a glass slipper. You name it — Peruvian textiles from the fourth century, exquisite Southwestern Indian baskets, nineteenth-century tools, a mummified hand from Egypt, miniature furniture — you'll find it somewhere here, and chances are Fred will hand it to you for a closer look.

The Miner Museum has been in a time warp for decades, but a new conservation program is underway to preserve fragile items. There's an extensive amount of rare paper — letters from Washington and Lincoln, for example — that has never been shared with the public, and a document room is planned for the third floor so that researchers can have access to these materials.

If You Go: Allow about two hours for a visit; call ahead for times for scheduled tours. Access for the mobility impaired is a problem; an elevator intended for the original structure was never built.

Be sure to ask questions if something catches your eye or if you're a collector. Bring the school-age children; at first glance this place may seem for grown-ups only, but Fred makes it fun.

Special Events: The third-floor ballroom, which houses the china and glass, is occasionally used for concerts and lectures. A popular summer program introduces local youngsters to the museum. In November, there's an open house that sometimes includes the Miner chapel and mausoleum.

Exploring Further: Save half an hour or so to stroll around Chazy, which has several fine early stone buildings within an easy walk. You can spot other buildings put up with Miner money, too: some are California Mission Revival style and look pretty incongruous; one, Gray Gables, is a towering concrete monstrosity built to house schoolteachers. Heart's Delight Farm, once the Miners' showplace for raising exotic game and fine farm stock, and now the Miner Agricultural Research Institute, is a short distance away and is occasionally open for tours and events; call 518-846-7121.

Elsewhere in this chapter, look for the Hyde Collection (page 162) and the Georgi Museum (page 165) for sketches of other lady collectors. If you're interested in decorative arts, the Potsdam Public Museum (page 129) has an excellent permanent display of English ceramics.

PEMBER MUSEUM OF NATURAL HISTORY
33 West Main Street
Granville NY 12832
Open: Year-round Tues.–Fri. 1–5pm and Sat. 10am–3pm; Hebron Nature
  Preserve open dawn to dusk daily
Admission: Donation
518-642-1515

Franklin Pember, born in South Granville, New York, in 1841, had become an amateur naturalist of great repute by the time he was twenty-one. He also had a good head for business, which enabled him to travel throughout the Americas collecting birds, eggs, nests, butterflies, and mammals. In 1909, he opened his museum — located above the town library — to the public, displaying case after case of colorful creatures, from tiny rainbow-hued hummingbirds to a full-size polar bear. But, just two decades later, after Pember died, the museum was quietly locked up and forgotten, with only occasional visitors let in to marvel at bright feathers and sleek furs.

In 1973, some townspeople brought the collection back to life, and today the Pember is a meticulously preserved gem, a museum true to its Victorian origins. Besides showcasing an astonishing array of creatures in gleaming floor-to-ceiling cherry cases, the exhibit hall gives us plenty to think about as we're face to face with passenger pigeons, Carolina paroquets, and great auk eggs.

Cases of stuffed carnivores and flocks of birds lurk behind glass at the Pember Museum.
Phil Haggerty

If You Go: The Pember Museum and Library is easy to find in downtown Granville. Allow about an hour for a visit, and do check out the historic photographs showing the slate-mining industry displayed in the library downstairs. Bring the kids; this is a place where they're encouraged to open drawers to peek at scores of exotic beetles and butterflies.

Special Events: The Hebron Nature Preserve is operated by the Pember Museum, and together the organizations sponsor a wide variety of ecology, astronomy, and wildlife conservation programs and field trips. Local youngsters join in a nature day camp in the summer.

Exploring Further: The Pember Museum is like a smaller cousin to the Fairbanks Museum, in St. Johnsbury, Vermont (802-748-2373), which has countless curiosities from around the globe. For an in-depth look at natural history, visit the New York State Museum, in Albany (page 4), which has permanent exhibits of minerals, birds, and mammals. The Charles Dickert Museum (page 161), in the Saranac Lake Free Library, has a collection of North American taxidermy specimens, as does the Bradt's Wildlife Museum (518-863-4040), in Northville.

Also in Granville, stop by the Slate Valley Museum (page 60) for an excellent overview of still-active regional industry.

MARGARET REANEY MEMORIAL LIBRARY/MUSEUM
19 Kingsbury Avenue, off Main Street (Route 5)
St. Johnsville NY 13452
Open: Year-round, Mon. and Fri., 9:30am–5pm, 6:30–8:30pm;
   Tues. and Weds. 9:30am–5pm; Thurs. 1–5pm; Sat. 9:30am–12 noon
Admission: Free
518-568-7822

Small museums — monuments and collections that testify to the largesse of some local industrialist-turned-hometown benefactor — are a long-standing and deservedly beloved American tradition. As to whether the collection is in and of itself any *good*, or whether its main purpose is to showcase the donor's worldliness and wealth, is another question. Happily for the town of St. Johnsville, the local library-cum-museum not only bespeaks Joseph Reaney's dramatic rise to riches from furniture salesman to mill owner, it also reveals an aesthetic sensibility as eclectic as it is pedagogically intriguing.

Here, in the lower floors of a yellow-brick Greek Revival building a block or two off Main Street, is a gold mine of assorted artifacts: nineteenth-century bronzes (thirty-two of them), heavy-framed oil paintings, weird collections of everything from flasks and cruets to walking canes to whale oil lamps. Military buffs gravitate toward cases crammed with Civil War artifacts like drumsticks, powder flasks, bullet casings from Chancellorsville, and heaps of buttons, each identified by regiment and battle. Lovers of odd Americana pause over early arithmetic-exercise books ("If 47 bags of indigo weigh . . .") and an 1868 tinted daguerreotype of the Eagle Baseball Club. Children scrutinize gas masks and hand grenades in the World War I case, along with the coconut carved like an owl.

There is a room full of carpenters' tools, another fixed up like an old-time doctor's office (eye chart, stethoscope, and all), and a third, a sort of community room, lined with wonderful St. Johnsville photographs of dancing-class garden parties, the hook-and-ladder company's fife-and-drum corps, family clambakes, and Shriners. No mere self-aggrandizing booster, Joseph H. Reaney, the businessman who founded this library and museum as a tribute to his mother, was a natural-born curator of American culture, high *and* low. All the diverse, interwoven strata of pre-World War II small-town life are proudly exposed in this ambitious collection. And when the legs weary and eyes blear, there are a couple of Cadillac-size leather couches near the massive hearth.

If You Go: Coming from the west, exit the Thruway at Little Falls, and take Route 5 east. From the east, take the Canajoharie exit and follow Route 5 west. St. Johnsville is a modest place with a quiet, intact Main Street and some fine old houses that bespeak its heyday as a thriving mill town a century ago. Call ahead for help with wheelchair access.

Special Events: Like many upstate libraries, the Margaret Reaney Memorial Library serves as a community arts center, regularly hosting all kinds of performances, lectures, and readings. The third Tuesday in July brings the annual band concert and ice-cream social, a much-loved community event.

Exploring Further: Fort Klock (page 33), the Palatine Church, and Fort Plain Museum (page 121) are all close at hand a few miles to the east. Also on Route 5, just east of St. Johnsville, is the historic colonial Nellis Tavern, open to the public in summer months. The way west leads to the Oriskany Battlefield, in Oriskany (page 36), and Fort Stanwix, in Rome (page 38). Either way, the state road is much preferable to the Thruway and dotted with farmstands along its length.

CHARLES DICKERT MEMORIAL WILDLIFE MUSEUM
Saranac Lake Free Library
100 Main Street
Saranac Lake NY 12983
Open: July–Aug. 10am–12 noon, 1–4pm
Admission: Free
518-891-4190

Duck into the downstairs of the Saranac Lake library and amaze your friends with this one: a cathedral-ceilinged room packed with more than 250 stuffed birds, mammals, and fish, all of them mounted by Charles Dickert, a local taxidermist who died in 1942. There are several moose, enormous wolves, a couple of leaping foxes, mink, muskrat, deer, beavers, polar bears, plus a few African trophies tossed in for good measure. Hanging from the ceiling is a flight of geese and up in the balcony lurk even more critters. There's a nicely restored guideboat and a birch-bark canoe.

Some people might find all these dead animals depressing, but there's a kind of goofy, exuberant innocence to the whole thing. Some of the animals look positively jaunty; others are artfully arranged with tails fanned and legs uplifted, no doubt intended as decorative accents for rustic retreats.

Allow about a half hour to check out this unusual collection, and bring the kids. And as long as you're there, stop into the William Chapman White room downstairs and admire its magnificent collection of Adirondack literature and ephemera; open by appointment.

THE HYDE COLLECTION
161 Warren Street
Glens Falls NY 12801
Open: Year-round, Tues.–Sun., 10am–5pm
Admission: Free
518-792-1761

From the beginning, Charlotte Pruyn Hyde intended her home on the banks of the Hudson River to be a showcase for fine art, rare books, and European furniture. The house, designed by Bigelow and Wadsworth from Boston and finished in 1912, is in the style of a Florentine Renaissance villa. The collection was influenced by Isabella Stewart Gardner's personal museum, also in Boston.

Mrs. Hyde's father was Samuel Pruyn, a co-founder and later owner of Finch Pruyn and Company, a manufacturer of quality paper just across the river from the museum. The family fortune allowed the Hydes to collect paintings, tapestries, small sculptures, and other artifacts, guided by the best art historians of the day such as Bernard

Among the remarkable works of art in the Hyde Collection is this "Cartoon for the Mona Lisa," circa 1503, by Leonardo da Vinci. Joseph Levy, for the Hyde Collection, Glens Falls

Berenson, William Valentiner, and R. Langston Douglas. The Hyde Collection was founded in 1952 and the museum was permanently established after Mrs. Hyde's death in 1963.

The entrance is through a new wing designed by Edward Larrabee Barnes in 1989. A large gallery houses major changing exhibits such as contemporary artists Dorothy Dehner (who was David Smith's wife) and Joseph C. Parker (a sculptor from Hadley, New York, who studied with Fernand Leger) or important traveling shows from other institutions; smaller galleries have displayed Winslow Homer engravings, beautiful examples of paper money, illuminated manuscripts, and so on.

The house itself is elegant, warm, and wonderfully lit, in marked contrast to the heavy industry visible just across the river. The bedrooms, library, dining room, hallways, stairwells, and courtyard are all packed with exquisite furniture and hung with works of art that come as quite a surprise. Paintings by Rembrandt (*Portrait of Christ*), Rubens (*Head of a Negro* — perhaps one of the Hyde's best-known oils), El Greco, Botticelli, Tintoretto, and many more Old Masters are joined by a selection of late nineteenth- and early twentieth-century works by Renoir, Degas, Seurat, Picasso, Whistler, Hassam, and Homer. The pictures are hung modestly, with discreet lighting and a minimum of labels; the overall effect remains that of visiting a private home where the lady of the house has just stepped out for a minute.

The music room, on the second floor, contains several fine tapestries, including a lovely scene with birds and deer. The library, a richly paneled room with leather-bound volumes and numerous small sculptures, is a beautiful space; it's for savoring with your eyes, though, not sampling the books.

If You Go: The Hyde Collection is just a few blocks from downtown Glens Falls on Warren Street, one of the main arteries that meets Glen Street in front of the Civic Center. Allow about two hours for a visit.

Guided tours are available from 1–3pm on most days the museum is open. Join one especially if furniture is a particular interest. Do pick up a free copy of *Hyde House: A Guide to the Collection* by W. Sheldon Hurst, whether or not you take a tour.

The atmosphere at the Hyde Collection is hushed but not pretentious; this museum is suited to older children and teenagers who are comfortable looking at art. The new wing and ground-floor portions of the Hyde House are easily accessible; there is an elevator to reach several rooms on the upper floor. A gift shop near the entrance has art reference books and biographies, fine art prints and cards, jewelry and accessories.

Special Events: The Hyde Collection schedules art workshops for children and adults, tours to other museums, numerous lectures by art history scholars, and a chamber music series, all publicized in an attractive bimonthly calendar. Recent exhibitions include "Inventions of Leonardo," "Women of Hope," and oil sketches of Thomas Hill. As for the Hyde's annual late spring dress-up-as-your-favorite-artist-or-work-of-art costume gala and dance, it has emerged as one of the hippest, most hilarious bashes of the season; winners have included a two-person Calder mobile, and St. Sebastian. Call for times.

Exploring Further: The Alice T. Miner Museum, in Chazy, represents another woman's highly individualistic museum (see page 156). The Georgi Museum, in Shushan, about forty minutes from Glens Falls, likewise showcases a private collection: Russian icons, Renaissance art, and decorative arts (see page 165).

In Glens Falls, visit the Chapman Museum (page 107) for a solid overview of city lore and great nineteenth-century images by photographer Seneca Ray Stoddard.

MUSICAL MUSEUM
Route 12B
Deansboro NY 13328
Mail: PO Box 223
Open: May–Nov. Thurs.–Sat. 11am–3pm
Admission: $5.40 adults, $4 age 3–12
315-841-8774

In a nondescript building at the edge of a small town settled in 1784 by Christian Indians and named after Quaker missionary Thomas Dean is the cluttered, loving, and altogether remarkable legacy of the Sanders family, passionate collectors of musical instruments and mechanical devices that the lucky visitor is actually invited to crank, pump, and play. Here are hand-crank organs, dulciphones, Yankee bass viols, and music boxes by the busload, pump organs of every size and description, banjos, harmoniums, vintage juke-boxes, musical toys like Zilotones and wind-up ukuleles, even a case of brass train whistles from old-time locomotives.

Somewhere there may be another collection that rivals this in bulk and ambition, but surely not in accessibility. A video introduction in a dim chapel-like room launches the adventure. Here, the late Arthur Sanders, owlish, bow-tied son of museum founders Hardie and Esther Sanders, demonstrates a few of the more unusual artifacts (a mechanical nightingale just like the one in the Chinese emperor's fairy tale, an organ that painstakingly teaches birds how to sing) and invites us to "go through the red door . . . and play with my toys for the rest of the day!" Not all these toys are user-friendly: many are delicate and only for looking. But where else can you play a sonorous "Dixie" on a Victorian reed organ without fear of some glowering guard telling you "hands off!" or crank away at a massive Mississippi steamboat organ that calls up the brassy sounds of a German street band from the 1880s.

Best of all is the mock ice-cream parlor full of gorgeous player pianos. Two bits will get you an ear-splitting, lushly orchestrated waltz on one of these marvelous machines, and better still, thanks to glass panels that let you peek into their innards, a chance to see how they actually work. A great many devices here exemplify the weird American zeal for trying to squeeze two or three functions into one — like a liquor bottle that plays a tune when it's lifted, or a pocket phonograph that looks like a camera, or the short-lived Marxophone that combines the sounds of the piano, guitar, mandolin, and harp. And for embodying the national genius for compulsive mechanical economizing, nothing compares to the player piano. In a Co Coinola model from Chicago, ingenious mechanisms power not just the piano roll but cymbal, snares, mandolin, piccolo, clarinet, bass drum, and triangle. On top of a 1916 Seeburg is an animated seven-piece orchestra, with a horn section, a violinist, even a tiny conductor waving his baton.

Captions that explain the uses of the instruments are always helpful, but occasional and inconsistent. Better notes are in the two-dollar pamphlet that provides the history of many of the instruments, how they worked, and how the Sanders family came into their possession (buy it before you start; it's worth it). While the Musical Museum is obviously geared toward players and lovers of homemade music, there is much here to captivate scholars of folk art, mechanical design, material culture, and ethnic, social, and industrial history as well. Indeed, the technological wizardry of these early musical devices is no less a celebration of the golden age of American mechanical design and ingenuity than any collection of farm tools or domestic implements in the historical societies and small museums noted elsewhere in this book.

If You Go: Patience is its own reward here. Children will be tempted to race in and out of the long rooms, sampling briefly and charging on. But all the instruments have a story to tell and many need a moment or two to understand. Take pains to explain to kids (as no signs do) that these instruments are old, fragile, easily damaged, and not readily repaired, and should be sampled with heaps of tender loving care. Parts of the museum are wheelchair accessible; call to check.

Exploring Further: Rome, with its plethora of museums, forts, and historic sites, is only twenty minutes away; the Children's Museum in Utica (page 178) is likewise within striking distance. Akin in spirit — if not in artifacts — is the Clark's Broadalbin Heritage and Camera Museum (page 167), in Broadalbin.

GEORGI MUSEUM AND PARK CENTER
Adams Street
Shushan NY 12873
Mail: Box 150
Open: Thurs.–Sun. 1–4pm; museum grounds open dawn to dusk
Admission: Donation
518-854-3773

Flanked by the winding Battenkill, set in a modern home, Shushan's Georgi Museum can boast surely the most offbeat and unlikely collection in all of museum-rich Washington County. The cool, river-hugging house was built by English-born New Yorkers Maria and William Georgi in 1955 for their son Henry, an engineering geologist, but Henry never lived here. His widow *did*, however; and it was Jessie who, with Henry's blessing, finally gave the rather elegant structure and its curious collections to the town of Shushan as a museum at her death.

And that's why at the end of a back road in rural Shushan a passerby might stumble on a house full of chunks of malachite or lumps of agate in Henry Georgi's minerals collection, a library with a small but impressive

European paintings, furniture, and decorative arts collected by Maria and William Georgi are displayed in their late son's home in Shushan. Phil Haggerty

collection of serious art books, and a gallery of fine European art, such as landscapes and portraits done "in the manner of the School of Cologne," "the Sienese School," "the Dutch School," and so on. Disregard the capricious lighting, the lack of labels, and the unconvincingly solemn handwritten notes ("We have our eyes on you!") in lieu of museum guards. At the Metropolitan Museum these paintings would raise nary an eyebrow, but this isn't Manhattan, it's Shushan, and to happen on such a zealous cache of Old World culture after numberless country museum displays of pitchforks, milk bottles, and maple-syrup buckets is a thrill, maybe even a relief. Country life wasn't all milking, haying, and logging, after all. It was also the story of city dwellers who turned to the hinterlands for a change of pace, and their culture, ranging from the high rustic style of the Adirondack Great Camps to the Georgi family's private passion for European art, is also a part of the rural experience, and deserves its day in the sun.

If You Go: Allow an hour or more. The house isn't particularly accessible for the mobility impaired.

Special Events: Band and folk concerts are scheduled on the Georgi's lawn through the summer. The last weekend of September brings a fall festival with games and food. Christmas open house in the museum falls on a weekend afternoon in early December. Lectures by local experts on subjects as diverse as old toys, rare books, and fine arts are scheduled through the year.

Exploring Further: The newly revived Batten Kill Rambler offers a scenic three-hour round-trip train ride along the trout-filled Battenkill River that includes a one-hour layover in Shushan. A marked path on your map leads directly from the station to the Georgi, or you can get there via Main Street, or skip the train and take some time to explore not just the Georgi, but the little shops on Main Street, the old churches, acres of picnic grounds at the Georgi, and the Shushan Covered Bridge Museum (page 63) at the other end of town.

To the east is Arlington, Vermont, with a wealth of historical sites of its own, and a bustling antique center. Due north is the way to Granville, home to the impressive new Slate Museum (see page 60). And the back roads of Washington County, among the most beautiful and least-celebrated in the region, will steer you toward other historical homes and museums in Fort Edward (page 109), and farther north, in Whitehall (page 106).

Henry Georgi wrote an odd but likable travel book, *The Bow-Wows of Bimini*, which you can thumb through at the museum.

CLARK'S BROADALBIN HERITAGE AND PHOTOGRAPHY MUSEUM
Extension S. Second Avenue
Broadalbin NY
Mail: 141 Midline Road, Amsterdam NY 12010
Hours: Seven days a week, at Mr. Clark's discretion
Admission: No admission, no donation; "If you gotta buy it, it's not
    worth it."
518-883-3357

On a country road in Broadalbin is a lawn bordered by a line of pickets, each bearing a small sign. The signs mark off ten-year intervals over the past two centuries, and bristle with names of U.S. Presidents, years each state was admitted to the Union, years when Broadalbin got its first hospital, telegraph, or water tower. Swing left into the driveway so you're looking at the silver-painted windmill, the sundials, and a row of small hand-cobbled wooden structures topped with weather vanes and lightning rods. This is Clark's Broadalbin Heritage Museum. Mr. Clark will probably be outside to meet you before you can climb out of your car.

The tour starts with the exhibits in the garage next to Clark's own house. This is the oldest part of the museum, the part that holds Mr. Clark's twenty-year-old museum of photography. On low shelves in the first room are ancient cameras in bits and pieces, and that's the way Clark wants it. In this room, he says, "the kids can touch anything they want. Because if you can't touch it, you won't learn anything." Next door is his camera "shop" (nothing is for sale) with all the old-time paraphernalia, flash guns, vintage bulbs, scales, timers, plate polish, even wooden racks for glass plates. But the nucleus of the museum is the chamber packed with Clark's prized collection of fifteen hundred cameras, from the earliest kerosene-fueled magic lanterns to the latest in junky, landfill-packing disposable.

Mr. Clark is not a snob. He loves them all. He knows them all. On one side of the room are his four-by-five press cameras, on the other box cameras and Brownies (also Kewpie, Bolsey, Agfa, Geno, Churchill, and Empire models). A middle case is full of toy cameras, and from the ceiling points a rack of early Super 8s. One proud, if somewhat haphazard display, are daguerreotypes, ambrotypes, and tintypes, and army combat cameras from World War II.

In this room Clark teaches local schoolchildren how to fall in love with cameras and take good pictures, and in the next room how to develop them and print them. He also teaches them how to fashion usable photography equipment out of furnace filters and tin foil, or old milking machines, or chemicals you mix yourself instead of buy. "I show the kids how you don't have to spend anything," he says. Some of his students' work has made it to the Fulton County Fair. The minimum age is five years old.

Martin Clark is a thin-haired man of seventy-something in gold-rim glasses and a well-worn tee shirt. He learned to love what a camera could do from his shutterbug father, a gladioli farmer with a talent for finding swarms of bees. Clark himself worked two factory jobs before he retired — "and nothing came up the driveway unless it was paid for."

It's only natural his love of cameras and photography would translate into an interest in local history, or that his own family's history in rural Fulton County figures so boldly in the model village that makes up the second part of his museum. Because Clark's uncle was a blacksmith, here is a model 1920s smithy. Because of his own reverence for public education, his schoolhouse is full of admonitions like, "Don't be a Dunce and Quit School!" For thirty years Clark has served as a volunteer fireman, and here, in a firehouse not big enough to swing a cat in, is a 1989 certificate he was awarded for saving two neighbors from a burning house. His love of local history means one of the buildings is a small working library, full of books by local authors and scrapbooks on Broadalbin lore. There is also a grocery store, a church-cum-military exhibit, with badges, medals, flags, uniforms, antique K-rations, Clark's own bronze star, a Purple Heart he salvaged from a flea market, and a windmill rescued from the former estate of Brooklynite and Broadalbin benefactor Katherine Husted.

Clark is not a folk artist in any usual sense. He doesn't make artifacts, draw, weave, or bang things together out of bottle caps and wire. The cabins may be fun to poke around in but there's nothing novel about the way they're built or organized. Still, to the extent that his collections reveal at least as much about his own experience and notions as they do about history, and celebrate his own cherished values of thrift, ingenuity, and memory, and embody an original and highly quirky point of view, they work on us like folk art, and in any case force us to consider how a private vision can inform and bind the curatorial impulse, and what that impulse means. When other historical museums exhibit an early wire minnow trap, for instance, it's to show how people used to fish. When Clark displays one, it's because it puts him in mind of skipping school and going fishing, which he did and regretted, as suggested in the scrawled caption, "Get caught in the cage — minimum wage!"

That's why this is one museum you want to tour with the director/owner/curator. He'll help you connect the seemingly indiscriminate artifacts with their rightful meaning. He'll help you see what you're looking at the way he intended it to be understood.

If You Go: Call ahead and make a date, not because Mr. Clark is averse to drop-ins, but because you'll get a lot more out of it if he's there to show you the ropes. This could take an hour. It could take two. And if you ask, Martin Clark's genial wife, Florence, would probably show you her Betty Boop collection, too.

Exploring Further: Broadalbin itself, like so many other northern Mohawk Valley settlements found by Scots or Scotch-Irish immigrants (the name is from the Scottish place name Breadalbane), is a handsome farming and one-time mill village with several fine early nineteenth-century churches and a historic old hotel that once served as a glove factory and hospital. East from Broadalbin is the way to the Rice Homestead (see page 73), Johnstown, Amsterdam, and Gloversville, a nexus of historic sites described elsewhere in these pages.

MUNSON-WILLIAMS-PROCTOR INSTITUTE
310 Genesee Street
Utica NY 13502
Open: Tues.–Sat. 10am–5pm, Sun. 1–5pm
Admission: Donation
315-797-0000

In Utica is a first-rate arts center with three distinct divisions: a museum, a performing arts center, and an art school. Named after its city benefactors and founded in 1919, the "Munstitute" has emerged as the cultural mecca of Oneida County. Between the two main buildings, an International-style edifice designed by Philip Johnson, and the former Proctor family home, Fountain Elms, are some two dozen galleries appealing to tastes both conservative and avant-garde. Here are lovingly curated works by Hudson River landscapists like Thomas Cole; paintings by modern masters Willem de Kooning, Vasili Kandinski, and Mark Rothko; and a mural-size major Jackson Pollock.

Aficionados of American cabinetmaking and craftsmanship will surely appreciate the four discrete Victorian-period settings in Fountain Elms, and marvel at the unique Troy-made Galusha secretary in the bedroom, the rare Quervelle secretary in the study, and the suite of Belter furniture in the florid Rococo Revival style. Changing exhibits are in the decorative arts galleries upstairs. Don't miss the four hundred pieces of Oneida stoneware on display in the study storage galleries, the Alexander Calder in the sculpture grove outside, or the Victorian garden when you crave a break from serious art.

If You Go: Most visitors spend at least two and a half hours. The art museum is very accessible; portions of Fountain Elms are not.

Special Events: Because of its three different program areas, this joint is jumping with more than two hundred events a year. For a full week around Independence Day, a festival runs from ten in the morning to ten at night, with performances, activities for children, and even a vintage car show. Fountain Elms is decked in Christmas finery from Thanksgiving weekend through the first of the year.

Exploring Further: Just down the street is the Oneida County Historical Society (page 147).

THE ANTIQUE BOAT MUSEUM
750 Mary Street
Clayton NY 13624
Open: Daily, May 15–Oct. 15 9am–4pm
Admission: $6 adults, $2 children 5–17
315-686-4104

Clayton is an old-fashioned river town with the main street paralleling the St. Lawrence and a small, sheltered harbor. In that harbor is the Antique Boat Museum, a collection of sheds, barns, docks, and a stone building holding scores of old freshwater craft ranging from dozens of the region's trademark vessel, the St. Lawrence skiff, to the monstrous *Pardon Me,* a forty-eight-foot-long runabout. Said boat — a vast expanse of luminous mahogany that required 150 gallons of gas per hour to fuel its massive engines — dominates the Cleveland A. Dodge Launch House, towering above the other sizable craft beneath it.

Beyond numerous inboards, outboards, hydroplanes, sailboats, rowboats, and canoes — in fair to Bristol condition — the museum offers a good social history of the river, from descriptions of fishing traditions to an exhibit on bootlegging complete with a detailed map showing rum-running routes from Canada to New York and a handy diagram illustrating where to hide liquor on a small boat. There are models, trophies, posters, burgees, dioramas.

This is an informal kind of place. Boats are displayed simply, with short descriptions listing basic information, but you can get right up close to check out the finish, examine the oarlocks, peer into the motor; they're presented as working artifacts, not works of art.

If You Go: The Antique Boat Museum is easy to find if you head for the river. Parking is along the street or in public lots a short walk from the entrance. Allow about two hours for a visit. Most of the site is accessible, although getting on the floating docks to see some of the boats may be difficult. Children will find plenty to do here and there are some displays with hands-on activities.

If you're planning to attend one of the antique-boat gatherings arrive in plenty of time to find a parking space. Clayton really comes alive for these affairs, so you can peruse flea markets and yard sales once you've overloaded on watercraft.

Special Events: The museum is thronged with activity during two classic-boat weekends. In early August is the annual Antique Boat Show, featuring vintage Chris Crafts, cabin cruisers, and human-powered boats, plus old outboard engines. A highlight of the show is a boat auction, where it's possible to find a nicely restored wooden boat in running condition for a song. Later in August is the biennial Antique Raceboat Show, which showcases Gold Cup racers slicing through the waves; boats from the museum collection take to the waters to rumble and roar in a parade down the river.

From June through September, the museum offers boat-building classes for adults led by craftsmen from across the Northeast. Courses — which range from two-day to week-long sessions — include refinishing, wood bending, and canvassing for folks who have old boats to repair, and classes in building rowing skiffs, guideboats, paddles, and so forth. Nautical and regional historians should note there is a research library here available by appointment.

Exploring Further: Within walking distance is Clayton's Thousand Islands Museum (see page 128), and Boldt Castle (page 91) is a short cruise offshore.

Boat fans wishing to do a Northeastern tour can visit the Lake Champlain Maritime Museum, at Basin Harbor, near Vergennes, Vermont. The museum is open year-round; call 802-475-2022 for more information. The boat collection at the Adirondack Museum is regarded as one of the finest in the country (see page 183). The book *Boats and Boating in the Adirondacks* (Syracuse University Press/Adirondack Museum, 1995) by Hallie Bond is the perfect companion to visits to these sites.

NATIONAL MUSEUM OF RACING
191 Union Avenue
Saratoga Springs NY 12866
Open: Year-round, Mon.–Sat. 10am–4:30pm, Sun. 12 noon–4:30pm;
   racing season daily 9am–5pm
Admission: $3 adults, $2 students
518-584-0400

A real starting gate with a life-size lunging steed sets the stage as you enter the National Museum of Racing. Suddenly shouts and whinnies ring out from an audio tape recorded during a race. The attendants yell, "Whoa! Whoa!" The bell clangs and hooves thunder. It's a fitting introduction to this elegant institution dedicated to thoroughbred racing in America.

The museum was founded in 1950 and completely redesigned in 1988. The story of racing is presented in chronological order, in thematic galleries that are packed with oil paintings of famous stallions, portraits of owners, gleaming trophies, colorful silks, and quaint ephemera.

After the human history of horse racing, comes a high-tech gallery all about the thoroughbred, showing a real skeleton and a video about the life of a racehorse. A circular exhibit of the Stud Book allows visitors to trace certain horses, like Seattle Slew or Northern Dancer, all the way back to the foundation sire, the Darley Arabian.

The Racing Day gallery brings visitors up to modern times, with a full-size diorama of a shed row, with horses peering out from their stalls. On the rail nearby, audiophones divulge the secrets of top trainers Wayne Lukas, Shug McGaughey, Jonathan Sheppard, and Jack Van Berg. In its own alcove is the Racing Hall of Fame, a tasteful auditorium lined with eighty sets of racing silks. Six computer terminals introduce visitors to the careers of hall of fame members, describing hundreds of horses, jockeys, and trainers. The film "Race America" is shown here at regular intervals.

Among all the computer-assisted razzle dazzle, and glimpses of the rich and famous, are fascinating artifacts, like the boots Eddie Arcaro wore when he rode Citation to win the Triple Crown in 1948, and an unbelievably petite saddle worn by Man O' War as a two year old. (Man O' War, Big Red himself, is buried across the street, in the lovely park that surrounds Saratoga Racetrack.) Another life-size diorama shows the jockeys' room with silks, caps, and saddle cloths all arranged in numerical order; from audiophones, Angel Cordero, Eddie Maple, and other winning jocks talk about racing strategy. This part of the museum helps demystify exactly what happens between the stalls and the starting gate, explaining the role of jockeys' valets, the weigh-in procedure, and so forth.

Another room celebrates the leading racing families, many of whom helped fund renovations at the museum. Although racing across the country is discussed, there's background on the neighboring track and the town

The National Museum of Racing and Hall of Fame is across the street from Saratoga's acclaimed thoroughbred racetrack. Courtesy of the National Museum of Racing and Hall of Fame, Saratoga Springs

itself: high society in Saratoga reached its opulent peak in the 1890s, at the same time that the track was acquired by a particularly unscrupulous bookie and its reputation became sordid. (William C. Whitney and August Belmont resurrected the track in 1901 with their purchase.) A panel entitled "Saratoga Swells" gives a glimpse of the high life: a man named Marcus Daly won a cool million on one race, and William Collins Whitney reportedly lost $385,000 at the casino while he was waiting for his wife to dress for dinner.

If You Go: To find the National Museum of Racing, take Exit 14 from the Northway. Follow the signs for the thoroughbred racetrack, which will take you along Union Avenue. The museum is across the street from the main entrance to the track, and parking is in the back.

Allow at least an hour and a half for a visit, more if you're with a horse-crazy youngster. The mix of audio, video, computers, dioramas, and artifacts is a good one for well-behaved, independent kids who can read; younger children will need a lot of lifting, pointing, and watching. All of the facility is accessible. There's a gift shop featuring lots of tasteful items with a horsy motif.

During racing season in August, the museum can be quite busy.

Special Events: The best Kentucky Derby celebration outside of Louisville is held here; you can party hearty for a price. On the first Monday in

August, new inductees are welcomed into the hall of fame. Call for information about lectures, films, and other events.

Exploring Further: The Saratoga Racecourse, less than a furlong from the front door, is one of the loveliest tracks in the country. The grandstand is full of amusing architectural details, with ornate towers, gables, and wrought-iron horsehead embellishments. During late July and August special tours of the track are available every day but Tuesday (518-584-6200). Another accumulation of equine artifacts can be found at the Saratoga Harness Hall of Fame (518-587-4210), in the Saratoga Raceway and open May–November.

Also in Saratoga are the National Museum of Dance (below), the Saratoga Springs Historical Society (page 111), and several self-guided walking tours available from the Urban Cultural Park's visitor center on Broadway (518-587-3241).

Edward Hotaling's *They're Off! Horse Racing at Saratoga* (Syracuse University Press, 1995) is a must-read for thoroughbred fans.

NATIONAL MUSEUM OF DANCE
99 South Broadway
Saratoga Springs NY 12866
Open: Late May–Aug. 31, Tues.–Sun. 10am–5pm
Admission: $3.50 adults; $2.50 seniors, students
518-584-2225

Next to Saratoga Spa State Park in a lavish building that was once a bathhouse, the National Museum of Dance is a newcomer to the list of North Country museums. The institution was established in 1991 to complement the New York City Ballet performances at Saratoga Performing Arts Center, which are held practically at the museum's back door.

The museum is simply stunning, laid out in an I-shape with long passageways and wonderful natural light. The permanent exhibit, the Hall of Fame, was completed in 1994 and is just beyond the marble foyer in the center of the building.

The hall honors American dance stars like Alvin Ailey, Katherine Dunham, Isadora Duncan, Ruth St. Denis, and Bill "Bojangles" Robinson in biographic sketches and photos. The bios are lively, in tune with what visitors might like to know: Catherine Littlefield, for example, whose company became the Philadelphia Ballet, choreographed a piece with dancers on bicycles for the 1939 World's Fair and staged an avant-garde ice show the next year. Bill Robinson went through twenty to thirty pairs of dance shoes per year during the height of his career.

Interspersed with the panels are video monitors showing trademark dance routines, from Busby Berkeley's "Lullaby of Broadway" — with tiered squadrons of dancers tapping away — to scenes from *West Side Story*, to a 1926 film of Ted Shawn performing the mysterious "Cosmic Dance of Shiva." Next to the monitor is the actual set from the piece, a rectangular platform with a circular frame made at a foundry in Calcutta. There's also a thirty-five-minute program in an alcove with chairs that shows clips of Fred Astaire and Ginger Rogers from *The Gay Divorcee*; Martha Graham; Bill Robinson and Shirley Temple in the staircase scene from *The Little Colonel*; and other highlights.

Changing exhibits are mounted in the first gallery visitors enter and in the wing beyond the hall of fame. In 1996, shows included "Igor Stravinsky's *Firebird* and the New York City Ballet," with marvelous costumes, stage sketches, posters, and photographs, and "Paul Sanasardo in Max Waldman's View," showing dramatic backstage and performance photographs of the Sanasardo dance company.

If You Go: Allow at least an hour for a visit. An interesting day might be to tour the museum, then attend a matinee ballet performance or a rehearsal. The building is accessible.

Special Events: Lectures relating the exhibits and demonstrations are scheduled from time to time.

Exploring Further: Saratoga's celebrated Roosevelt Baths are within walking distance; by all means reserve part of the afternoon for a dip and a massage (call 518-584-2011) and assure yourself you're having a historically accurate experience. Thus rejuvenated, proceed to Saratoga's other cultural institutions, like the Racing Museum (page 172) and the museum in Canfield Casino (page 112).

NATIONAL BOTTLE MUSEUM
76 Milton Avenue
Ballston Spa NY 12020
Open: Daily June 1–Sept. 30; Mon.–Fri. remainder of year, 10am–4pm
Admission: $2
518-885-7589

The spring-water industry of Saratoga Springs and Ballston Spa required countless millions of bottles, and the local manufacture of glass bottles has been well documented. The National Bottle Museum, in a former hardware store on Ballston's main street, showcases vessels made with lung power and hand tools in the eighteenth and nineteenth centuries. There are shelves and shelves full of assorted bottles, a diorama showing a typical glass factory, an intact pharmacy counter, and hundreds of bottles in open storage, stretching upward toward the ceiling. Visitors are often greeted by Jan Rutland, who

Decanters, flasks, and containers of all descriptions can be found at the National Bottle Museum, Ballston Spa. Courtesy of the National Bottle Museum, Ballston Spa

serves as curator, tour guide, fund-raiser, and publicist; she's quite knowledgeable and interested in sharing her enthusiasm for the subject with others young and old.

If You Go: Milton Avenue is Route 50. Parking on the street can be a problem, but there's a large public lot around the corner from the museum. Allow about thirty minutes for a visit if you're casually interested in the subject or traveling with children. Bottle collectors will find ample material here to peruse. They can also contact the museum for information on dating and identifying bottles; a research library is available by appointment.

Special Events: The museum's annual auction and bottle show, usually the first weekend in June in Saratoga Springs at the City Center, is an affair that attracts a widespread audience.

Exploring Further: Brookside (see page 142), the Saratoga County museum, is only a few blocks away. If you're interested in sampling local spring water, the Old Iron Spring is across from Brookside, and there's a walking tour of springs in downtown Saratoga available from the Urban Cultural Park Visitor Center on Broadway.

1932 & 1980 LAKE PLACID WINTER OLYMPIC MUSEUM

216 Main Street
Olympic Center
Lake Placid NY 12946
Open: Daily, Memorial Day–Columbus Day, late Nov.–early Mar. 10am–5pm;
 call for off-season hours
Admission: $3 adults, $2 seniors, $1 students
518-523-1655 ext. 263

Hometown pride is the invisible glue that holds most local museums together, but here in the Olympic village it's raised on a pedestal and festooned with medals. There's a "Gee whiz, look what we've done" feel to this place, but the message is proclaimed by giving credit where credit is due, to local heroes and small steps taken gradually.

This Olympic museum underwent a much-needed redesign in 1996. The space is modest, but well thought out; the exhibit begins with a short video mixing historic clips with current footage and proceeds to explain how this tiny Adirondack town was named the site of the third Olympic Games — mainly due to the efforts of winter-sports maven Godfrey Dewey, of the Lake Placid Club. There's an amusing assortment of artifacts: bobsledders in 1932 wore red, white, and blue full-face masks, while hockey goalies protected just their eyes with wire gizmos that look like a cross between a bridge and a brassiere. You'll see lots of medallions, old skates, duffel coats that would make Ralph Lauren envious, and even elegant wooden skis manufactured in Lake Placid.

The 1980 section pays tribute to modern stars — Eric Heiden, with his thirty-one-inch waist and twenty-nine-inch thighs, and the U.S. hockey team — and has displays on each of the modern sports, with a real bobsled you can sit in for picture-taking. Most impressive is the list of athletes from the region who competed in winter games, beginning with Charles Jewtraw, a Saranac Lake speed skater, who won the very first gold medal in the first Winter Olympics.

If You Go: The admission price includes a tour of the Olympic Center; by all means take advantage of it — you may catch world-famous figure skaters practicing. Bring the kids. There's a "Go for the Gold" quiz that sends them scurrying from case to case looking for answers, and correct ones earn a "gold" medal. Allow an hour or two for the museum and tour. The museum is wheelchair accessible.

Special Events: During February and March, local athletes and photographers speak on sports competitions and training. Call the Olympic Regional Development Authority (518-523-1655) for information on competitions and open training sessions.

Exploring Further: If you're in an Olympic mood, check out the Kodak Sports Park, where ski jumpers practice year-round. You can ride the elevator to the top of the jump for an awesome view, too. At Mount Van Hoevenberg, about six miles from downtown Lake Placid, you can walk up the luge and bobsled runs in the summer and watch training and races in the winter. Eastman Kodak offers a package that gets you into all the venues plus the Whiteface Memorial Highway, for about $16 for adults; call 1-800-462-6236 for details.

The bobsledding Stevens Brothers were heroes of the 1932 Winter Olympics. Courtesy of the Adirondack Museum, Blue Mountain Lake

CHILDREN'S MUSEUM OF HISTORY, NATURAL HISTORY, AND SCIENCE
311 Main Street
Utica NY 13501
Open: Sept.–June 10am–4:30pm; July–Aug. 9am–3:30pm
Admission: $2.50 adults, children
315-724-6129; 724-6128 for information recording

On a dead-end street near a highway overpass is a former three-story dry-goods emporium that now houses the Children's Museum of Utica. As everybody knows, children's museums come in two flavors: the unashamedly pedagogical kind that aims to improve you with lots of meticulous historical dioramas and glass-topped cases full of china dolls and exotic butterflies, and the newer-fangled, gaily experiential kind that lets you learn by doing, playing, and generally running yourself ragged. The Utica Children's Museum manages to have it both ways.

Here is an "Automotive Safety Exhibit" comprised of a see-through full-size Saturn sedan, not unlike the Visible Man of yore. Press a button on the control panel and hear the engine *vroom* to life. Press another and watch the air bag bloom into life-saving action. Here's the giant bubble wand on a pulley that lets you make a bubble big enough to stand in, a hyperbolic funnel that imitates something called Kepler's Laws of Planetary Motion, and a stationary bike that helps you see exactly how you turn muscle power into energy.

One side of the ground floor is laid out like a miniature Main Street, complete with police station where you stand against a wall and get measured for a mug shot, and grocery store with shelves of toy cartons, tins, and boxes, and a child-size shopping cart to wheel your stuff around. At the doctor's office, weigh yourself. At the Moola Moola Banking Center, make fake withdrawals with a pretend ATM card. If you're too young to savor the thrill of the ATM, spread out with a wide assortment of building blocks, or mess around with an old telephone switchboard, or race upstairs and stamp out a war dance in the model Iroquois longhouse while your parents admire the wizardry of the WPA-sponsored historical dioramas of local rural scenes.

Youngsters will particularly delight in the delectably gruesome dioramas of dinosaurs at war and play from the hand-fashioned collection of curator-anthropologist Lewis S. Brown. Here a *Tyrannosaurus Rex* munches bloodily on a hapless *Scelidosaurus*, and a triceratops makes a messy feast of some absentee rival's eggs. The notes are marvelously unpedantic: T-Rex, we learn, had a mouth "big enough to swallow a human in one bite," while the *Comsognathus* "was about the size of a chicken," and the largest dinosaurs "were too long to fit inside this building." Also on the second floor is a display on "Toys Before Computers" and the mysteries of their manufacture (no joke! Silly Putty is produced in thousand-part batches "somewhere near New Haven . . . the exact location of the plant a company secret"), and a small children's theater with stage and curtain.

Don't neglect the third floor with its two displays: batons and bugs. Here, in the New York State Twirlers Hall of Fame, are press clips and photographs galore on perennial crowd-pleasers like the Millerette Metronomes, Roseanna's Robillaires, and the newly inducted Desperado Debs and Drum Corps of Hornell, New York. On loan to the museum from collector Louis Kravetz are a dozen glass cases full of New York State insects. Big magnifying glasses attached to the cases help you zero in on giant glittering dragonflies, moths, and roaches. More delicious still, tarantulas are regularly fed in the "Live Insect Zoo" around the corner.

If You Go: Just to see it all takes probably an hour and a half. To soak it in from soup to nuts, allow for half a day. The building is handicap accessible throughout.

Special Events: The museum publishes a packed calendar of events every month. Call for news of upcoming play activities, concerts, storytelling, Jell-o-eating contests, and so on.

Exploring Further: Utica is also home to the Oneida County Historical Society (see page 147) and Munson-Williams-Proctor Institute (page 169) and only minutes away from numerous historic sites in Rome via the New York State Thruway (see page 126). If you've got young ones in tow, it's a short drive to the Musical Museum (see page 164), where hands-on is the rule rather than the exception.

CHILDREN'S MUSEUM AT SARATOGA

36 Phila Street
Saratoga Springs NY 12866
Open: Tues., Fri., Sat. 10am–4:30pm; Weds. 12 noon–6pm;
   Thurs. and Sun. 12 noon–4:30pm
Admission: $3; under 2 free
518-584-5540

Young children especially will cotton to the touch-and-clutch stations in this experiential museum. A few shelves of old-time store goods in the mock general store aside, pristine artifacts are at a minimum. The idea is to learn by doing, and for such a relatively small space — just one floor of a brick building wedged between Ben & Jerry's and a produce market — what an awful lot there is to do! In the karaoke room, you can sing along with "Alouette" on a video; throw your voice all over the place and drive everybody crazy (boxes of glittering costumes at the ready for your big debut); lasso yourself with a giant soap bubble; try on real firemen's bunker pants, boots, and helmet; ring up a buddy on an antique telephone, for starters.

For local history, there's a make-believe street front of the one-time (now demolished) biggest hotel in the world, Saratoga's thousand-room Grand Union. There you learn that 1890s tourists ate differently than we do now, and you can test yourself on what might have been on the Grand Union's menu — tacos, burgers, or calf's head *poele*. Hit the right button and see a light flash on in the window behind the dining room. Hit another and you'll see a bustle or a Saratoga trunk.

A particularly neat exhibit, "Many People, One World," sets you to the task of matching seven cut-out pasteboard children with their "missing" luggage by matching up the contents of the suitcases with their descriptions of their trips aboard. Example: "We had lots of fun sailing here and found some lava rocks. . . . The people speak English but it doesn't sound the same to me." Now, which valise belongs to Charlie — the one with all the souvenirs from the tropical rain forest or the one with a toy penguin, Weetabix, and Marmite? It's a set-up that appeals to grown-ups every bit as much as kids.

If You Go: The more fun the kids are having, the higher the decibel level: on Saturdays, consider earplugs. A half an hour might suffice, but if your child develops a sudden yen for performing karaoke or trying on firemen's helmets or learning world geography, it could be weeks.

Special Events: Plenty of classes and activities for children are on the roster every week, but one annual museum-sponsored event that caters to adults equally well is the doll house and miniatures show in late October (call for dates and directions to the armory).

Exploring Further: Behind the museum and past the parking lot is Congress Park, with lots of famous springs, sculptures, fountains, and an elegant casino, now the city's historical society (page 112). At the former trolley depot on Broadway, just across from the entrance to the park, is the visitor center of the Urban Cultural Park (518-587-3241). Up the road, in Glens Falls, the new World Awareness Cultural Museum (518-793-2773), beckons youngsters with changing exhibits and scores of events.

CHAPTER EIGHT

THE ADIRONDACK MUSEUM

■■

A ll kinds of themes represented elsewhere in this book converge at the Adirondack Museum, in Blue Mountain Lake: the heritage of the region can't be separated from the scattered potsherds of native Americans; the narratives of soldiers; the dollars-and-cents data of mining, logging, and farming; the embellished tales of guides and sports; and the impressions of visitors who painted, sketched, and wrote about the wilderness. Key figures in the Mohawk Valley, like Sir William Johnson, knew the region and its resources well. Others, like the Constable clan, not only owned thousands of acres in the St. Lawrence lowlands but also explored millions more on early wilderness hunting and fishing expeditions. Developments in one section of the region — the Erie Canal, for example — had lasting impact on settlement in the park and helped lure would-be Adirondackers westward with the promise of fertile land and a more temperate climate. These threads weave together here, in a twenty-acre campus overlooking one of the Adirondack Park's most famous waterways.

ADIRONDACK MUSEUM

Route 28 North and 30
Blue Mountain Lake NY 12812
Open: Memorial Day weekend–mid-October, daily 9:30am–5:30pm
Admission: $10 adults; special rates for families, seniors, and groups
518-352-7311

The Adirondack Museum's extensive photographic archives document people, places, and events, including these African-American musicians performing at an 1890s canoe meet in Lake George. Courtesy of the Adirondack Museum, Blue Mountain Lake

Some forty years ago, in a clearing high above Blue Mountain Lake, a museum opened that was modest in size but ambitious in vision. The guiding hand behind the project was Harold K. Hochschild, author of *Township 34*, an exhaustively researched history of the central Adirondacks privately published in 1952. Fate might have had a role in his abiding connection to the region: Hochschild was born on May 20, 1892, the very day the Adirondack Park was created.

Hochschild first came to Blue Mountain Lake in 1904, when stagecoaches and steamboats still brought guests to grand hotels. Lumberjacks used horses and rivers to send logs to mill and market; miners toiled with pick and shovel; guides took city men into woods and waters in search of trout and venison; farm families were nearly self sufficient, growing food for man and beast. An astute observer, Hochschild saw these ways of life disappear and wished to capture his experiences. And while his long, distinguished career with the American Metal Company led him to Mexico, China, Siberia, Rhodesia, South West Africa, and across the globe, Eagle Nest, an estate on the shore of nearby Eagle Lake, remained ever his home.

In 1957, as now, the institution's mission was to interpret the human relationship to the Adirondacks as expressed in fine arts, folk artifacts, photographs, and countless examples of material culture both large (a private railroad car) and small (trout flies named after famous Adirondack anglers). Over the years, though, how the place has grown and changed. The original exhibit buildings, an 1876 log hotel and a hall designed specially for the boat collection, have been joined by more than twenty historic and modern structures. Today the Adirondack Museum is widely regarded as one of the finest regional museums anywhere, with permanent exhibits covering the legacy of tourism, the economic and social impact of logging and mining, the role of transportation, and the popularity of outdoor recreation, all enhanced by glimpses of simple daily life in the woods, in towns, and on the farm.

Most people begin their visit by watching *The Adirondacks*, an award-winning documentary by Florentine Films, creators of the PBS series *The Civil War*. It's a peppy, thoughtful presentation that sets the stage for exhibits to come, with interviews of mountain folk and vintage footage of happy vacationers; you may find yourself humming the tune "Mountain Greenery" for days to come. From there, you can go by the numbers or look at your map to choose your next step. It's not critical to see exhibits in any particular order and you may be happier following your impulses instead.

Canoe camping, 1880s style, in the Adirondack Museum's permanent exhibition on regional boats and boating. Courtesy of the Adirondack Museum, Blue Mountain Lake

Building number one houses the permanent exhibit "Boats and Boating in the Adirondacks 1840–1940," which is for many an all-time favorite spot. Loaded from stem to stern with watercraft in unimpeachable condition, the space enthralls fans of canoes and guideboats every bit as much as Gold Cup motorheads. Of course, there's more here than boats, paddles, oars, and the like; an entire culture arose around canoeing, a sport as popular at the turn of the century as, say, snowboarding is today. Canoe caps, canoe tents, canoe songs illustrate the point. If the Adirondack guideboat is your vessel of choice, you'll find fine examples here and rare footage of one of the last traditional builders in his Saranac Lake shop.

Next, two tall pine pillars flank the entrance to the main building, which houses changing exhibits. In its center is a three-dimensional map of the Adirondack Park; a tiny blue light marks Blue Mountain. Buttons illuminate rivers, peaks, and major towns, and help orient visitors to the region's topography. (Yes, the map is tilted slightly to make viewing easier, and you can rest assured that water does not trickle uphill. Many rivers flow north to the St. Lawrence, though, a fact that visually confounds some folks.) Galleries with changing exhibits flank this interactive display; in 1997 three new exhibits celebrate the museum's fortieth anniversary. "These Glorious Mountains: Masterworks of the Adirondacks" showcases superb paintings from the museum's holdings, other institutions, and individual collections. "Small Things Remembered: Four Decades of Collecting Adirondack History" displays and interprets a range of unusual and rarely exhibited objects. The museum's founding and development are explained in the exhibit "A Mirror of the Mountains: The Adirondack Museum 1957–1997." In years to come, these galleries will hold selections from the museum's particularly fine reserves of nineteenth- and twentieth-century artworks and changing history exhibits.

Thematic permanent exhibits resume with a five-bedroom log structure that began life as Merwin's Blue Mountain House, and it's hard to imagine that this tiny building, with its cramped bedrooms and chamberpots, attracted an elite clientele from the Northeast's major cities. An annex — " Hotels, Camps, and Clubs" — depicts this temporary life in the woods, with menus of elaborate seven-course meals (dating from the Precholesterol Epoch), pictures of long-disappeared hostelries, a chambermaid's closet complete with spare Edison light bulbs, and a primitive vacuum cleaner. Pass by a truly rustic two-seater outhouse to reach a small cottage that was original to the site and used by painter Gustav Wiegand as a studio in the early 1900s.

Down the hill, the twig mosaic walls of Sunset Cottage show rustic artistry on a truly grand scale. The building was part of Camp Cedars, built by William West Durant in 1880. Originally on Forked Lake, this gem was one of the few of the estate's structures to survive the Great Blowdown of 1950. Following a sandy path, you reach remnants of a cabin built for the author known as Ned Buntline (born Edward Z.C. Judson), who lived at Eagle Nest in the 1860s. Buntline cranked out dime novels — including titles that launched the career of Buffalo Bill Cody — and was a founder of the Know-Nothing Party. He wrote little about the Adirondacks, though, except for a few griping letters to his publisher, preferring to create swashbuckler fantasies. Next, all-weather panels discuss one-room schools, and the Rising Schoolhouse, which served students from 1907–45, lies ahead. The school, which never had electricity or running water, is filled with desks, benches, maps, and books; you can almost hear ghostly voices reciting their lessons. Back toward the cafeteria, Mike Virkler's hand-built log cabin, which stood on a pond near Old Forge until 1991, brings to mind how modern men and women still long for a little camp in the pines.

"Woods and Waters: Outdoor Recreation in the Adirondacks" is more than the title suggests; the deceptively large space also introduces ecology, natural history, and mapping, and is permanent home to one of the icons of Adirondack art, A.F. Tait's *A Good Time Coming*. The 1850s oil painting shows hearty, florid sports dressed in coats and ties imbibing vintage port as their guides labor around the lakeside campsite. The entire exhibit is a dream come true for anglers and hunters, with a fine assortment of rods, lures, flies, and guns. A long case — adjacent to the gun room — displays antique specimens of extirpated and rare species: wolf, lynx, moose, mountain lion, pine marten, fisher. Here, too, is hermit Noah John Rondeau's cabin from a remote spot on the Cold River; push a button and his quavery voice moans "I died in the fifth grade. . . ." That's not his literal demise, of course; it's a comment on how he gave up on schooling.

Directly above is the huge "Road and Rail" building, which opened in 1969. Here is the complete and compelling story of how the region was developed; a section on agriculture points out the importance of an economy that has virtually vanished. Essex County, for example, once produced 280,000 bushels of oats per year, and Hamilton County, 43,000 bushels of potatoes. Practically every farm raised sheep for wool (can't have too many blankets or mittens in this climate), and a surprising number of North Country plots grew tobacco. Numerous vehicles — from ornate sleighs with brass finials to heavy-duty freight wagons — underline the vital role of horses. But the artifact that captures everyone's attention is the *Oriental*, a private railroad car that once belonged to August Belmont; wandering through its walnut-paneled corridors and gazing down at marble bathrooms makes the Gilded Age real.

On Merwin Hill, dotted by turn-of-the-century cottages that were once part of the Blue Mountain House complex, native plantings lead the way to Bull Cottage, the best assortment of rustic furniture you'll find anywhere. A secretary desk covered with white birch bark has a definite Louis Quatorze look; big, burly benches seem Gothic; twig mosaic tables and smalls reflect Arts-and-Crafts styles. The artisans of many of these pieces are now forgotten, but the styles and sensitivity of their work show true creativity and craftsmanship.

The logging buildings ("Work in the Woods") follow on a by-the-numbers tour, logical if you've got all that wood and bark on your mind and wonder how it got from the stump to the parlor. These spaces are packed with dioramas explaining felling, skidding, and kedging trees, along with life-size settings: piles of hemlock bark for tanning, a sprinkler wagon for icing roads, a river-drive cook camp, a Barrienger brake for controlling the downhill slide of logs. A large section deals with the life of a lumberjack — including (under Plexiglas) actual vermin that plagued lumber camps: bedbug and body louse.

The mining building, a recent addition to the campus, depicts the region's other primary industry. A light-up map shows mineral deposits (iron, garnet, feldspar, graphite, and zinc) and the eras when mines were active, creating a quick context for the concise social history that follows. Compared with transitory lumber camps, mining towns were full-blown communities, with schools, stores, homes, and even churches supplied by the company. Tools, ore samples, products, maps, scrip, and other artifacts are juxtaposed on impressive blown-up photographs that show mines and furnaces.

Some visitors get exhausted just from being exposed to a miner's rugged, dangerous life, and the Photo Belt, down the hill, is a favorite spot because it offers a place to sit and absorb some history. Hundreds of vintage photographs — Paulina Brandreth, hunting rifle across her lap; young girls at the sewing machines of a long-gone North Creek shirt factory; marching bands on dusty main streets — pass right beneath your nose on a motorized track; a mere fraction, though, of the museum's seventy thousand images.

At the Marion River Carry Pavilion, the steam locomotive that once ran on the world's shortest standard-gauge track sits quietly; this is one antiquarian object that will withstand active kid exploration. Inside the adjacent replica of a train station is a charming mechanized diorama that explains train and steamboat connections between Raquette Lake and Blue Mountain Lake; the voice-over is Harold Hochschild's brother, describing a route he traveled dozens of times.

The museum's most recent large acquisition, the Bill Gates Diner, is at the easternmost end of the campus. The former trolley is still equipped with chrome stools, really hard donuts, and signs that read "Don't Make Fun of Our Coffee — You May Be Old and Weak Yourself Someday."

If You Go: A couple of tips: allow plenty of time, at least three or four hours for a visit. A leisurely trip is more decidedly enjoyable than rushing from spot to spot trying to cram it all in. Don't put off this jaunt for a rainy day, either. You'll be far happier when you can see the magnificent views and lovely plantings. Children are welcome, although active ones need to be well in hand. Wheelchair access to exhibit spaces is excellent, although in the transportation building you may need help finding the circuitous route. Strollers are available.

Plan to spend some time in the museum shop, in the gatehouse; you won't find a better source for Adirondack books, prints, maps, videos, music, cards, and gifts. If you'd like paperback excerpts from *Township 34,*

Hochschild's landmark local history that provides excellent background on railroads, steamboats, mining, and early resorts, you'll find them here.

Youngsters with felt hats and pack baskets try "I'd Rather Be Camping," one of the Adirondack Museum's educational programs. Courtesy of the Adirondack Museum, Blue Mountain Lake

Special Events: Eclectic activities are planned for day and night, from old-time games that children can play to oral-history sessions with local old-timers to academic lectures and conferences. Educational programs range from special school tours to Elderhostel weeks. Three annual events attract devoted crowds: the No-Octane Regatta, featuring antique boats of all descriptions, held on Blue Mountain Lake in June; the Rustic Furniture Makers' Fair, showcasing the best contemporary furniture artisans from around the country, on the museum campus in September; and the Adirondack Antiques Fair, with more than a hundred dealers in tents and booths on the main lawns, in late September. Call or write for a schedule.

Exploring Further: While many places portrayed in permanent exhibits are difficult — or even impossible — to find today, you can capture a bit more of the Adirondack past if you're willing to cover some miles. For example, few of the massive wood-frame hotels survive from the nineteenth century, but what used to be the St. Hubert's Inn, near Keene Valley, still stands. It's part of the private Ausable Club; you can drive in and take a look, but don't

The Ausable Club, near Keene Valley (formerly St. Hubert's Inn), is one of a handful of nineteenth-century hotel structures that survive today. Courtesy of the Adirondack Museum, Blue Mountain Lake

wander about. On Mirror Lake, the lake you see from downtown Lake Placid, portions of the huge Lake Placid Club remain; a high stone wall marks where the multi-storied hotel once stood.

To capture the age of horses in the Adirondacks and see a Great Camp to boot, you can hire a horse and wagon to trek the ten-mile round-trip into Santanoni Great Camp, near Newcomb. Call the Newcomb town clerk (518-582-3131) for information about wagon trips and to find out about upcoming guided tours of the site. If you'd like to sleep in a Great Camp, Sagamore (page 84) takes paying guests midweek and when space allows during weekend workshops and conferences.

On several lakes you can taste the age of steamboats: Lake George has a fleet of tour boats, including a couple that really look like vintage paddlewheelers; Lake Placid has the *Doris* and the *Lady of the Lake*, which cruise by camps great and small; narrated boats ply the Fulton Chain of Lakes starting in Old Forge; the *Carillon* shuttles between Fort Ticonderoga and other historic sites on Lake Champlain's western shore; the *William West Durant* gives a fine view of Raquette Lake Great Camps and kids' camps, and serves lunch and dinner. Check with local tourism offices or at the museum gatehouse for brochures and schedules.

Railroads — once the major transportation link between far-flung hamlets — are enjoying a regional renaissance. The Adirondack Scenic Railroad, in Thendara, makes short, pleasant excursions along the Moose River and may eventually extend to Saranac Lake and Lake Placid. The former Delaware & Hudson tracks that parallel the Hudson River between Lake Luzerne and North Creek are expected to have a tourist train sometime in 1997. Amtrak's Adirondack route, which goes from New York City to Montreal, can be used for short hops between Port Henry and Westport and other towns. Again, check with local information centers for the details.

It's tough to find remains of logging camps unless you really do some digging (Barbara McMartin's *Discover the Adirondacks* hiking guidebooks are a big help, and her *Hides, Hemlocks and Adirondack History* will lead you to tannery sites), but to catch the living traditions of lumberjacks, woodsmen's field days are held in Tupper Lake in July and Boonville in August. Both venues feature skidding with horses, chopping with axes, and speed slicing with crosscut saws — plus more modern competitions, like precision skidding. The Paul Smith's College Woodsmen occasionally sponsor events at the college, at the Adirondack Park Visitor Interpretive Centers, and at the Adirondack Museum that show off old-time techniques and draft teams.

One of the best relics that you can find — just off a country road — is the 1854 blast furnace at Tahawus, near Newcomb. Follow Route 28N past Newcomb to a turnoff for High Peaks hiking trails marked by a large brown-and-yellow sign and keep driving north. En route, you can detour to gaze into the awesome open pit mine that once supplied titanium dioxide for paint pigments and ceramics. Continue on toward the "Upper Works"; the massive stone tower is surprisingly intact, and below it, on the bank of the Hudson River, you'll see the squashed and jumbled iron pieces that were blowers that supplied air to the furnace. At Lyon Mountain, in the far northern reaches of the Adirondack Park, homes and buildings from Republic Steel's huge underground mine offer a glimpse of a company town. Likewise, the rock piles around Witherbee and Moriah and company-built houses and offices evoke days of iron. Yet another site you can visit — and take home samples from — is Barton's garnet mine, near North River. Call 518-251-2296.

From the museum's view deck, you can see down Blue Mountain Lake to Eagle and Utowana lakes. This chain — which includes portions of the Marion River — makes an excellent canoe trip. Study the moving diorama by the Carry Pavilion and you'll be able to trace the steamboat route and even walk the shady trail that was once the shortest standard-gauge rail line in the world.

The easiest exploring you can do, though, is a spin through the bookstore at the entrance and exit to the museum. Countless guides and histories there can lead you to Adirondack odysseys of your own.

CHAPTER NINE

PARTICULARS
AND POTPOURRI

■■■■■■■■■■■■■■■■■■■■■■■■■■■■■■■■■■■■■■

ANNUAL EVENTS

Most museums and historic sites schedule lectures, antiques shows, fall festivals, holiday open houses, and so forth every year. Listed here in rough chronological order is a brief selection of popular annual affairs from around the region. Call for exact dates and times. Weekly papers often contain lengthy calendars of events, as do *Adirondack Life* magazine and the *I Love NY* travel guides. For details on other happenings, check the "Special Events" section following the individual site descriptions.

Sugaring-Off Party, Herkimer Home State Historic Site, Little Falls
        (315-823-0398), late March or early April.
Military Musicians Weekend, Fort Stanwix National Historic Site, Rome
        (315-336-2090), early May.
American Maple Festival, American Maple Museum, Croghan
        (315-346-1107), early May.
Third Tryon County Militia at Fort Klock, St. Johnsville (518-568-7779),
        Memorial Day weekend.
Eighteenth-Century Market Fair, Johnson Hall, Johnstown (518-762-8712),
        second weekend in June.
No-Octane Regatta, Adirondack Museum, Blue Mountain Lake
        (518-352-7311), mid-June.
Battle of Sackets Harbor Reenactment, Sackets Harbor (315-646-2321),
        late June.
Grand Encampment of the French and Indian War, Fort Ticonderoga,
        Ticonderoga (518-585-2821), late June.

Memorial Military Tattoo, Fort Ticonderoga, Ticonderoga (518-585-2821), July 4 weekend.

Woodsmen's Field Days, Tupper Lake (518-359-3328), early July.

Old-Time Fiddlers Jamboree, Horicon Museum, Brant Lake (518-494-7286), mid-July.

Candlelight Concert, Constable Hall, Constableville (315-397-2323), mid-July and mid-August.

Essex Maritime Festival, Essex (518-963-7504), mid-July.

Old-Time Folkcraft Fair, Paine Memorial Library, Willsboro (518-963-4478), late July.

Civil War Encampment, Almanzo and Laura Ingalls Wilder Association, Burke (518-483-1207), late July.

Antique Boat Show, Antique Boat Museum, Clayton (315-686-4104), late July.

Valcour Island Lighthouse Tours, Valcour (518-561-0340), July or August.

Historic House Tours, Kent-Delord House, Plattsburgh (518-561-1035), early August.

Heritage Day and Adirondack Memorabilia Show, Ticonderoga (518-585-6366), early August.

Battle of Oriskany Reenactment, Fort Stanwix, Rome (315-336-2090), early August.

Civil War Encampment, John Brown Farm, Lake Placid (518-523-3900), early August.

Native American Festival, Whiteface Mountain Ski Center, Wilmington (518-946-2223), early August.

Eighteenth-Century Day, Philip Schuyler House, Schuylerville (518-664-9821), mid-August.

Heritage Day, Penfield Homestead Museum, Ironville (518-597-3804), late August.

Grant Remembrance Day, U.S. Grant Cottage, Wilton (518-587-8277), late August.

Harvest Festival, Erie Canal Village, Rome (315-337-3999), Labor Day weekend.

Rustic Furniture Makers' Fair, Adirondack Museum, Blue Mountain Lake (518-352-7311), early September.

Lumberjack Festival, American Maple Museum, Croghan (315-346-1107), early September.

General Steuben's Birthday Party, Steuben Memorial State Historic Site, Remsen (315-831-5528), mid-September.

Historic House Tours, Herkimer County Historical Society, Herkimer (315-866-6413), September.

Civil War Encampment, Speculator (518-548-4521), mid-September.

Forest, Field and Stream Day, Adirondack Center Museum, Elizabethtown (518-962-8778), late September.

Old-Time Gas and Steam Engine Show, Agricultural Museum at Stone Mills,
La Fargeville (315-658-2353), late September.
Portage Day, Herkimer Home State Historic Site, Little Falls
(315-823-0398), late September.
Apple Folkfest, Penfield Homestead Museum, Ironville (518-597-3804),
early October.

RESOURCES

A wide variety of organizations — while not museums or historic sites
— offer historical programs and educational services to the public, mainly
during late spring, summer, and fall.

Adirondack Architectural Heritage (518-834-9328), based in Keeseville,
covers the entire Adirondack Park and sponsors more than a dozen outings
to noteworthy structures and communities, led by experts in the field. In
1996 AARCH trips visited Great Camps, the Dannemora prison, and rustic
buildings around Big Moose Lake; similar destinations are planned for future seasons.

Adirondack Discovery (315-357-3598) has its headquarters in Inlet and
offers more than a hundred programs during July and August in Tupper Lake,
Speculator, Old Forge, and many other towns. The organization is the offi-
cial outreach entity for the Adirondack Park Visitor Interpretive Centers; his-
tory-themed talks and tours range from hikes to tannery ruins led by historian
Barbara McMartin to Adirondack hermit Noah John Rondeau's mysterious
coded diaries.

Adirondack Park Visitor Interpretive Centers are in Newcomb (518-582-
2000) and Paul Smiths (518-327-3000); both highlight the region's natural
history through exhibits, lectures, workshops, concerts, and interpretive trails
for hiking, skiing, and showshoeing. The permanent exhibit in Newcomb
describes the origins of the Adirondack Park and the wilderness-preservation
movement.

Beth Joseph Synagogue (518-359-7229) in Tupper Lake, a lovely turn-of-
the-century building, has been recently restored by community volunteers
and hosts art exhibitions, concerts, and lectures in warm weather months.

While the **Boquet River Association** (c/o Essex County Government Center, Elizabethtown NY 12932) is primarily interested in watershed preservation, the group has published a fascinating tour suitable for cycling or driving;
send a legal-size self-addressed stamped envelope and a dollar for a copy of
Historic Boquet River Bike Trails or look for it in Westport and Essex.

The **Center for Folklife, History and Cultural Programs** (518-792-6508), at
Crandall Public Library, in Glens Falls, offers a variety of events year-round,
such as children's workshops, music and dance performances, and lectures.
There's a small space in the library devoted to changing exhibits, and developing traveling shows for schools and small museums is a goal for future

years. Topics have ranged from balsam traditions, all about the Adirondacks' sweetest-smelling industry, to Indian camps and upstate tourism of the nineteenth century.

Essex Community Heritage Organization (518-963-7088), in Essex, specializes in hands-on restoration of historical properties, education about local cultural resources, and other programs. The group has published two excellent walking tours of the town, available as a simple brochure or a more informative booklet.

Numerous **Elderhostel** (75 Federal Street, Boston MA 02110) programs covering regional history are held in New York's North Country, at Fort Ticonderoga, Sagamore Great Camp, and other locations. Courses are open to people over sixty and usually last five days.

Friends of the North Country (518-834-9606), in Keeseville, has produced an excellent booklet, *Crossing the River*, which describes historic bridges over the Ausable River, in the eastern Adirondacks. It makes a fine driving excursion and is available for five dollars. *A Wide Awake Little Village*, a superbly detailed history and walking tour of Keeseville, was published in 1996 and is free for the asking.

Historic Saranac Lake (518-891-0971), in Saranac Lake, hosts informal lectures, tours, and workshops from time to time; the history of health care in the region is a specialty. The organization has published two books: *Cure Cottages of Saranac Lake* (1985) by Philip Gallos and *Saranac Lake: Pioneer Health Resort* by Mark Caldwell (1993).

The **Northern Frontier Project** (Box 1, Vernon NY 13476; 315-829-3090) helps preserve and promote historic sites in the Mohawk and Susquehanna valleys. Greenway trails and recreational facilities linking these locations are in development.

As its name suggests, the **Preservation League of New York State** (518-462-5658), based in Albany, covers a huge area. Of special interest here is its 1993 book *The National Register of Historic Places in New York State*, which contains a county-by-county listing of noteworthy structures. Also, the *Preservation Directory* — as thick as a big-city phone book — lists national, state, and local preservation groups, historical societies, and programs.

The **Saratoga Springs Preservation Foundation** (518-587-5030) is a very active group, sponsoring house tours, lectures, school programs, traveling exhibits, and workshops all year.

Traditional Arts of Upstate New York (315-386-4289), in Canton, has been documenting folk arts and music for many years, pulling together fascinating traveling exhibitions of little-known works and regional customs for museums and arts centers and presenting shows in its downtown gallery. TAUNY sponsors concerts, lectures, and tours year-round and is working on a resource guide to traditional culture of the region.

WORKS IN PROGRESS

The country's bicentennial in 1976 launched many community museums and local-heritage projects, and now, 20-some years later, it seems that New York's North Country is poised on another burst of historical appreciation. Maybe it's the looming millennium; maybe it's the desire to pull off the information superhighway to capture the last remnants of bygone days. Whatever the reason, watch for the creation, expansion, and significant renovations of these sites and more to come. Check local papers and regional publications for updates.

In Glens Falls, portions of the former downtown YMCA are becoming exhibit space for **IACA World Awareness Children's Museum** (518-793-2773). For many years the organization has offered participatory programs for children in various locations; this permanent home offers space for workshops and events that complement well-planned temporary shows on life in other lands.

Construction and renovation has been ongoing in Port Henry for a new local museum called **The Iron Center** (518-546-3606), housed in a carriage barn near the town hall. Exhibits already include a locomotive and rail car; plans are to incorporate self-guided tours of mining sites and important structures in the vicinity.

The library in Keeseville's old high school is the home of the collections of the **Anderson Falls Heritage Society**, presently open by appointment. The group is hard at work cataloging its photographs, papers, books, and artifacts, including materials on the "Peanut Line," a railroad spur that once chugged into town.

Speaking of trains, **North Creek's railroad station** has been undergoing restoration since 1995, with plans for future interpretive displays. At the depot, in 1901, Teddy Roosevelt learned of William McKinley's death and sped off to become president of the United States. Along the same line — railroad, that is — there's a small historic display in the Riparius depot, and Warren County hopes to launch a tourist train on the scenic tracks paralleling the Hudson River by summer 1997. Contact Warren County Tourism (518-761-6366) for the latest information.

Also in that corner of the region, **Johnsburg Historical Society** (518-251-5811/251-2733) maintains changing historic displays on the communities of North Creek, North River, Bakers Mills, Wevertown, and Johnsburg at the Wevertown Community Center. Recently the group published *River, Rails and Ski Trails*, an illustrated local history.

A stately Greek Revival church in Wells is the home of the **Hamilton County Historical Society**. Restoration work is ongoing; the group sponsors lectures occasionally in the summer.

Two sites in Northville, **Bradt's Wildlife Museum** and **Northville Northampton Historical Museum** (518-863-4040), are housed in offices currently under renovation and should be open by 1997.

BEST BETS

Travel authors are frequently asked to supply readers with a short list of their favorite spots and, truthfully, we couldn't come up with just a couple. Instead, we brainstormed for places that we felt were great for specific activities, like entertaining older parents or active children. Our highly subjective list follows.

Best places to picnic: Crown Point State Historic Site, Erie Canal Village

Best guides in period character: Fort Stanwix

Best places to take your mom: Alice Miner Museum, Constable Hall

Best places to take your dad: Antique Boat Museum, Agricultural Museum at Stone Mills

Best places for shutterbugs: Clark's Broadalbin Heritage and Camera Museum, Adirondack Museum, Chapman Historical Society

Best place to take a retired engineer: Log Village Gristmill, Jefferson County Historical Society's turbine collection

Best place for boat nuts: Adirondack Museum, Antique Boat Museum

Best places to take ten-year-old boys: Fort Ticonderoga, Utica Children's Museum

Best places to take six-year-old girls: Saratoga Children's Museum, Herkimer County Historical Society doll display

Best places for a natural history lesson: Pember Museum, New York State Museum, Dickert Wildlife Museum

Best place for sights and smells of old-time kitchens: 1812 Homestead, Herkimer Home State Historic Site

Best historic communities for an overnight: Sackets Harbor, Essex, Thousand Island Park

Best formal gardens: King's Garden at Fort Ticonderoga, Colonial Garden at Adirondack History Center

Best spots for music lovers: Musical Museum, Marcella Sembrich Studio

Best places to contemplate fine art: Hyde Collection, Munson-Williams-Proctor Institute

Best place for Wild West fans: Frederic Remington Art Museum

Best battlefield for biking: Saratoga National Historic Park

Best rustic decor: Adirondack Museum, Sagamore Great Camp

Most poignant tragedies: Boldt Castle, Oriskany Battlefield

TRAVEL INFORMATION

It's beyond the scope of this book to suggest places to stay and eat, but that information is readily available from state and regional tourism agencies, *I Love NY* guides (1-800-225-5697), *Adirondack Life* magazine, *The Adirondack Book* (Berkshire House Publishers, 1996), and other publications. Here are some useful numbers to get you started:

Adirondack Regional Tourism Council: 518-846-8016
Lake Placid–Essex County Visitors Bureau: 518-523-2445, 1-800-275-2243
Franklin County Tourism: 518-483-2900, 1-800-709-4895
Leatherstocking Country: 315-866-1500, 1-800-233-8778
Lewis County Chamber of Commerce: 315-376-2213, 1-800-724-0242
Oneida County Convention and Visitors Bureau: 1-800-426-3132,
    315-724-7221
New York State Department of Environmental Conservation Campground
    Information: 1-800-456-CAMP
Saratoga County Chamber of Commerce: 518-584-3255
St. Lawrence County Chamber of Commerce: 315-386-4000
Seaway Trail Incorporated: 315-646-1000, 1-800-732-9298
Thousand Islands International Council: 315-482-2520, 1-800-847-5263
Warren County Tourism: 518-761-6366, 1-800-365-1050
Washington County Tourism: 518-746-2290

MUSEUMS AND HISTORIC PLACES DESCRIBED IN THIS BOOK

Albany
New York State Museum (pp. 4-7).

Alexandria Bay
Boldt Castle (pp. 91-93).

Amsterdam
Walter Elwood Museum
(pp. 119-121).

Ballston Spa
Brookside, Saratoga County
History Center (p. 142).
National Bottle Museum
(pp. 175-76).

Blue Mountain Lake
Adirondack Museum (pp. 183-91).

Bolton Landing
Bolton Historical Museum (pp. 102).
Marcella Sembrich Opera Museum
(pp. 86-88).

Brant Lake
Horicon Museum (pp. 101-02).

Broadalbin
Clark's Broadalbin Heritage and
Photography Museum
(pp. 167-69).

Burke
Almanzo and Laura Ingalls Wilder
Association, Farmer Boy's Home
(pp. 80-82).

Canton
Silas Wright House, St. Lawrence
County Historical Association
(pp. 151-52).

Cape Vincent
Cape Vincent Historical Museum
(pp. 127-28).

Caroga Lake
Caroga Historical Association and
Museum (pp. 122-23).

Chazy
Alice T. Miner Museum
(pp. 156-58).

Chestertown
Museum of Local History, Town of
Chester Historical Society
(pp. 103-04).

Clayton
The Antique Boat Museum
(pp. 170-71).
Thousand Islands Museum of
Clayton (pp. 128-29).

Constableville
Constable Hall (pp. 75-77).

Corinth
Corinth Museum (pp. 115-16).

Croghan
American Maple Museum
(pp. 66-67).

Crown Point
Crown Point State Historic Site
(pp. 18-21).
Penfield Homestead Museum
(pp. 58-59).

Deansboro
Musical Museum (pp. 164-65).

East Hartford
Log Village Gristmill (pp. 62-63).

Edinburg
Nellie Tyrell Edinburg Museum
and Rural Museum (pp. 116-17).

Stillwater
Saratoga Battlefield National
Historical Park (pp. 41-43).

Ticonderoga
Fort Ticonderoga (pp. 22-24).
Ticonderoga Heritage Museum
(pp. 59-60).
Ticonderoga Historical Society
(pp. 99-100).

Utica
Children's Museum of History,
Natural History, and Science
(pp. 178-80).
Munson-Williams-Proctor
Institute (pp. 169-70).
Oneida County Historical Society
(pp. 147-48).

Warrensburg
Museum of Local History (p. 104).

Watertown
Jefferson County Historical
Society Museum (pp. 149-50).

Wellesley Island
Thousand Island Park (pp. 90-91).

Whitehall
Skenesborough Museum and
Urban Cultural Park (pp. 106-07).

Willsboro
1812 Homestead (p. 55).

Wilton
Grant Cottage State Historic Site
(pp. 82-83).
Wilton Heritage Society (p. 114).

INDEX

ABOUT THE AUTHORS

Elizabeth Folwell arrived in the Adirondacks during the Bicentennial and got her first taste of regional history as education coordinator of the Adirondack Museum, where she assembled a directory called *Cultural Resources in New York's North County*. From there, she's been manager of a general store, a human-services staffer during the 1980 Winter Olympics, and administrator of a local arts center. Now she's editor of the award-winning regional magazine *Adirondack Life* and author of *The Adirondack Book* (Berkshire House).

She lives in Blue Mountain Lake with her husband, Tom Warrington, and assorted pets.

Amy Godine uses her Saratoga Springs home as a base for North Country research in ethnic and social history. She's an accomplished free-lance writer with features in national travel, scholarly, and general-interest magazines, and is a regular contributor to *Adirondack Life*. A graduate of the Iowa Masters of Fine Arts program in writing, she has taught fiction, nonfiction, and literature courses in arts centers, libraries, and prisons.